THE GIRLS WHO STEPPED OUT OF LINE

THE GIRLS WHO STEPPED OUT OF LINE

UNTOLD STORIES OF THE WOMEN WHO CHANGED THE COURSE OF WORLD WAR II

MAJOR GENERAL MARI K. EDER
U.S. ARMY, RETIRED

THORNDIKE PRESS
A part of Gale, a Cengage Company

GALE
A Cengage Company

Thorndike Press® Large Print History Fact and Fiction.

The text of this Large Print edition is unabridged.

Other aspects of the book may vary from the original edition.

Set in 16 pt. Plantin.

LIBRARY OF CONGRESS CIP DATA ON FILE.
CATALOGUING IN PUBLICATION FOR THIS BOOK
IS AVAILABLE FROM THE LIBRARY OF CONGRESS.

ISBN-13: 978-1-4328-9532-7 (hardcover alk. paper).

Published in 2022 by arrangement with Sourcebooks, LLC

Printed in Mexico
Print Number: 02   Print Year: 2022

"My grandmother turned toward a guard — she was in line to be shot into a pit — and said, 'What happens if I step out of line?' And he said, 'I don't have the heart to shoot you, but somebody will.' And she stepped out of line. And for that, I am here. And for that, my children are here. So step out of line, ladies. Step out of line!' "

Alex Borstein
2019 Emmy Awards Acceptance Speech

For my great grandmother
Harriett E. Patterson Greer

CONTENTS

INTRODUCTION 11

Chapter 1: Wonder Woman 25
Chapter 2: What the Next Day Brings 52
Chapter 3: The Life of a Warrior . . . 81
Chapter 4: A Good Influence 107
Chapter 5: The Limping Lady 133
Chapter 6: Falling Angels 163
Chapter 7: Inside of Time 192
Chapter 8: The Torchbearer
of Freedom 222
Chapter 9: Love Conquers All 242
Chapter 10: We Followed Our Stars 265
Chapter 11: Power Maps 292
Chapter 12: Code Secrets 311
Chapter 13: Wind and Sand 335
Chapter 14: The Golden Hour 366

Chapter 15: High Morale 392

Chapter 16: Return to Normal. . . . 417

Chapter 17: No More Firsts 434

Chapter 18: It Starts Today 459

ACKNOWLEDGMENTS 473

NOTES 475

BIBLIOGRAPHY AND
    REFERENCES 549

ABOUT THE AUTHOR 583

INTRODUCTION

In 1943, *Mass Transportation* magazine published an article entitled "Eleven Tips on Getting More Efficiency Out of Women Employees." It provided "insights" into the psyche of the working woman of the day and offered advice to male managers on how to deal with the wartime influx of women into the workplace. As one such tip stated: "Women make excellent workers when they have their work cut out for them, but they lack initiative in finding work themselves."

Hiring women during World War II was a difficult and unwelcome chore for many male managers. However, they had little choice. With one third of working age men in uniform, accepting a substitute appeared to be an unfortunate necessity. The U.S. population at the time was 140 million people. Over 16 million men were in uniform, representing 11 percent of the population. But the stores still had to stay open; the factories had to run. While the men were away at war, women needed to save the home front and the economy at the same time. An act of bravery for many. Prepared or not, they took up the challenge. How would women adjust to being in the workforce, many for the first time in their lives?

Their male supervisors worried about the same thing. How would they adjust? Could they handle the stress of nine to five? The *Mass Transportation* article offered tips to remember when selecting new hires. "Pick young married women. They usually have more of a sense of responsibility than their unmarried sisters." Then there was the gentle reminder, "Husky girls are more even tempered and efficient." These baldly condescending guidelines were typical of the times. According to L. H. Sanders, author of the *Mass Transportation* piece, women were essentially invisible in society. They appeared destined to shuffle along in their predetermined roles and along the narrow cultural paths set out for them. At best, they might aspire to a secretarial job, or a teaching career . . . at least until they married and had children.

While this was a common view of women at the time, it was also an incomplete picture. There were other women, those who chose to ignore convention, disregard established roles, and step out of line. They served, fought, struggled, and made things happen, in and out of uniform. They embraced any opportunity to serve, to test their limits, make a difference, and experience a world more worthy of their skills and abilities. They weren't concerned with lipstick or their hair — they were concerned with doing their job and doing it well.

Most weren't even trailblazers by choice. Some were merely trying to survive from one day to the next. Others just wanted to make a contribution to the war effort. They didn't target the glass or even the brass ceiling. These brave ladies, mostly unknown today, did not benefit from the strength of feminist movements, women's marches, and technological advances that connect and empower so many women across the globe in the twenty-first century. Many carried on in isolation, imprisoned in a concentration camp, operating alone in a foreign country under an assumed name, or in a unique, individual role that offered no safety net whatsoever. For them, failure wasn't even an option. Success was a matter of survival. Others were constricted by the blunt force of their security clearances and the need for silence or hemmed in by the pressure of being both brilliant and an anomaly.

This book isn't about what these women were forbidden to do. Or how they were discriminated against. This is the story of who these women were and what they did do. Their achievements have shaped our opportunities today, gifted us with role models and mentors who speak to us even now, seventy-five years down the line.

The actions of these amazing women put comic book heroines to shame. But their lives aren't just stand-alone testimonials to courage, determination, and drive. While their achievements are considerable, their legacy is even greater. As we look at their stories, we can see ourselves in those who dream of flying one day, earning a degree in chemistry or education, nursing the ill or injured, and serving as witness to history, speaking up for others who may not be able to speak for themselves.

Despite being groundbreaking at the time, none of this is new. Women have served their country since the Revolutionary War. They simply were not acknowledged then, much less accepted. For hundreds of years, women have served in other conflicts around the globe. Some undercover, in disguise, others openly, but all of them with courage.

In fact, within the United States, women also served in the Civil War. One history book set out to remedy the misconception that only men had served. It was a thick volume entitled *Women of the War* by Frank Moore, first published in 1867. His book tells the stories of forty-three women who contributed to the war effort. Some followed their husbands and sons along the way, hoping to provide comfort, to care for them, and picking up a rifle out of necessity. Others fought side by side with the men from day one. As the author noted in his introduction, "There are many hundreds of women whose shining deeds have honored their country, and wherever they are known, the nation holds them in equal honor with its brave men." He continues, "The story of the war will never be fully or fairly written if the achievements of women in it are untold. They do not figure in official reports; they are not gazette for deeds as gallant as ever were done; the names of thousands are unknown beyond the neighborhood where they live . . . yet there is no feature in our war more creditable to us as a nation, none . . . so worthy of record."

Those words shock: *thousands of them.* Thousands who made a difference, who did more than sew bandages or cook. They contributed in significant, life-changing ways — fought, suffered, and were killed in action. And I'd never known this. I, an Army major general, who served her country for thirty-six years, studied military strategy, the great captains of history, and famous battles — I knew *nothing* of how legions of women volunteered their time, and sometimes their lives, in defense of freedom. Sure, I knew the general statistics, maybe even recalled an example or two. But no more — it wasn't taught; it wasn't in the books. History did an injustice to these women, wiping the slate clean of not just their service, but their very names.

These stories matter. Not just because of what they did then. But because of their impacts today. Every one of them had an influence that echoed down through the generations, even if we don't recall, aren't taught, or try to ignore the doors they opened. They still affect us, connect us, and as we connect to them, still inspire us.

The U.S. Armed Services began recruiting women in 1917 to serve in World War I. In 1918, the Army followed the example of the Marine Corps and the Navy and began admitting women, initially as nurses. Then General John Pershing said he needed women to serve as telephone operators.

They were faster than male operators and more accurate. And, yes, they also had to be fluent in French. Recruiting began in earnest, and there were 223 of Pershing's "Hello Girls" on the front lines in France by the time the war ended. More were in the pipeline, waiting to ship out when the cease-fire was called. Yet following the war, the Army refused to acknowledge the women were indeed veterans, or that they deserved any service benefits. It took sixty years for that wrong to be righted. By that time, the majority of the "Hello Girls" had passed away, but those who remained relished their long-awaited moment of victory. They were recognized, called veterans, given discharge papers, able *at last* to stand beside the men who had served. They had earned the right to be buried under the flag.

World War II started out in much the same vein of indifference and intolerance, with women tucked away in the background. And yet they did it all: flew planes, broke codes, smuggled refugees from Germany, fought with the Resistance, and survived persecution, concentration camps, and enemy attacks. Those women in uniform did everything the men did, except combat. Those who fought with the Resistance or engaged the Nazis independently picked up weapons

17

of their own. All the while, they endured indifference from others who could have helped their efforts, grinding racial and gender prejudice from the institutions they served, and the effects of peers who tried to undermine them each and every day. Stephen Ambrose, author of *D-Day June 6, 1944,* said of servicewomen, "They did not have an easy time. Cruel and vicious jokes were told about them — although not by the wounded about the nurses. These pioneering women persevered and triumphed."

Even after the war, they humbly remained in the background. They knew what they had done. These women did not need or expect thanks and shied away from medals and recognition.

But that recognition was important, if not to them, then to the generations to follow. These women didn't realize that at the time, but they were role models not only for their own children but also for cohorts of pioneering women who followed them. They influenced Army desegregation, stood as role models for entrepreneurs, were admired by generations of intelligence professionals and cartographers. They served as mentors to generations of pilots and astronauts and scientists. They inspired legions of leaders in technology and engineering, having proved that mathematics was the backbone of a career in the hard sciences. Those who continued to serve as executives in intelligence and cryptanalysis demonstrated daily their critical contributions to national defense. Perhaps these women veterans didn't want or need the recognition, but future generations needed them.

Early in the postwar years, when society and culture tried to turn back the clock and restrict women's opportunities once again, many who had discovered their capabilities during the war found a way to continue to defy expectations, step out of line, and go on to contribute in other ways to society and make a difference in the lives of others. One went on to fight prejudice in professional sports. Another ran for public office. Others went on to careers in the Central Intelligence Agency (CIA) or National Security Agency (NSA). Some preferred to live a simple quiet life, basking in their freedom and ever thankful for their survival. Several were recognized as Righteous Among Nations. A few received a warrior's burial at Arlington National Cemetery.

By stepping out of line, the trailblazing women of World War II were able to achieve remarkable things. Every contribution, no matter how limited, no matter how short the period of actual service or sacrifice, was significant to the greater whole — preserving freedom. In today's politically and culturally divisive society, these stories are not just about hidden history. These are real people who overcame their doubts and fears, who were scarred by imprisonment and torture of war, who witnessed unspeakable acts of terror, who tried and sometimes failed. They kept going.

Today more women are stepping out of line, moving beyond bland expectations, and setting their own high bar for success. They are demanding opportunities, defying odds, and they are doing it in greater numbers than in the past. There are still unicorns, the "firsts" in fields previously closed to women or unaccepting of those who aspire to join. But the once rare "firsts" are falling away. Young career women in all fields have mentors, current leaders to serve as role models, cohorts to join, and professional associations and groups to support and enable them. They and their peers have the ability to go further and faster than ever before — together, helping each other and pulling each other up. Their male counterparts have evolved too, supporting and encouraging women to succeed.

That's what brought me to this project.

I'd heard a few abbreviated histories before — in women's history month celebrations, through presentations for African American history month, in a speech about the contributions of Native Americans, at a remembrance for victims of the Holocaust, but those stories were typically brief and oversimplified. I couldn't relate to those women as real people without getting to know them. I needed to learn their stories and understand what drove them, how they fought, what they loved and valued, how they had tried and failed, and fell and got up again. I needed to see them in color and in 3-D, as women of their time, not just as quotes in a speech or article. I feel honored to know them now.

In October 2017, the Army Women's Foundation invited me to give a presentation on "Leading in a Complex World" at the Association of the U.S. Army's (AUSA) annual symposium in Washington. I was a last-minute substitute; the main speaker had dropped out. I scrambled to find a few stories about unknowns who had influenced the development of future opportunities for women through their unconventional service. One was Virginia Hall, a World War II spy who fought with the Office of Strategic Services (OSS) in France, after having failed multiple times to enter the State Department as a Foreign Service Officer. The other was Captain Stephanie Czech Rader, a first-generation Polish American who served as a counterintelligence agent. I found her story through the *Washington Post* as the OSS Society was fighting to get her the medal the Army had denied her. Then I found the *Wall Street Journal* obituary for Hilda Eisen and was transfixed by the story of her courage.

Yes, I found many of these women first through reading their obituaries. As the women of the Greatest Generation continued to pass in large numbers, I found more incredible people and became hooked on their stories. The more I learned about them, the more I admired them. I wanted to meet them all. World War II, which once seemed to lie in the distant past, moved up in my consciousness. These trailblazers lived just yesterday. They were like today's younger women, hopeful, afraid, yearning. I also came to realize how incredibly young they were when they took that first step towards their future. Some were only seventeen, eighteen, or twenty.

By 2019, I was awestruck by how many of them had reached, or nearly reached, the age of one hundred. It wasn't just Stephanie Czech Rader, but Diet Eman,

Ruth Gruber, Hilda Eisen, Kate Nolan, Millie Rexroat, and Dame Mary Barraco. Unbelievable.

Further, my research showed how many of them were connected in unusual and unexpected ways. The succeeding chapters will attempt to highlight those connections and show how we all touch and influence lives far beyond what we can realize at the moment.

On November 14, 2008, the U.S. Army promoted Ann Dunwoody to the rank of four-star general, the first woman to achieve the rank in U.S. military history. On February 7, 2009, the Women in Military Service for America (WIMSA) Memorial Foundation hosted a luncheon in her honor. Women general officers, currently serving and retired, from all services attended. The author is in the second row, second from the right. Photo courtesy of the Women in Military Service for America Memorial Foundation/Donna Parry.

I wanted to take each one of these ladies by the hand and welcome them back to the forefront of our formation and grant them all respect due. By remembering their achievements and their sacrifices, we acknowledge our foundation and give thanks for their gifts to us.

When they were needed, each of them understood what they had to do. They stepped out of line. They saved themselves, and they saved the lives of thousands of others. We are all here because of them.

CHAPTER 1

WONDER WOMAN

"When my life was in danger, I did what I've always done. I fought."

ALICE MARBLE

The headlights bounced up and down on the narrow mountain road like a tennis ball. The dark car screeched back and forth around hairpin curves lined with firs, then sped up along short straightaways, only to have to brake hard at the next bend. A speeding roadster was gaining ground. Alice stole a glance in the rearview mirror, her Rolls nearly careening off the wet pavement. Gravel sprayed as she fought the steering wheel, and she gasped as blinding headlights bounced at her again in the mirror, closer now. Alice glanced over at the passenger seat and shook her pistol out of the holster. They were going to overtake her. Whoever they were.

She wiped a tear from her cheek. Ten

25

minutes ago, Alice had been heartbroken. She'd betrayed an old lover, a man she still cared for. Too late now. She had broken into the safe at his home and took photos of the journals he kept, records of his Nazi clients and benefactors. She left the gold bars, the cash, and all the jewels — she wanted nothing of the banker's stolen wealth. The evidence was locked in her camera. And in her memory.

A serious Alice Marble looking every bit the international spy. Photo © The National Portrait Gallery, London.

It was early March in the Swiss Alps, 1945. Alice Marble, international tennis star, had been in neutral Switzerland for weeks, playing in a tennis exhibition and reuniting with old friends and one special man. He would come to be called Hans Steinmetz (Alice never revealed his real name), and he was a wealthy Swiss banker when they were first involved years earlier. Now he was a millionaire, sitting on a mountain of dirty money. Alice knew him long before he had built his wealth; she had even loved him back then . . . but not enough to stay. Returning now, during the war, everything was different. They were different. She'd fallen in love and married in their time apart, and suddenly she was now a widow. Her husband had been dead for only a few short months, and while it felt wrong to pick up again with Hans, it felt familiar at the same time. It was strange, like being back at the height of her tennis career, when her relationship with him was new. It was almost as though the last eight years had been erased. That she found it so easy to fall back into that old rhythm staggered her. It felt surreal. The spark between them still burned. She believed him when he said he wanted to marry her, and that he'd take care of her for the rest of her life. It hurt to lie to him in response. She almost backed out of the task at hand. Part of her wanted to say yes, marry him, and bury the rest. But Alice had never quit anything in her life. She'd taken an oath, after all.

The chase car pulled alongside her. Slowing the Rolls-Royce, she reached for her gun, then realized with a gulp of relief that it was her Army handler who had been following her escape from Hans's mansion. Major Al Jones smiled faintly and waved from the passenger seat. She carefully eased her car onto the side of the narrow road behind Al and flew out of the door into his arms.

"Al, thank God it's you! I have the film!" She held up the camera like a prize. She'd made it.

"Wonderful," he said flatly, his tone saying something different.

Alice looked back. Headlights from another car were shining brightly in the distance. "We've got to get out of here, Al. Hans or the Russians or God knows who is following us! We can leave the car. He'll find it." She didn't want to have to face Hans.

"There's been a change of plans. Give me the film!" He demanded.

Something was off. This wasn't like him. Al never spoke to her like this. Alice took a step back. "No. I'll give it to you in Geneva. Like we planned." Her stomach lurched. What was going on? Alice tightened her grip on the camera.

He lunged for the dangling strap, but before he could grab her wrist, a thick voice shouted from the driver's side of the car, "Stop wasting time on that bitch! Get the film *now*!"

Alice wasn't letting go even as she strug-gled to realize that the driver had a thick Russian accent. And Al, who had been with her throughout her training and prepara-tions for this mission . . . What was he doing with a Russian? What did that make him? A traitor, she realized.

"You bastard!" Alice screamed in his face. The camera clattered to the ground between them, and Al pulled out a pistol. It looked huge in the mist from the headlights, a can-non aimed at her face. Alice turned and ran. Behind her, she heard the other man.

"You fool! Kill her! Hurry!" Behind her, she heard brakes squeal, doors slam, and then the sounds of gunfire. A white-hot streak of pain pushed Alice to the ground. Then the light was gone.

"When my life was in danger, I did what I've always done. I fought," Alice said later. "My mother didn't raise a quitter."

She woke up in an Army hospital in Ger-many, the colonel who'd sent her on this mission sitting at her bedside.

"What happened?" she asked, wincing in pain. She reached up to touch her immobi-lized left shoulder, but the lightning bolt of pain was enough to stop her.

"Al shot you," Colonel Linden replied. His mouth worked like he wanted to say more but couldn't get the words out. "We had to kill him and the Russian before anyone else showed up. But before he died, he opened the camera. Alice, I hate to tell you this, but the film was exposed. We lost everything. All the evidence is gone." Linden looked down at the floor. "I'm sorry, Allie. After everything we put you through."

Alice carefully pulled herself up into a sitting position. "I can still help you," she said. "Remember, Colonel, I have a photographic memory. And I recall every name and the exact amount of every deposit listed in that bank ledger."

The colonel smiled with relief, astonished. "My God, Alice. What would we do without you?"

Alice's sense of purpose returned. The war was winding down, and she'd finally made a contribution. Alice recognized those names from Hans's ledger a year later, while watching a news reel. The names and amounts of their deposits were read out one by one, listed as evidence at the Nuremberg trials. She was proud of her role in helping prosecute those Nazi war criminals. Her evidence had *definitely* helped.

Alice Marble grew up in San Francisco. She moved there with her parents and five siblings in 1919, just as the Spanish Flu struck. Her father died on Christmas Eve that year, ruining Christmas for Alice forever. Her mother began to clean houses in 1920, and Alice's older brothers left school to get jobs. Meanwhile, Alice was a natural athlete from an early age. She was a young mascot for the San Francisco Seals baseball team and enjoyed catching fly balls in the outfield to entertain the crowds. Even Joe DiMaggio admitted, "She had a pretty good arm."

Her brothers thought she needed to take up a different sport — there definitely wasn't a future for her in professional baseball. They steered her toward tennis, giving Alice her first racket for her fifteenth birthday. She stomped her foot, disappointed. Alice thought tennis was for "sissies," until her first competitive match when she discovered the game was actually much harder than it looked. It was a challenge, and it took much more than strength. It took finesse. The new challenge had her hooked. Alice's nickname in the California junior tournament league was "Queen of Swat." It was a fitting title. Alice never backed down from a challenge. She had the talent and the drive. Beyond that, she had sheer guts. Alice just didn't know how to quit.

One summer day in 1933, she was playing in a qualifying tournament in East Hampton, New York. The day was exceedingly hot — 100 degrees Fahrenheit — and Alice played from 10:00 a.m. until 7:00 p.m., 108 games in all. It was too much for a body to take. She collapsed with heatstroke, and her season was over. It taught her to recognize when she had gone over the limit of what she could, or should, endure.

Next year, she collapsed again on a court in Paris. Doctors discovered she was suffering from not just anemia but also tuberculosis. They told her she would never play tennis again. She didn't listen. That couldn't be true. She would make sure it wouldn't come true.

It took two long years, but Alice clawed her way back to the highest amateur rankings, making the Top Ten in the World list, then Number One. She listened to her coaches, honed new skills, and refined her game along the way. She adopted the serve-and-volley, adding to her already aggressive attacking game. Some commentators disapproved, sneering that she "played like a man." Alice shrugged, fired that cannonball, and kept on winning. She wore shorts as well, not a skirt, further scandalizing the commentators. And those naysayers who

Alice Marble, number one in the world, leaps over the net, victorious again. Photo by Gjon Mili/The LIFE picture collection via Getty Images.

thought she was a one-hit wonder earlier in her career had to eat their words.

Alice Marble won an unprecedented eighteen Grand Slam championships in her nine-year amateur career: five singles, six in women's doubles, and seven in mixed doubles. Alice was ranked number one in the world in 1939. The Associated Press named her Athlete of the Year in 1939 and again in 1940. She was the first woman ever to win both the British and U.S. women's singles, doubles, and mixed doubles in the same year. She was on the cover of *Life* magazine, a superstar.

Alice Marble led a glamorous lifestyle, enjoying casual tennis with friends who were Hollywood A-list stars. She was often seen with the Hearsts and her good friends, the famous couple Carole Lombard and Clark Gable. Or maybe on the arm of Errol Flynn or Cesar Romero. The 1930s were full of heady moments in the public eye. Born to stand out, Allie was platinum-blonde gorgeous, famous, and at the height of her game. She even attended the premiere of Clark's new movie, *Gone with the Wind,* with the couple. It was an incredible time, exciting and magical. Despite her fame, Alice stayed grounded with her sport and learned that the work it took to get to be number one didn't end at the top of that mountain. In fact, it took even more to stay number one.

With a little help from Carole, plus a bit of star power of her own, she even had her own part-time career designing women's sportswear. Young girls everywhere wanted the new Alice Marble tennis racket. That special didn't help her friends improve their game, though.

"C'mon, Allie. Play nice for once." Carole Lombard, star of stage and screen, licked her lips nervously. The two played tennis often, although Carole constantly reminded Alice to take it easy on her.

"Don't you like my design for a new tennis outfit?" Alice teased. *Pock!* She hit the ball with her racket and palmed it again.

Slap! Hesitation. Alice had faked her out. Carole was leaning so far forward she nearly fell over in anticipation of the serve.

Alice ticked up the edge of her lip, just the hint of a smile. She knew Carole was worried. Alice watched her friend twirl her racket, squinting in the sharp California sun. *Not yet,* Alice thought. She wasn't ready to serve until Carole was teetering on the edge of panic.

The bright yellow tennis ball smacked the ground again. *Pock!* Alice snapped her fingers. *Click!* Then she palmed the ball and grinned. *Slap!* Alice bounced the ball again.

"Set, match," she crowed. Across the net, her opponent gulped in anticipation. Carole should have known what was coming.

Wham! Alice's renowned thundering serve

rocketed by Carole's head, just a blur. Carole didn't even have time to react. It was too easy, sure. But it was still fun to fool her. Alice grinned at her friend's open mouth.

By 1940, Alice had indeed won it all, and had gone 145 amateur matches without a single loss. At the time, she had accomplished every challenge the sport had to offer her. War was rumbling from Europe to the United States, and Alice asked herself, "What's left to challenge me? There may not even be a national tournament next year."

She played in one final tournament before turning pro. It was the U.S. National Women's Singles Championship, her last major title. She'd won it three years in a row. Later she donated that special trophy to the International Tennis Hall of Fame.

Turning pro meant she could no longer play major matches like Wimbledon. Professionals weren't permitted to play there until 1968. But Alice needed to make some money. In 1941, pioneer tennis promoter Jack Harris signed her to his inaugural tour. It featured the biggest names in the sport, all friends of Alice. The first match took place in New York City in January 1941. Alice spent the next eighteen weeks playing sixty-one matches across the U.S., with additional stops in three Canadian cities plus Havana, Cuba, and Nassau, Bahamas. She was thrilled to meet the Duke and Duchess of Windsor at a Red Cross benefit in Nassau. It was an enjoyable tour. She played with the likes of Don Budge, Bobby Riggs, and Mary Hardwick, but Alice was really the headliner. Her loss to Mary in Phoenix was her first in over two hundred amateur and pro matches. She should have been able to enjoy a long and profitable run as a pro tennis player, but then the war got in the way of travel and sponsorship for pro tours, and exhibition matches all but dried up.

The attack on Pearl Harbor in December 1941 changed everything. Allie went ahead with her opening match at Madison Square Garden in January 1942, but there wasn't the turnout she had hoped for. She played badly, perhaps tired. In addition to playing tennis professionally, Alice was also singing in a couple of Broadway shows. She was trying to do too much.

For Alice, the 1940s were vastly different from the 1930s: tougher, more dangerous, and packed with failures, tragic love, and loss, though it didn't seem that way at first. In the fall of 1941, Alice met publisher Max Gaines at a cocktail party. A writer and editor with All American Comics Inc., he wanted to pioneer a new character — Wonder Woman. And he knew Alice Marble, the famous international tennis player, was just the right celebrity to endorse his new effort. At that time, All-American Publications published *All-American Comics, Sensation Comics, All Star Comics,* and more.

"So, what do you think? This comic is great, isn't it? *Wonder Woman Arrives in Man's World!* First issue will come out in January of '42. And I'll tell you, having your stamp of approval on it will get a lot of young girls interested in Wonder Woman and her amazing adventures." He tapped the draft comic book to emphasize each word. It would be a bestseller. He was sure of it.

"Mmm." Alice pulled the book back from Max's hands. She was still reading. But beyond a female comic superhero, which was unique enough on its own, she saw other opportunities. She leaned forward, ready to serve.

"I'll tell you what, Max. I like it, but what your *Sensation Comics* series really needs is a solid dose of reality. I think that there needs to be some other stories included with Wonder Woman, stories about *real* women heroes from history." Alice sat back and waited.

"Such as?" he finally asked, looking confused.

"Clara Barton, Dolly Madison, Eleanor Roosevelt . . ." She flipped her wrist. There were hundreds more female role models. Thousands, probably. "Do I have to spell it out for you?" Alice could definitely turn on the charm when she wanted to.

Max Gaines was a savvy entrepreneur, and he knew a good deal when he saw one. "Sold!" He stuck out his hand. By the time the party ended, Alice Marble was an associate editor for the *Wonder Woman* comic series.

Alice's influence was instrumental in the comic's success. In the second issue, published in the fall of 1942, she wrote, "The first issue was a complete sell-out, and we all want to thank you for giving 'Wonder Woman' such a swell reception." Her creation, stories of real "wonder women" from American history, ran from 1941 to 1946. The comic continued to be a bestseller.

It still wasn't enough for Alice. She was frustrated by her inability to do anything truly meaningful. She wasn't sacrificing anything, giving enough. Alice wanted to make a contribution to her country. A real contribution. Something meaningful. The rest of the world was involved in the war effort, and yet here she was, playing tennis and editing comic books.

The tuberculosis diagnosis meant she wasn't eligible to enlist in the military. She tried, but every service turned her down. She did her best, though, speaking to youth groups, Scouts, and high school students — all part of her work to promote fitness for young girls through the Civilian Defense Corps. She also entertained troops, playing more than five hundred tennis exhibition matches at military bases, and gave tennis clinics for interested soldiers.

Alice Marble and British tennis player Mary Hardwick at Fort Oglethorpe, Georgia. They were visiting the WAC Training Center with Subaltern Mary Churchill (British Prime Minister Winston Churchill's daughter). Alice and Mary were ready to play an exhibition match for the WAC troops. U.S. Army photo.

The exhibition matches felt superficial. Alice wasn't an entertainer; she was a doer. She turned to her friend Carole Lombard for advice.

"What else can I do, Carole? I can't get in the Army." Alice flopped on the lounger beside Carole's pool. She threw an arm over her eyes dramatically.

"You could support War Bonds. I do," Carole replied. Like regular savings bonds, the sale of war bonds was helping the U.S. finance the war effort. "You know, we all have our place. You are doing a lot for the troops already."

"It doesn't feel like I'm doing enough," Alice said. "It just doesn't. I'll think about those war bonds tours."

Carole didn't press. Alice would come around when she was ready. Several months later, Carole finished another long war bonds rally tour, providing her celebrity presence to the cause. She was headed home when her plane took off from a Las Vegas airport on a dark, cold evening in 1942. There were no lights on the field due to wartime restrictions. The plane flew straight into the mountainside at the far end of the field, exploding on impact. No one survived.

Alice was devastated by the loss of her friend. However, starting with the death of her father, she'd had to learn early how to gut her way forward from terrible challenges. As a teenager, Alice had been raped and assaulted, strangled, and left to die near the courts where she played in San Francisco. When she regained consciousness, she managed to stagger to her aunt's house, where she finally let herself fall apart. But she never told her mother, and it wasn't until years later that she was comfortable telling anyone else. She lived with that pain until she could transform it into a hardened piece of steel in her gut. It drove her forward. Every achievement, it seemed, wasn't enough. She wanted more. She needed to do more.

A few months after Carole's death, Alice started visiting military hospitals near New York, taking time to visit the injured soldiers. She kept singing too, often performing at the Stage Door Canteen. One evening, while she was singing for the troops, she was surprised when a rich baritone voice joined in on the chorus. Her eyes sought him out, standing at the back of the room. From the shadows, deep brown eyes looked straight through her. Alice felt a chill on the back of her neck when the song ended, and the room erupted in applause. A good-looking young man in an Army uniform smiled at her, and Alice found herself smiling back.

Captain Joe Crowley walked Alice home that night. The handsome pilot spoke five languages and worked for Army intelligence, but he wouldn't tell her any more than that. They said good night at the door, but Alice couldn't get him out of her mind. Three months later, he was back from a mission, and they met for dinner. The two became fast friends, then lovers, and just months later, husband and wife. It was wartime. They had to grab whatever bits of normal life they could get.

"My husband and I were to spend two and a half years living on notes, phone calls, and days stolen from the war," she recalled later. Every visit was special, and the reunions were always too short. They sometimes took place in New York, sometimes at other Army posts around the world. Occasionally, she'd travel just to be with him. At other times, she managed to fit in a tennis exhibition. But the time with Joe was always too short.

After one too-short interlude in Panama, Alice was thrilled to discover she was pregnant. Joe was overjoyed and wrote he couldn't wait to see her again so they could celebrate. But when she was five months along, she was driving home from a cocktail party in New York when she was hit by a drunk driver who had swerved into her lane. Alice wasn't badly hurt, but the impact had been harsh enough that she lost the baby. Alice swore her friends to secrecy, knowing that Joe would be home for leave just after New Year's. She'd tell him then about their loss. She needed to have that conversation in person.

On Christmas Eve 1944, Alice and some friends were in her apartment singing carols when a telegram arrived from the War Department. Alice thought it was from Joe. She'd already received a gift from him, a bottle of her favorite perfume and a lovely letter. Alice tore the envelope open and read those words that made her heart die. "We regret to inform you that Captain Joseph Crowley was killed in action when his plane was shot down over Germany."

A black blanket of depression fell over her immediately. It was so heavy, it brought her to the floor. Alice didn't want to *be* anymore. How could she go on without him? Days later, she attempted to end her life by overdosing on sleeping pills. Her old friend, Clark Gable, heard what happened. He sent her three dozen red roses while she was recovering.

"If I can do it, so can you," he wrote in the card, referring to his own loss. Clark was still mourning Carole's death, and Alice was deeply sad over losing Joe, but his words gave her the first rung on the ladder back. She was released from the hospital on Christmas morning, took one step forward, and then another. It was time to pull herself up and start over again.

She was still recovering, having good days and bad, when Uncle Sam came calling with a carrot and a stick. The carrot was an offer to play in a tennis exhibition in Switzerland. The stick was a little more difficult. Colonel Linden, Army intelligence, wanted Alice to renew an old acquaintance, a Swiss banker and her former lover, Hans. They wanted to learn about his Nazi connections and investors. "I felt I had nothing to lose but my life," she wrote, "and at that time I didn't care about living."

Unknown to Alice, the Allies created "Operation Safehaven" in 1944, an intelligence-gathering operation focused on preventing Nazi Germany from laundering money through neutral countries, specifically Switzerland. In December, while Alice was at home waiting for Joe, Bern OSS Chief Allen Dulles (later CIA director) sent a memo to headquarters, stating, "At present, we do not have adequate personnel to do an effective job in this field and meet other demands."

That's where Alice came in. Now she had the opportunity to do something meaningful. And when that door opened, she jumped right in. Once that painful mission was over, Alice finally felt as though she'd served her country and made a difference through doing more than just playing exhibition matches and entertaining the troops. Fully recovered from the gunshot wound, she started to play tennis again and even took up golf.

Alice never shied away from a fight, and following the war, she took on a new opponent, one she thought was destroying her sport: institutional racism. Alice had met twenty-three-year-old Althea Gibson at an exhibition and was impressed with the young player. At that time Gibson was barred from playing in U.S. Lawn Tennis Association competitions because she was African American. Alice was furious at their blatant discrimination. She didn't make calls to organizers of the U.S. Open. She didn't talk to influential friends or sports commentators. Instead, Alice hit a powerful serve, a first, right into the heart of the American tennis establishment. She called out their racist practices in a letter that was published in the July 1950 issue of *American Lawn Tennis Magazine*.

"We can accept the evasions," she wrote, "or we can face the issue squarely and honestly." She called them out, bluntly and with the same aggressive attack that had always

Althea Gibson and Alice Marble at Forest Hills August 28, 1950, for the U.S. National Championships (now the U.S. Open). Photo by Bettman via Getty Images.

marked her game. "If tennis is a game for ladies and gentlemen, it's also time we acted a little more like gentlepeople and less like sanctimonious hypocrites."

The sharp words stung on impact, just as Alice intended. If Gibson were banned from playing, she added, "then there is an ineradicable mark against a game to which I have devoted most of my life, and I would be bitterly ashamed." Shortly after the letter was published, Althea Gibson was admitted to the U.S. Open, winning it just a few years later.

Alice Marble was blessed with a natural athletic ability and the inborn drive to play and win. A world champion tennis player, she parlayed that natural talent into eighteen Grand Slam Championships and a professional career on the pro circuit. She taught and she led by example, knowing full well how her actions represented her sport. She promoted Wonder Woman comics and insisted the publishers feature the achievements of *real* wonder women from history. Recruited to spy for the United States in World War II, she provided the U.S. Army with information that was used to convict Nazi war criminals in the Nuremberg trials.

After the war, she continued to fight for what was right.

The love of the game never left her. Alice continued to teach and coach tennis. In 1960, sixteen-year-old Billie Jean King was ranked nineteenth in the country. She was fortunate to have Alice Marble work with her every weekend to develop her game. Alice coached a number of promising young players, even nine-year-old Sally Ride, who would go on to become an astronaut. Alice could always pick a winner.

But she also knew what it was like to lose: "I have been a loser before and have had to learn through hard work, patience, and faith . . . the way to overcome defeat . . . And I know that everyone is endowed with qualities of the champion and can succeed despite handicaps in the most important game of all — the game of life."

She lived an incredible life that brought her many unique opportunities. But it was also a life that provided powerful personal lessons — in love, loss, friendship, physical trials, and betrayal of trust. Alice was the type of friend, teacher, mentor, and lover that people wanted to learn from, to admire, to simply be close to — to absorb some of her talent, insights, and maybe just a touch of her greatness, if not her guts.

Her story has been termed "both perfectly plausible and utterly impossible at the same time." Those who have tried to dig deeper and confirm the details of her marriage to a handsome pilot or her role as a spy have been unable to find records that would corroborate her claims. But neither can those stories be disproved. "Nuance and enigma and shades of gray — are what Alice and her story are all about."

The legacy and the mystery of Alice Marble endure within and far beyond the game she loved. Generations of young women were inspired by her athleticism on the court, and the young hopefuls she coached cherished her advice. Thousands of young girls were influenced by her stories of real American wonder women and given hope for their own dreams and aspirations. The tennis establishment itself owes her a debt of gratitude for her willingness to stand up and be counted — a champion for fairness and equal opportunity for all in making certain the game occurred on a level playing field. Lastly, America itself owes her eternal thanks for her service in World War II, taking risks and putting her own safety on the line to help bring Nazi war criminals to justice.

Alice Marble *was* a wonder of a woman.

A natural athlete with the ability to use her success for the greater good, a champion who led with her heart and soul. She fought hard for everything she got. Alice Marble didn't just step out of line. She leapt over it.

CHAPTER 2

WHAT THE NEXT DAY BRINGS

"Now you're going to see what the next day brings."

HILDA GIMPEL EISEN

The dark ashes fell slowly onto the still-smoking rubble, dead snowflakes softly blanketing the earth, hiding the death of an entire town. Below, two young people looked up at the dull sky. Like lost children, they made their way home after the end of the war, only to find — nothing. Their families and other Jewish people from Izbica-Kujawska had been murdered in the Chelmno death camp in December 1942. At the time, they didn't know what had happened — everyone was just gone.

The abandoned houses stood empty, mere shells. Both had struggled to find their way, but the hope that brought them lay buried under a pile of rubble. There was no one and nothing to come home to. When she was a girl, Hilda had loved to catch the sparkling snowflakes on her eyelashes and tongue. Now she was twenty-eight, five long years of her life gone to war. She tasted one of the bitter ash flakes that floated by. It felt like a last goodbye.

The Gimpels had been wiped out. Hilda's husband had been murdered by a vengeful Polish farmer. Harry Eisen was the last of his family, too, with the exception of his stepbrother, Abe, and his older brother, Mosche. Harry had never been good at schoolwork; he ran away from home at age thirteen. Hilda remembered him from those days, had seen him occasionally on his visits home, but she had been popular as a teenager. She didn't have time for shy boys then. Now it was as though she saw him for the first time.

"Hello, Harry. It is good to see you." She recognized him immediately, that wide smile, the dimpled cheeks. He was too thin, though, and nervous. She glanced at the man standing beside her, never quite looking him in the eye. He shifted back and forth, seemingly unable to stand still.

"It is good to see you too, Hilda. Thank God you survived. I've thought about you . . . I've thought about you a lot in these last long years." He didn't look at her either. In her

53

hand Hilda held a scrap of dirty cloth she'd found in what had been the kitchen, in the ruins of her family home. The small decoration she'd embroidered as a teenager was all she had left of her family. She used the dirty cloth to dab her eyes.

What did the next day bring? There was Harry, that was true. But there was no life for them to rebuild in their hometown. Hilda knew they would have to keep looking. It wasn't safe to stay there. The Poles were still hunting down Jews.

Hilda was born April 25, 1917, in Izbica, about 100 miles west of Warsaw, Poland. She was the second of seven children. Her father ran a small bakery in the Jewish neighborhood. While he was sleeping during the day, the children had to be quiet indoors and not disturb him. Her mother made sure each of the seven had their own chores to do. Because Hilda was older, she helped look after the younger ones. "We were spaced three years apart," she recalled. The younger children had chores like polishing shoes, doing dishes, and sweeping the floor. The others made the beds, cleaned floors in the bakery, and helped their mother haul sacks of grain.

Hilda's mother came from an entire family of grain dealers. As was expected, she went into the family business. She bought wheat, rye, barley, and oats from local farmers and sold them to mills in the area. There was a good rhythm to the family's life in the little town, where the smell of baking bread always made Hilda feel at home and safe. With seven children, there were times when money was tight, but they got by. Hilda and her brothers and sisters went to public school through the sixth grade. Their classes were comprised of about half Jewish and half German-Polish children.

Hilda didn't have any non-Jewish friends. The two communities kept to themselves, but that they didn't mix wasn't unusual. It was just how things were. As teenagers, Hilda and her friends would go to dances and the occasional movie. Sometimes they would go to nearby Lodz for the day. It was a big, bustling city to young Hilda, full of energy and spirit. Even if the girls didn't have a lot of money, Hilda and her friends enjoyed people-watching and looking in shop windows at all the fancy clothes. Her family spoke Yiddish at home, kept kosher, and observed Shabbat. Religion for them was more tradition than religion, Hilda recalled. It was just who they were, how they lived, and simply part of life in their neighborhood. Everyone Hilda knew spoke Yiddish.

Their childhoods, while far from perfect,

were still the stuff of good memories — of home and safety. Following World War I, the little town of Izbica prospered, growing to nearly six thousand inhabitants, over five thousand of them Jewish. That all changed in 1939, when both Russia and Germany invaded Poland, dividing the spoils between them. The Germans occupied western Poland. Russia took the eastern half.

By 1940, German soldiers began to occupy Hilda's hometown. Jewish businesses were shut down. Religious rites had to be hidden. The discrimination was blatant. Hilda and her family had to wear the yellow star, both on the front and the back of their clothes. "We just closed ourselves up in the house," she said.

But as the occupation took hold, the terror escalated. Hilda recalled with horror how German soldiers took the town's Torah and threw it into the street, forcing the older religious men (those with beards, she said) to spit and step on the sacred text before setting it on fire. Then the invaders destroyed the local Jewish cemetery and established a ghetto in the middle of town. The ghetto transformed the little town into a prison, enclosing the entire Jewish population, restricting movement, limiting food access, instilling fear, and slowly squeezing not only life but also the will to live from the inhabitants inside.

Hilda was twenty-two then, newly married, living with her husband David in their own small apartment. When her parents and siblings were taken from their home by German soldiers in the middle of the night, the couple decided to flee. They moved from town to town, scavenging for food, hoping David could get work as an auto mechanic. David's blonde good looks often proved to be an advantage. "He looked like a Goy," Hilda said. He didn't look like a Jew. For a while, a sympathetic German soldier hid the young couple in a barn.

Unfortunately, their freedom didn't last. While on the move to another small town, they were picked up by a Nazi patrol and forced into the Jewish ghetto in nearby Lublin. Hilda once described the ghetto as though she could still see the horrors happening in front of her. It was a movie that ran nonstop in her memory. "It was filth, it was hunger, fear." She shook her head as though to push the film from the screen in her mind. "You just couldn't believe what was happening around you."

Daily, she witnessed others being shipped out to concentration or extermination camps. Hilda was determined to do whatever it took to survive. And she took risks because she knew that she couldn't simply wait for help. No one was going to rescue her. She had to rescue herself. Of the more than forty thousand Jews living in the Lublin ghetto, only two hundred survived the Holocaust. More than three million Polish Jews were murdered in the Holocaust. Nearly two million non-Jewish Poles were also slaughtered, many as punishment for helping Jews escape or for hiding them. The killing often extended to the rescuer's family, neighbors, or an entire village.

But in 1940, no one could have predicted what was to come. There were thousands of people in the Lublin ghetto waiting, worrying, and wringing their hands with fear and indecision. They were trapped because they waited. The longer they waited, the tighter the Germans pulled the cinch on the trap. Hilda could see it coming. One day the Germans would come for them, and she had to make something happen for herself. "You survive if you have to," she said. "There's no other way."

Early in 1942, she talked a Nazi guard into opening the main gates to the ghetto, just so she could run an errand, she said — something she couldn't find at the market. It was a big risk and a poor excuse, but then,

German soldiers watch as women shop at the outdoor market in the Lublin ghetto. 1941. Photo credit: The U.S. Holocaust Memorial Museum courtesy of Evan Bukey.

he didn't appear to be a very smart guard. The guard opened the gate just far enough for Hilda to slip out, and she started to run. David squeezed through the gate behind her, just before it slammed shut with a final clang.

They kept moving, watching for random patrols, banking on the rumors they'd heard in the ghetto about where to go. The couple ended up in the nearby Parczew Forest, joining one of the growing ragtag groups of resistance fighters. The forest was thick with towering firs and had few roads, serving as an ideal location for organizing refugees,

Jewish fighters, and partisans to conduct guerrilla warfare against the Nazis. The forest was huge, Hilda recalled, about 500 to 600 miles in diameter. At night there were no birds calling to each other, no sounds at all. It was as though even the wind was afraid to push so deeply into the trees. Hilda, David, and their companions moved further and further into the deep woods, moving as far away from the outside world as they could. Inside the deep forest, time slowed. Hilda didn't know what month it was. She was aware of the seasons only because of the rush of a chill wind, a snowstorm, or a bloom of crocuses. Summer was pleasant, and Hilda wasn't cold at night.

In later years, she often said she could never be cold again. The partisans slept on the ground in the rain and snow for two winters, using the embers from the daily fires to keep warm at night. They did this by spreading the embers on the ground and then covering them with branches. It was tricky keeping the embers from catching fire again, but the coals kept them warm.

Their group emerged often to take on the Germans. There were many intense engagements with Nazi troops. The partisan group's organizers were former Polish soldiers and had access to weapons. They knew how to train civilians to use them correctly and execute small team tactical maneuvers. The partisans also used machine guns and had dynamite for blowing up railway tracks and bridges. They had Russian suppliers who sent ammunition, more guns, and of course, vodka.

A partisan unit in the Parczew Forest. Photo credit: The U.S. Holocaust Memorial Museum courtesy of Michael Temchin.

They picked up air-dropped Russian supply packages and requisitioned food from local farmers. Yet it never seemed they had enough. The women worked to steal beets or potatoes from local farmers, making potato soup in buckets over a small fire. They lived each day with the fear of capture, not just by soldiers but also by regular Polish citizens who hated Jews. They were afraid and always on alert, hyperaware for suspicious noises and always watchful on all sides for informants and spies. In recalling those days, Hilda said, "You never knew who to trust and who not to trust. There was so much espionage going on . . ." She sighed, remembering. "You either make it or you don't. You have nothing to lose."

It was early afternoon on Christmas Eve in 1943, or maybe 1944, Hilda couldn't recall. She had lost all sense of time since coming to the forest. She recalled that particular day because she could hear church bells in the distance, but the months fell away from her memory.

That afternoon, Hilda went off alone into the woods to get a bucket of water from a nearby stream. A Nazi patrol was lying in wait, ready to pounce on a woman out alone in the forest. She was quickly captured and searched. Once the soldiers found she was carrying a pistol, they tied her hands behind her back.

"How many Germans have you killed with this?" they screamed, waving the pistol in her face.

"None," she replied defiantly. They spun her around and marched her over to the next town, where a former schoolhouse had been transformed into a Nazi police station. The officers there gave her food, she recalled, and asked her if she had lice. "I haven't got no lice," Hilda replied in German.

The officer seemed puzzled. If she didn't come from the lice-infested ghetto, then she must have been hiding somewhere else. "So, where do you people sleep?" he asked. They couldn't possibly survive a Polish winter in the forests. No one could.

"Why, we sleep in the empty houses in all the villages," she lied. Hilda knew that explanation would sound logical to him, since all the Jews had been chased out of their homes or taken away to the camps. She would never lead the Germans back to the forest where her husband and the other partisans were.

She was given the opportunity to have a bath and change into some clean clothes the Germans kept in a storage closet. The next morning a guard brought her a large cloth bag full of straw. "Your bed," he said and pointed to the floor with a harsh laugh.

When he slammed the door behind him and locked it, Hilda had an uneasy feeling that there was another gift in store, one she wouldn't like. Leaning on the door, she heard sounds from the room next to hers and realized that the German officer was forcing himself on another woman prisoner.

She looked down at the lumpy straw mattress and with a sudden realization, she knew she would be next. If not that night, then the following night he would come for her. Or one of them would. Or more.

That absolutely wasn't going to happen, Hilda vowed. She opened the window in her room, climbed up on the windowsill, took a deep breath, and before she could rethink it, jumped from the second story of the old schoolhouse, breaking a bone in her foot upon landing in the courtyard. She stifled a scream and hobbled towards the perimeter fence, twenty meters away.

A Russian guard saw her, but he didn't appear to be overly concerned by her attempt to escape. "The Russians did their dirty work," Hilda explained. The Germans used Russian troops for work they didn't want to do, like guard duty. "They didn't like the Germans either." The guard watched her casually for a moment, then set his cigarette down on the ground, a red dot glowing behind Hilda as she hobbled away.

Time slowed. She could actually hear the rifle click as the safety snapped off.

Hilda sprinted for the fence, running now, skipping as fast as her broken foot would allow. The guard raised his rifle and took aim, then jerked the weapon down as he opened fire. Just a warning. Two shots echoed in the darkness. They didn't sound close at all, Hilda thought distractedly. She hit the fence and started to climb. The soldier continued to fire a few more rounds, aiming high over her head. Hilda didn't even hesitate, pulling herself up and over. She went down on one knee on the other side, got up and kept on running, ignoring the pain in her foot. The final shot sailed over Hilda's head. She knew he'd just decided to let her get away for some reason, but she didn't look back. There was no time to thank him.

Hilda ran on through the night, the full fifteen miles back to the edge of the forest. It was cold, and while she had socks, she had no shoes. The cold kept her moving. When she finally stopped, she realized that she didn't recognize her surroundings. She'd come to the edge of the forest, but which edge?

Hilda blinked. "Where am I?" She said aloud, her breath heaving clouds of mist out into the chill night. Hilda felt all alone in the world. But then she saw a light in the distance, and headed towards it.

Her foot was swelling and her side was bleeding. It was on fire where she'd slammed into the fence top before jumping. By the time she arrived at a Polish farmhouse, it was morning. The farmer saw her approaching and called his wife and son out of the farmhouse to look at the young woman with no shoes and ragged clothes. He asked her, "Are you the girl who jumped out of the police station?"

"What police station?" Hilda replied stoutly. The Germans must have been out searching for her during the night.

She bent over, her bravado fading quickly as the pain in her side surged. She knew she needed help. Reaching into a deep pocket, she pulled out her only bargaining chip, a 10 ruble coin, one David had given her after they'd stolen some money and guns from Russian soldiers. It was all she had. She paid the farmer to keep her secret and to get her back to the forest the next day.

He agreed, and she spent that night and the next morning hidden in a warm haystack. The farmer's wife brought her cheese and bread. By the following afternoon, he led two horses out from his barn and guided her back towards the edge of the forest, not far from her partisan group. She reminded him of his promise. After all, if anything happened to her, the "boys" in her group would come for him. They knew everything, she emphasized, including how to find him.

"I was pretty beat up," Hilda said, that

admission a massive understatement. Besides the broken bone in her foot, a tear in her side, and the damage to her feet, she was exhausted. Hilda fell off the horse into David's arms. He was overjoyed. He took the other horse, and they continued back to the camp. Once they arrived, David let the horses go. He was unwilling to leave her for even a moment. Hilda later said he thought that, like most horses, these two would know how to find their way back to the barn.

They didn't. Even horses got lost in the massive forest. These two ended up in a little lake at the edge of the forest and tried to ford it. They drowned. The Polish farmer found them the next morning, beyond angry at the loss of his horses. This was a major setback for his farm, his family, and his livelihood. He went into the town and talked about how the Jewish partisans had killed his horses. He got sympathy from the locals and promises of help with his plan for revenge. Unaware of the danger he was in, when David next went to town for bread and salt, the Polish townspeople took him hostage, then beat him to death.

Hilda was devastated. After all this time, all of the running, hiding, and fighting, for him to die this way was gut-wrenching. She kept to herself for a long time, staying in the camp and offering to sit with the few children while the others ventured out. It comforted her to be with them, though she feared what lay ahead for them all. She was still struggling to get her strength back, and even more difficult, to build up her will to go on. Despite the constant fear, the deprivations, and the tragedies, including the death of her husband David, she said, "There was no time for grieving."

By spring, the partisans got word that the war was near its end. German occupiers were being replaced with Russians. One spring day, Hilda was back on her feet and out scavenging for food with other women when she heard a girl in the fields nearby praying, exulting, and singing praises to God that the war was over. Was that true? Hilda wasn't certain. The partisans scattered when there was no longer any reason to keep fighting. Or rather, when there was no one to fight. The Germans were gone, the Russians on the move.

However, it still wasn't safe to travel, not for any of them. The Poles wanted their former Jewish neighbors gone completely. When it seemed that the countryside was settling down, Hilda traveled alone to Warsaw to ask for help. Warsaw, in the spring of 1945, was a city divided: half under Russian control and half under German control. Hilda went to the Soviet sector, where she met with a Russian general and pleaded with him to allow two regular Russian troops to escort her to visit her husband's grave, near that small town where the Polish people still hated her. She couldn't risk going alone. The Russian looked at her through narrowed eyes, then lit a cigarette. He pointed it at Hilda and replied, Hilda said, in "the dirtiest language a woman could ever hear." Fifty years later, she still remembered his exact words.

"You could walk out of here right now and die like a dog. Then another dog could come along and crap on your grave."

Even after everything she'd been through, the casual vulgarity still shocked her.

"What was your husband's name?" The general sucked hard on the cigarette.

"David," Hilda replied in a near whisper.

"David, hah. He was one lucky son of a bitch, that husband of yours. To have someone to grieve for him. No one is going to cry for you, you know. Or visit your grave. So why the hell should you even bother? The answer is *no*. I'll be damned if I let you use my men just to visit his grave. Now get out of here, you damned whore." The officer cursed her again in Russian, flung his cigarette butt at her feet, and walked away. She'd been dismissed.

Hilda was stunned speechless, but the slap of his words stung enough to dry her tears. His brutal response had the awful ring of truth. This was no different from her escape from the police station. If she were going to survive, she couldn't afford to let herself look back. She couldn't expect help or wait for someone to save her. Just like before, she had to save herself. It was time to look ahead to the future because what was done was done. "Day is day and night is night. Now you're going to see what the next day brings."

Later that summer, after the war's end, when she stood in the ashes of her hometown, surrounded by nothing but loss and death, she thought the next day had brought her nothing. Nothing but a scrap of cloth she'd decorated as a teenager and hung in the kitchen. She couldn't see any hope. Any future.

But Harry was there, standing right in front of her. Harry Eisen was born a month after Hilda, on May 15, 1917. His mother died of the Spanish flu when he was only three. His father remarried, and Harry was unhappy in the melded family. He had difficulty reading Hebrew and struggled against his father's wishes that he grow up to become a rabbi. According to Hilda and Harry's daughter Mary Eisen Cramer, he was probably dyslexic. Later, he ran away and ended up in Warsaw where he learned a trade, working in a factory that produced processed meats for delicatessens.

He had escaped from Auschwitz in January 1945 during a death march to another camp. Harry and his stepbrother Abe faded to the back of the column of marching prisoners and then sprinted into the woods at the first opportunity. They found a small cabin to hide in and stayed there for a few days, until it was safe to move on. Harry headed back to Izbica where there was no family waiting for him either. He was emaciated and scarred. Hilda was traumatized and alone.

Hilda knew when they were reunited that day in Izbica that they were among the few survivors in their town. As they stood side by side in the ashes, their eyes met. It was the summer of 1945. Poland was devastated. They were lost. The only way to go forward was together. They were determined to honor those they had lost and make their lives count for something. Hilda had stepped out of line to get a guard to open the ghetto gates and jumped out of a police station window to survive. Harry was ensnared and sent to the death camps but hung on until he could finally escape. They had made it to the other side of war. They found peace in each other. Hilda and Harry married immediately.

"I'll tell you the truth." Hilda recalled. "I got married out of fear; being scared to be alone in this world, no family, no friends," she said in an interview years later. "He had the same feeling. He didn't love me. I didn't love him." They moved on, searching for somewhere safe to settle. The couple made it to the border with Germany, and American soldiers admitted them. Russian soldiers gave them a ride to Munich, where Hilda's cousins lived.

Hilda and Harry Eisen's wedding photo.
Photo courtesy of Michael Rubinstein.

Together they shuffled from one displaced persons (DP) camp to another for three long years. The U.S. military had rushed to set up the DP camps, commandeering former Nazi troop barracks, concentration camps, even horse stables. When President Truman heard of the terrible conditions, he sent an expert on refugees, Dr. Earl Harrison, Dean of Law at the University of Pennsylvania, to investigate. According to the renowned correspondent Ruth Gruber, Harrison reported his shock at seeing some DPs sleeping twenty to thirty in a room, in bunks where thousands of Jews had slept before being gassed. He said American soldiers were treating the Jews much like the Germans had. The situation was deplorable.

Hilda knew they had to do something to pull themselves out of the situation. It was impossible to climb up and out of abject poverty in postwar Germany. Hundreds of thousands of people were barely surviving at the bottom of that same cliff. No food, no jobs, no homes.

She was determined to find a way out. Hilda managed to track down a distant cousin who was living in California. He offered to sponsor them so they could immigrate. There were quotas at the time, and immigrants had to show that they could be self-sufficient. Hilda's cousin generously sent enough money for their passage, and a new life could begin at last. It was the third time she escaped from the Germans. At last, freedom was going to stick.

In May 1948, the couple sailed to New York on the SS *Marine Flasher.* Hilda was pregnant with their first child, a daughter. After arriving at Ellis Island, they took a train to Los Angeles. They had no money; they didn't know any English. But they had the drive and the will to survive, which had long sustained them both. In America, as a non-English speaker, the only job Harry could get was cleaning out meat barrels in a hot dog factory in Vernon, California. They were staying with Hilda's cousin then. A life-long bachelor, he was wary at the thought of a crying baby in his home and wanted them to find their own home. The Jewish Federation helped the young couple find an apartment and got them started in their new life. Hilda and Harry saved their pennies until they had finally scraped together $5,000.

Once they had enough money, they bought one hundred chickens and started a backyard farm in Arcadia, near Los Angeles. Harry looked after the chickens. "I talked Jewish to my chickens and they laid eggs," he later said with a smile. Always organized and efficient, Hilda washed and packaged the eggs and Harry loaded them onto the back of his bicycle, selling them on street corners around the neighborhood.

There were many firsts in America. On their first Christmas morning in their first house together, Hilda opened the front door that morning to pick up the newspaper and discovered that their new neighbors had delivered an armload of toys for their young daughter. Hilda stepped back in surprise.

Suspicion and fear had been her only neighbors for years. She didn't know what to think. They hadn't tried to make friends, too afraid the neighbors wouldn't welcome her and Harry to the neighborhood. Their English was still clumsy, their accents thick. They were foreigners, alone in a strange new world.

"How did they know who we were? How did they know where we came from?" Hilda was amazed. She was still struggling to learn English and how to read the newspaper. "And then I realized it didn't matter. We were part of the community," she said. Kindness was another first to experience. Being accepted was a brand-new feeling.

Hilda and Harry would go on to have two more children. They continued to build their American life and worked hard to establish their business. They were natural entrepreneurs and quickly became successful. In the 1950s, they moved again. The town of Norco was only forty miles away but gave them the opportunity to buy more land so they could expand operations.

Now Harry managed the growing business while Hilda oversaw the chickens and egg production. It was a perfect partnership. Over time, their company, Norco Ranch Inc., became one of the largest egg distributors in the area. When they sold the business in 2000, it had over 800,000 chickens, approximately 450 employees, and annual sales of $100 million. Their major customers included Kroger, Safeway, Albertson's, Costco, Trader Joe's, and Jack in the Box. Until 2005, Norco Ranch was the largest egg producer west of the Mississippi.

But Hilda and Harry never forgot where they came from or how they got there. They became part of the Beverly Hills 1939 Club, the first organization in the area comprised of Holocaust survivors. The fourteen founders were Polish, like Hilda and Harry, and their goal was to care for each other, a "family forged out of hardship, perseverance, and hope." In 2014, the organization changed its name to the 1939 Society; it remains active in Holocaust education and witness.

Hilda and Harry also ran the Lodzer Organization of Southern California. For twenty-five years, the group, comprised of Holocaust survivors, gathered for social occasions and philanthropic events. The nonprofit donated to a long list of American and Jewish causes.

In 1998, Hilda and Harry presented a $5,000 check on behalf of the Lodzer Organization to Christoph Meili when the 1939 Club sponsored his weekend visit to Los Angeles. One year earlier, Meili, then a security guard at a Swiss bank in Zurich, discovered the bank was destroying documentation of Holocaust era assets. Meili rescued documents and ledgers from the shredder and smuggled them out of the bank, later giving them to a local Jewish cultural organization. That act made Meili a criminal, and he and his family fled to the U.S., seeking asylum. They arrived with no money, no home, and not knowing any English. Hilda and Harry could certainly identify with their story.

Those ledgers were much like the ones Alice Marble had discovered hidden in the bank vault at her lover's home near Geneva. And they provided the same kind of evidence of wrongdoing on the part of Switzerland's banks. By 1998, a lawsuit against

Swiss banks by Holocaust survivors and their descendants prompted a $1.25-billion settlement.

The support to Christoph Meili was one more example of Hilda and Harry's philanthropy in action. Their children sometimes didn't know the rationale for their charity, perhaps because they didn't know the details of their parents' wartime suffering. Hilda didn't want to talk about it. "They didn't feel comfortable burdening their children with horror stories," her daughter Fran Miller told the *New York Times* in 2012. "They were able to take their grief and become very philanthropic about it and very Zionistic and very into giving back. They felt fortunate to be on the giving end of charity rather than the receiving end."

Hilda and Harry also contributed to the building of the new Holocaust Museum in Washington, DC, and attended its 1993 dedication ceremony. Theirs was the first $100,000 donation to the new museum. Harry's interview is now preserved in the museum's permanent oral history collection. "We are the eyewitnesses . . . We went through hell," he recounted.

In 2016, Hilda donated an ambulance to Magen David Adom, the national aid society of Israel, in honor of her ninety-ninth birthday and in memory of her husband, Harry, who died in 2012 at age ninety-five. When Hilda passed away in 2017 at age one hundred, she proved that Russian officer wrong when he said no one would cry for her when she passed. Her passing was mourned deeply — by her three children, eight grandchildren, and seven great-grandchildren. Thousands across the country read her story and felt her loss as well. They were touched by the sacrifices she had made and the generosity she bestowed in her life.

One of their daughters said that what others often viewed as huge problems in everyday life seemed like nothing to Hilda and Harry. "They always said, 'Thank God we live in America.'"

Hilda Eisen was a living example of the power of will, a woman of iron determination to survive and prevail against overwhelming odds. She escaped: from a ghetto, out of a cell, through a forest, and into a stark and destroyed landscape where she picked herself up, married again, and escaped again, to a new and very different welcoming world. If the definition of hope is the possibility of change, Hilda Gimpel Eisen charted that course from possibility to reality.

Given freedom and opportunity, nothing could stop her or her husband. Hilda Eisen didn't choose to step out of line; she was forced out of her home, the life she had, and the future she'd planned. That path was destroyed. Yet, she still had a choice. And she chose, with courage that exists beyond words, to take that next step towards the new day coming and see what it would bring to her. Whatever it was going to be, she would make something of it. And because of that drive, because she took that step, her children are here today along with her grandchildren and great-grandchildren. She gave them all the gift not only of life but also of life with hope and meaning, the example of perseverance. It is a legacy of fortitude and resilience.

Hilda and Harry Eisen at their grandson's bar mitzvah in 1996.
Photo courtesy of Michael Rubinstein.

CHAPTER 3

THE LIFE OF A WARRIOR

"They gave me a gun, but I never carried a gun. What the heck was I gonna do with a dumb gun?"

STEPHANIE CZECH RADER

"Please stand if you served in the OSS." A small number of people rose slowly to their feet and looked at each other, scanning the room. There was a smattering of applause across the Smithsonian Institution's auditorium. Started in World War II, the Office of Strategic Services (OSS) was the precursor to the CIA. This special event in 2012 was to educate the public about the OSS and to honor the veterans present.

"Now then," the speaker continued. "Tell us your story. What did you do in the OSS?" He pointed at a man standing in the front row. "You start."

Some of the men had been translators. Others were in logistics, research, legal

81

services, visual information, or finance and administration. Finally, it was her turn. Hundreds of heads turned towards the only woman veteran in the room, Stephanie Czech Rader.

"I was X-2," Stephanie said in a low voice. There was a collective gasp that rippled through the crowd, then total silence. It's an old cliché that you can hear a pin drop in a quiet room. At this moment, no one dared to drop the pin.

Ken Elder looked around at the stunned crowd. He and Stephanie were neighbors in nearby Alexandria, Virginia. Ken and his wife had been friends with Stephanie and her late husband, Bill, for years. He hadn't even known she had served in the war until the OSS Society found her and told him. Once OSS personnel files were declassified in 2008, Charles Pinck, OSS Society president, went hunting. He found Stephanie at home in Alexandria. Since Bill had passed away in 2003, Ken began to accompany her to OSS events. She was shy, hung back, and didn't tell war stories or try to hype a book about the war like many other veterans did.

He had no idea what X-2 meant, but by the crowd's reaction, it had to be something important. The stunned veterans around them obviously knew. Stephanie had shocked everyone there. What hadn't she told him?

There were approximately 4,500 men and women in the OSS during the war. But Stephanie was one of only 650 assigned to the OSS Counter Espionage branch known as X-2. The ninety-seven-year-old lady with the white hair, thick glasses, and two rows of military service ribbons on her modest dress was actually a spy.

The moment of silence ended abruptly with an explosion of applause. One elderly gentleman stood up from his wheelchair and gave her a shaky salute. Others crowded around, asking her to autograph their programs. Stephanie was overwhelmed by the attention.

One visitor asked breathlessly if she knew Julia Child during the war.

"Julia Child was a clerk," Stephanie snapped.

She grabbed Ken's arm and told him, "I've got to get the hell out of here."

Ken understood. All the attention was too much. "People in that generation didn't ask for awards or recognition. And I know that as a woman, it wasn't part of the culture for her to ask."

Silence about service was a definite part of the OSS culture as well. The OSS Society found in her file that she was nominated

Major Stephanie Czech Rader at the OSS Society's William J. Donovan Awards Dinner in 2012. Photo courtesy of Rebecca D'Angelo.

for the Legion of Merit not once, but twice. She never received it. She wasn't awarded the Bronze Star either. "Like many of those who served so heroically in the OSS, she was never properly recognized for her heroism," said Charles Pinck, president of the OSS Society.

The Legion of Merit is an Armed Forces award given for especially meritorious conduct in outstanding service or achievements. It is one of only two awards to be worn around the neck. The other is the Medal of Honor. The award is typically presented to senior officers or those serving in positions of significant responsibility.

Charles Pinck visited Stephanie several times. He told the OSS Society membership about her service. He told her friends and neighbors, like Ken Elder. He wrote to Senator Mark Warner. They began a concerted campaign to see her recognized. She didn't seek any recognition for what she'd done. In fact, she hadn't participated in any OSS events until she was found out. Then she began to tell her story.

Stephanie Czech was born in 1915 to Frances and Vincent Czech in Toledo, Ohio. Her parents were Polish immigrants. They barely spoke English, and the family later moved to an immigrant neighborhood in Poughkeepsie, New York, where there were other Polish families they could relate to. Growing up in a working-class immigrant neighborhood, Stephanie heard a variety of languages around her. But she had learned Polish first, English only when she started school.

"When you get to school and everyone is speaking something different, for survival you have to learn in a hurry." Stephanie not only learned her parents' language but also developed a perfect native accent, Polish mannerisms, and exact cultural awareness. She learned Polish history. If necessary, she could pass as a native Pole.

She was a good student in high school, and eventually, a teacher with a sharp eye for talent took a personal interest in her. What she saw in Stephanie was potential — ambition, intellectual curiosity, and drive, even if the girl couldn't see that for herself. The teacher, a Cornell graduate, submitted an application to Cornell on Stephanie's behalf, without telling her. Sponsorship and a personal recommendation were important. Cornell listened.

Stephanie was overcome with gratitude to learn she'd received a full four-year academic scholarship to Cornell. She knew she could have never afforded college otherwise and vowed to make her high school teacher proud. That scholarship, while generous, only covered her tuition. She waited tables in the cafeteria to earn a little more money for her books and living expenses. Her parents even sold their wedding rings to support her getting started. She had to pull all the other strings together for herself.

Stephanie graduated with a BA in chemistry in 1937, becoming the first member of her family to earn a college degree. She believed that her Cornell experience was instrumental in shaping her future life. The discipline, ability to meet deadlines, time management, and interpersonal skills she learned in college enabled her to take advantage of any opportunity that came her way.

Captain Stephanie Czech. Photo courtesy of *The Women in Military Service to America Foundation.*

Cornell was proud of Stephanie too. A trailblazer, they called her. A pioneer in the sciences. But as the Depression continued to hit the U.S. economy, Stephanie Czech had trouble finding a job. Finally, she landed a position as a translator of scientific studies with Texaco in New York City. It wasn't a path she would have chosen, but she knew other opportunities would come. When the

United States entered World War II, she decided to serve her country. As a first-generation American, she wanted to give back and thought military service offered a chance for her to prove herself. She raised her right hand on September 8, 1942, and was commissioned into the Women's Army Corps. At the time, Stephanie was twenty-seven years old, just five feet two inches tall, and a mere 111 pounds.

Over three thousand women applied to join the Women's Army Corps (WAC) in 1942. Only eight hundred were initially accepted, and Stephanie knew she was lucky to be one of them. She was sent straight to WAC training at Fort Des Moines, Iowa, and then helped train newly enlisted female soldiers. It was a fine job, but Stephanie wanted to do more that showcased her skills — whether in chemistry, analysis, or even her Polish language skills. She could do more than teach marching and military terminology to new soldiers. She had just been promoted to captain in 1944 when she learned the OSS was recruiting.

President Roosevelt established the new intelligence agency and put Major General William "Wild Bill" Donovan in place as the first director. Stephanie recalled, "They were interested in anybody with a language capability, and I spoke Polish." Stephanie applied and was accepted in 1944, then was assigned to the elite X-2 branch. It seemed like a perfect fit.

The OSS had two operational divisions. The Strategic Services Operations Division had oversight of Special Operations (SO). The Intelligence Services Branch X-2 was responsible for counterintelligence operations overseas.

Since she would be posted to Europe, her operational training took the usual seven months. It involved all of the skills she might need to observe and report on potential enemy agents. She learned how to surreptitiously pass messages, follow a target without being caught, and maintain her cover story under interrogation, and received more weapons training. Captain Stephanie Czech finally arrived in Warsaw in September 1945, one of only two OSS officers in the country and the only one who spoke Polish.

As the war had technically ended, the OSS was no longer a functional agency. President Truman had signed the order terminating the organization on September 20, 1945. By October, it was history. Only two branches were spared: Strategic Intelligence (SI) and X-2. Responsibility for Stephanie's mission fell to a temporary organization dubbed the Special Operations Unit. Unfortunately, the creation of the new Central Intelligence Agency (CIA) was still a year away. Stephanie was truly on her own.

She arrived in Warsaw just two weeks after General Eisenhower visited the destroyed city. He'd been shocked at the sight of block after block of flattened buildings and streets full of rubble, what the newly arrived U.S. ambassador had termed "a study in despair." Stephanie could see why. She went straight to the U.S. embassy where she was supposedly employed as a clerk. The embassy was housed in the Polonia Hotel, one of only a few surviving buildings in Warsaw's city center. It included the consular offices for eighteen other countries. The embassy staff also had rooms there. Given the housing shortage, Stephanie was glad her cover story included her within their ranks.

Inside the hotel there was electricity, heat, and food. Outside there was darkness, hunger, and chaos. The entire city of Warsaw was rubble; the ruins of the Warsaw ghetto were still smoldering. It smelled of death. Crime was rampant, violence was commonplace, and it wasn't safe to walk around at night. People lined up in the streets with buckets to get water from the public fountains. They averted their eyes from the frowning

Polish Security Police and clusters of bored Soviet soldiers. Deportations were common. Stephanie saw them, the dejected lines of ragged Poles, headed for the train station with guards pushing them onto cattle cars headed for Siberia.

Everyone in the embassy warned the new girl, told her to be careful, to look out for herself. Stephanie noticed there were no streetcars and only a few automobiles. Bicycles were at a premium. Arthur Lane, the U.S. ambassador, briefed her about the embassy's local nationals being harassed by the Soviets and threatened with death if they didn't spy on the Americans. He gave her an overview of the political situation and the upcoming supposedly free elections.

Everything about life in postwar Poland made her uneasy, but Stephanie set out to do her job. With a scientist's objectivity, she decided that the danger was a risk factor, but one that could be managed.

Her cover story, coupled with her native language skills, accent, and cultural knowledge, made her believable as young woman desperate to find members of her family in the chaos of postwar Poland. In a borrowed embassy car, she traveled north from Warsaw, reporting on Soviet troop movements, collecting data on the Russian and Polish

Security Services, and building her files on the country's economic and political situation. She traveled to the southeast, taking notes and searching.

Stephanie was often the first American to travel to some of the remote villages she visited. Occasionally, she actually found distant relatives of her parents and visited with them for several days, all the while continuing her observations. "You had to be very careful who you talked to," she remembered. "And the Russians were always watching."

Her parents had immigrated to the United States from Galicia, a region in southeast Poland, near Lublin. When she drove to southeastern Poland, she had to pass through areas where there had been death camps and towns were still burning from the destruction of ghettos, including Izbica, where Hilda Eisen's family had lived.

At times, it seemed like Poland was the crossroads of Europe. There were thousands of refugees and displaced persons on the roads. They weren't just Poles but came from every country, running from what had happened or trying to go home — sometimes to nothing. While the chaos made Stephanie's story about family seem more plausible, it also meant she had to stay hyperalert when asking questions. Mixed in with those refugees were former Nazis, spies, criminals, and killers.

Stephanie developed her own methodologies for gathering information. She had no parameters or specific directions for her actions. There were no rules for her to follow. There was no playbook. She set her own hours, planned her own travel. She didn't work for or with anyone in the embassy and filed her reports with OSS offices in Berlin or Paris. Her reports were thorough and detailed, objective and informed. They were generally well received. There was one exception though. Someone in the Paris office didn't like her reporting. Or perhaps more accurately, they didn't like that a woman could be such a good counterintelligence agent. While she would never find out their identity, her being female would ultimately be reason enough to betray her.

By December, the embassy moved to a new building in the city. Ambassador Lane was continuing to grow his staff, which would reach two hundred by the end of 1946. But tensions with the Soviets were increasing. In late December, the U.S. Naval attaché, Marine Lieutenant Colonel Andrew Wylie, died in a fall from a damaged bridge in western Poland. The fog was thick in the region, and an accident was likely — but there were rumors it wasn't an accident. At least he was in uniform. Stephanie didn't even have that protection. She traveled in civilian clothes with a false identity, and she refused to carry a weapon. "They gave me a gun, but I never carried a gun," she said. "What the heck was I gonna do with a dumb gun?"

In January 1946 she was asked to travel from Warsaw to Berlin, delivering classified documents to the OSS office in the U.S. embassy there. Stephanie agreed reluctantly. All travel was difficult, especially for a woman alone. As the Cold War was beginning to settle in, grievances and boundaries were both being aggravated and set in stone. Harassment of Americans at the embassy was ratcheting up. She didn't feel comfortable carrying a packet of materials she couldn't explain.

At first, the mission appeared to go well; Berlin was a welcome break from chaotic Warsaw, although her visit was short. Days later, when she was ready to head back to Warsaw, the OSS Station Chief called her to his office. When she entered, he handed her a package of highly classified documents.

"I'm not a courier," she said. "Don't give me that stuff. I don't want it." She took a step back.

"We just need you to take these. The

ambassador needs them. It's information he needs to have when he speaks to the Russians." The package was sealed. Stephanie shook her head. No. She didn't want to know what was inside.

"It's just too dangerous." She folded her arms, hands away from accepting the package. "Come on. Can't you find someone else?"

"There is no one else." The Berlin OSS chief held out the package, wagging it up and down.

"Don't ask me to do this again," Stephanie said, reluctantly taking the package from him. She meant it, too.

She tucked the packet of classified documents inside her trench coat. When the train stopped at the border checkpoint between Germany and Poland, she prepared to get off with the other passengers. Stephanie had a bad feeling. Her stomach hurt, a sign that something was off. As the train huffed to a stop, the nagging feeling intensified. She recognized it as an internal warning. It happened several times when she was driving in southeastern Poland, a sixth sense that told her a Russian patrol was ahead or bandits were around the next bend. She willed her breathing to slow.

Stephanie took her time exiting the train,

checking all the windows first. Her internal sensors were set on high. Scanning for danger, she stepped off the train and saw a cluster of Russian security agents observing each of the passengers. They weren't even checking papers, just waving them on by.

"They were looking for me. I just knew it." Stephanie didn't stop. She swallowed hard, straightened her collar, and stepped down, taking the conductor's arm. Eyes straight ahead, she maintained her casual pace. She couldn't run. They would chase her. Besides, there was nowhere to go. She couldn't keep the documents because they'd arrest her. She thought about the operatives who had disappeared, then thrust the thought away. No time for that. She wasn't going to let them send her to Siberia.

She calmly assessed her options and settled on a course of action. It only took a moment. When the agents glanced back at another train exit, she intentionally bumped into another passenger.

Stephanie cried out as she staggered and dropped her purse, going down on one knee. The man stopped and set his briefcase on the ground. He helped her up and took her arm.

"I'm so sorry," he said. "Are you all right?" Stephanie looked down at her ruined stocking.

"I'm just fine," she said and forced a tight smile. She looked around distractedly, patting her pockets. "Oh, I've left my glasses on the train. I'm going to have to go back. Look, would you mind taking this for me and dropping it off in the city? I'm going to be late," she said, holding out the package. "So late." She looked as though she might cry. "I'll be in trouble with my boss," she said. Stephanie sniffed.

He agreed immediately, red faced. Apparently, he thought he'd tripped her. *A little guilt never hurt anyone,* Stephanie thought. She gave him the package of documents and an address for delivery. She watched as the Good Samaritan disappeared into the crowd, probably eager to get away from her.

She straightened her coat and continued on, making certain she walked right past the Russians. "Stop!" one of them shouted. Two agents took her arms and arrested her. Stephanie played her part. She was the indignant American citizen who objected to being stopped and questioned. She was just a mere clerk who happened to work at the embassy.

The soldiers seemed disappointed to find nothing incriminating on her person or in her bag. Stephanie was relieved and glad, too, that she hadn't carried that dumb gun.

She was permitted to leave and reported the arrest as soon as she arrived back at the embassy proper.

Over the next few days Stephanie could tell that Russian surveillance of her activities had intensified. They followed her to work. They followed her home. She saw men on the street watching her apartment at night. What she didn't know at the time was that her cover had been blown by a superior officer in the Paris office. Official files referred to the event as "an act of gross negligence," but there was no mention of repercussions. Stephanie never found out who had outed her. She could have easily been killed because of the disclosure, and she never forgot it.

Her bosses wanted to immediately send her back to the states, where she would be safe. "I can still do my job," she insisted. She had started on a mission, and she was damn well going to finish it. Stephanie remained in Warsaw for several more weeks to complete her reports. She enjoyed leading her Russian watchmen around the city. They didn't try to stop her again.

A successful field operative, she was never captured. She was never wounded. She simply carried on, inspiring confidence and respect from everyone who worked with her.

Exterior view of the American Embassy in Warsaw.
Photo credit: The U.S. Holocaust Memorial Museum,
courtesy of Antionette Powell.

Despite the unknown traitor in the Paris office, Stephanie had a major fan club inside the European X-2 community. Her bosses were so impressed with what they termed her "unusual coolness and clear thinking" that they nominated her for the Legion of Merit, a high-level Army medal. It wasn't just for her performance at that risky border crossing, but for all of her other counterintelligence as well, the risks she had to take, and the dangers involved — everything she had to endure in order to get the job done. The nomination continued, "Her outstanding qualifications were such, that the

American Ambassador himself concurred and endorsed her assignment." Major General Donovan signed off on the recommendation on October 10, 1946.

She was back in the United States by the time the award was submitted, having returned in February 1946, but as she had insisted, it was on her own terms. She married Colonel William S. Rader that September. He was a decorated pilot who flew bombing runs in the Pacific and later in Germany. Stephanie retired at the rank of major and went back to school. She was working on her master of science degree in chemistry at George Washington University when Poland held parliamentary elections in January 1947 and the Soviet-backed Communist party took over. The Cold War was officially underway. Her job was done, and, to Stephanie at least, it looked like the Soviets had won.

Her husband continued on active duty with the Air Force, reaching the rank of brigadier general and earning the Legion of Merit himself. She traveled with him throughout the remainder of his Air Force career.

Bill retired in 1968, and they settled in Alexandria, Virginia. Together, Bill and Stephanie ran a car rental business in the 1970s and later invested in real estate and served as landlords for commercial properties in the city. They were both car lovers and in 1950 bought a baby-blue Cadillac. For the next forty-four years, they faithfully recorded every tank of gas, oil change, and repair made to their Caddy. In 1994, they had it restored to showroom condition, then donated it to a museum.

Stephanie and Bill were together for fifty-seven years until Bill passed away in 2003. He was buried at Arlington National Cemetery with full military honors.

Stephanie received only the Army Commendation Ribbon upon her retirement from active service in 1946. It was a relatively low-level award. That award was later redesignated as the Army Commendation Medal. But even that would have been nowhere near what she'd been recommended for, nowhere near what she deserved. The recommendations for her to receive the Legion of Merit and the Bronze Star were denied with no explanation given. As it was being dismembered, the OSS had neither the standing nor the political clout to push the award through. And there were internal comments that the War Department approving authorities didn't understand how dangerous her job really was.

"It was because she was a woman, that was

part of it," said Michael Golden, another of Stephanie's long-time neighbors in Alexandria. He didn't know about her history as a spy until the OSS Society came calling. She'd never said a word.

Once Golden knew, though, he had to tell. The secret was practically ready to burst out of his mouth. "After I found out, I outed her at her ninety-fifth birthday party" in 2010. Even so, it was hard for him to believe the "dog-loving, ukulele-playing senior citizen on his street had been a spy."

Even her family didn't know anything about her past. Her niece, Kathy Roxby, wasn't aware of her wartime service until her one-hundredth birthday. "She said she was supposed to keep it a secret." And she did. But the fierce warrior in her makeup occasionally peered out from behind the mask.

Another niece, Linda Hobbs, said that while she too was surprised by the news that her aunt was a spy, it actually made sense. "She was tough, let me tell you. As a kid, I was a little scared of her."

The campaign continued for Stephanie to receive the award she deserved. In her later years, she participated in events with the OSS Society and joined the Cayuga Society, a group of Cornell alumni donors who make major bequests to the university. In 2014, she was pleased to participate in Cornell's sesquicentennial celebration at the Warner Theatre in Washington, DC. There she was welcomed onstage to thunderous applause from her fellow graduates. Michael Golden and his wife Margie were with her to celebrate that day.

"Stephanie was a strong, intelligent, motivated, decent person with strong opinions masking her wonderful sense of humor, who believed that her Cornell experience created opportunities that she otherwise wouldn't have had," Golden said. "She paid that back full bore through her dedicated military service in World War II and afterward."

In 2012, the OSS Society recognized her with the inaugural Virginia Hall award, named for another trailblazer and spy who also served in the OSS. The OSS produced a video of Stephanie receiving the award and told the story of her service. She was also a life member of the Special Forces Association. Membership in this alumni group was very tightly controlled. Stephanie had to provide documentation of her wartime experiences. Once she cited her work with the OSS, there were no further questions.

As she neared one hundred years, her health began to fail. But the fight to get her the Legion of Merit continued. Virginia senator

Mark Warner took up the fight in the fall of 2015 to get her justice and worked with the Army to get the medal approved. "Stephanie Rader was a trailblazer for women in the 'old boy network' at the OSS, and we can find no legitimate reason why this commendation was denied, other than the pervasive gender discrimination which existed in the early days of the American intelligence community right after World War II."

He told it like it was.

The medal was finally approved on May 21, 2016. But it was four months too late. Stephanie Czech Rader had passed away on January 21. Senator Warner said, "Stephanie Rader was a patriot, and I am very, very pleased we were able to work with the Army, her family, friends and former OSS colleagues to right this historic wrong. Stephanie Rader will be buried at Arlington National Cemetery with the honor and respect of a grateful nation."

The Legion of Merit was presented at her funeral on June 1, 2016, at Fort Myer Old Post Chapel, just outside the gates of Arlington National Cemetery. It had taken seventy years for her to be recognized. The citation read, in part, "Captain Czech, charged with grave responsibilities, displayed outstanding abilities in the successful fulfillment of her assignment. Her courage, cool headedness, and foresight were of great benefit to the mission to which she was assigned."

The citation reads like many that were meant to award people whose work was classified or high risk. But there is no doubt about what she did and how much it meant to the OSS and the nation.

While a mentor opened the door for her to get into college, it was Stephanie's own tenacity and drive that pulled her through to graduation. She continued to forge her own way, carving out a path to service. She used every skill and talent she had to make a difference working in counterespionage for the United States. As one of only two OSS agents in Poland just after the end of the war, she understood the danger she was in but was determined to serve both the country of her birth and the home country of her parents. No one else could have done what she did the way she did it. Her cool mindset while traveling alone and unarmed through the most difficult and dangerous circumstances in Poland in the early postwar days with little to no guidance was a testament to her courage. With tenacity and objectivity, she completed the mission she was given — to observe, evaluate, calculate odds, and take necessary action. She set the stage for new generations of agents to follow in her footsteps — innovating and creating as she went along. She wrote the playbook for serving undercover in a volatile environment where allies were rapidly transforming into enemies. When threatened with arrest by Russian soldiers, she faced them down. Her time with the OSS may have been short, but her impact left a lasting legacy.

Army captain Azande Sasa, the chaplain who spoke at her funeral, summed it up best. "Stephanie chose the life of a warrior," she said. "She has earned her place among those honored here."

The final salute for a warrior. Photo credit: Rachelle Larue, Arlington National Cemetery.

CHAPTER 4

A GOOD INFLUENCE

"It was then that I realized how important women can be in a war-torn world."
ELIZABETH PEET MCINTOSH

"I've got it! An earthquake! That's what we need — an earthquake." Betty liked the idea. She liked it a lot. But around the table there were shaking heads. No one agreed? That didn't make sense. The guys always liked her ideas. She had ingenious, subversive ideas.

"Come on. What about having him predict an earthquake? That might shake up the Chinese and Japanese," Betty said. She was brainstorming a radio program with her team in the Morale Operations (MO) group of the OSS in Kunming, China, one hot summer afternoon. It was early August 1945. Betty fanned her face with a torn copy of *Yank* magazine and wiped a wet handkerchief across the back of her neck. The

Germans had already surrendered, and it was time to ratchet up the pressure on the Japanese to do the same. Maybe their little "black propaganda" radio station could play a role in killing Japanese morale.

Betty tapped a pencil on her desk like a Morse code message. She was still thinking about what their program host could say. The seer was a Chinese radio personality known simply as the Hermit. The Hermit was a hugely popular figure in the station's program lineup, telling stories based on his knowledge of astrology and making predictions about the future. The target audience for "Operation Hermit" was Japanese soldiers and collaborators in occupied China. His predictions were based on a combination of the stars, the Chinese calendar, the Japanese calendar, and any other sources Betty and her team could conjure up. The Hermit typically predicted something that had already happened and then congratulated himself on his prowess. His track record was 100 percent using this method, but now they needed something dark and frightening. Something brand-new

One of Betty's supervisors didn't agree with her idea about predicting an earthquake. "They're always having earthquakes in Japan." A prediction about another one, even if it were a big one, wouldn't impress anyone.

"Then let's have a tidal wave to go with it," she tried again.

"No, that's nothing either." The other team members threw their hands up. They didn't have any better ideas.

"Fine. I'll think of something," Betty replied.

In the end she didn't have to think of anything specific. She just told the Hermit to be vague and predict something truly disastrous. Something apocalyptic. He agreed. The Hermit went on the air and cautioned his legions of loyal listeners, "Something terrible is going to happen to Japan. We have checked the stars and there is something we can't even mention because it is so *very* dreadful, and it is going to eradicate one whole area of Japan." His hushed tone conveyed a deep sense of foreboding.

It sounded terrifically ominous. Betty was pleased.

The next day the United States dropped the atom bomb on Hiroshima.

Her boss, who would later become her second husband, Colonel Richard Heppner, came into the conference room, his face pale. Stuttering, he asked her, "How — how did you know about the bomb? That information was top secret."

"I didn't," she said. "We just made it up. It's what we do." Further up the chain of command, other bosses weren't so certain. It was a terrifically accurate guess, one that might well have compromised the entire operation.

There was some explaining to do, but Betty took it in stride. She'd been involved with the developing roles of information and influence since the beginning of the war and knew how to handle herself — with irreverence, just the right amount of wit, and sometimes, but only sometimes, a little humility.

Elizabeth (Betty) Peet grew up in Hawaii, the daughter of journalists. In 1940, she got her start writing for a Honolulu newspaper, covering sports, just like her father. Eventually, she found sports writing to be boring and asked to cover current events and general news. Instead, she found herself writing for the women's pages — fashion, recipes, and personal advice. Newly married, she and her first husband, Alex MacDonald, had been staying with a Japanese family in Honolulu, learning their language and customs. On December 7, 1941, they were listening to a Sunday morning radio music program when the broadcast was interrupted with a hysterical announcement of an attack at the nearby Navy base.

Betty got into her car and headed out to cover the story, whatever it might be.

Betty was twenty-six years old.

At first, she couldn't believe anything had happened at all. It was a typical warm Hawaiian day. The sun was shining brightly, the winds were calm, and the air sweet with bougainvillea. Along the highway, people were just coming out of church. As she drew closer to the city, she could see something was wrong.

"Then, from the neighborhood called Punchbowl, I saw a formation of black planes diving straight into the ocean off Pearl Harbor. The blue sky was punctured with anti-aircraft smoke puffs. Suddenly there was a sharp whistling sound, almost over my shoulder, and below, down on School Street, I saw a rooftop fly up into the air like a pasteboard movie set."

She spent the remainder of that day in a trance, witnessing death, carnage, and unbelievable scenes of destruction throughout her hometown. It was the random nature of the killing that somehow affected her the most. And people kept calling her — asking for information, guidance, wanting to know what they could do to help, whether or not

111

they should volunteer, and could she get a message to a loved one. It was overwhelming.

Betty wrote about what she'd seen that day in a column addressed to the women of Hawaii, exhorting them to find a way to help and make a difference. "It was then that I realized how important women can be in a war-torn world." She continued persuasively, "There is a job for every woman in Hawaii to do."

But her sharp descriptions of death and destruction were too much for Betty's editors to stomach. They refused to publish the opinion piece. It finally appeared in print for the first time in the *Washington Post* in 2012, seventy-one years later.

In 1942, she left the local paper for a new position with the Scripps Howard newspaper chain. Betty asked to serve as an overseas correspondent, but the media company sent her to its Washington bureau instead. Betty was disappointed. But she came to enjoy Washington, even as she chafed at its restraints. Her beat was covering the White House and First Lady Eleanor Roosevelt. The insights into Washington politics were eye-opening, and the potential to influence large audiences through her writing was a new and heady experience for Betty. She liked how the First Lady supported women, including programs such as Women Airforce Service Pilots (WASP). At the time, her views on women having their own careers was heady stuff.

One day in January 1943, Betty was assigned to interview an influential businessman from Hawaii. It was difficult to get in to see him, but she finally managed to snag time with the man. As they began talking, she learned he was a friend of her father, and the interview proceeded more easily as they chatted about mutual friends and the war situation in Honolulu. At the conclusion of their session, he asked Betty casually, "Wouldn't you like to get into something . . . more interesting than the work you're doing?"

"That depends," she said cautiously. "I want to serve overseas. Support our war with Japan. I witnessed Pearl Harbor, remember. And I speak Japanese."

"I think we can make that happen," he replied.

He didn't come right out and say "spying," and Betty didn't know he was really an influential friend of Major General Donovan, the founder of the Office of Strategic Services (OSS). But she was intrigued. When the offer came to join the OSS, she said yes without a moment's hesitation. It was a situation of mutual need: the OSS recognized what a catch they had in Betty, particularly given her language skills, writing ability, and news media connections, and Betty was looking forward to a real challenge that went beyond the newspaper's "Women's Page."

Several weeks later she reported to OSS Headquarters where she was fingerprinted, issued a badge, and told not to talk about anything she knew. Betty thought that was funny because she didn't know anything yet. But that would change very quickly. Training for new OSS members took place at several locations requisitioned by the agency, including state parks. Betty's field training occurred at the prestigious Congressional Country Club in nearby Potomac, Maryland. The OSS had requisitioned it for training and billeting agents newly returned from overseas.

Because of the OSS emphasis on self-reliance and self-confidence, there was considerable attention paid to "toughening up." Betty's physical stamina and endurance improved. She learned how to pass messages to other operatives in a clandestine manner, how to detect surveillance and lose a "tail," and how to handle explosives. And like Stephanie Czech, she also learned how to conduct an interrogation and handle a firearm. She later recalled, "We fired guns. We burrowed into sand traps for cover. I learned to throw grenades on one of the fairways." Betty admitted it had taken her a bit to get the hang of firing a machine gun. "The gun weighed more than I did."

But she definitely learned she was not the spy type. One instructor told her she was "an open-face-sandwich, with enough imagination to conceive a plausible MO cover story but with absolutely no histrionic ability to carry it out as an active agent." Undoubtedly, Stephanie Czech scored more highly in this aspect of the training, particularly since she knew she would need to use that training to survive in the field.

After Betty's experience with the machine gun left the Country Club fairways chewed up with .45 bullet holes, she was glad that part of the training was over. As a golfer, she was mortified at the sight of the pristine fairways transformed into a scarred battlefield, but as a trainee "undercover girl," she had to admit it had been great fun. Once dismissed from weapons training, Betty headed for familiar ground. "I went back to the club and directed all my attention lovingly to a two-and-a-half-pound offset agent press (a printing press) of bright aluminum. It didn't work well but I had it under control," she said dryly.

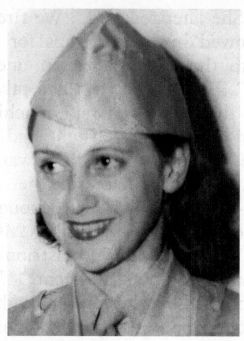

Betty in uniform. When she traveled, she used the cover of serving as a WAC second lieutenant. Photo courtesy of CIA.

Betty found herself assigned to the Morale Operations (MO) Division. Major General Donovan had earlier lost a political battle to retain control of the Defense Department's War Information Office, so he created a distinction between the "white" information — that which was intended for home audiences — and "black" information, which was intended to influence enemy actions through the spread of disinformation, lies, and psychological intimidation. Black information was most effective if appearing to originate within the enemy's homeland, so much of MO took place overseas. It looked as though Betty might get a chance to prove herself at last.

The MO Division had two branches, one for the Far East and the other for Europe. With her Japanese language skills, Betty knew where she would go. Her job title was intelligence agent, but today's moniker might be more descriptive — perhaps something in the arena of information operations specialist, or psychological warfare specialist, or even disinformation manager. But a title never mattered to her anyway.

Members of the Far East group at the OSS HQ were an eclectic bunch. They were cartoonists, artists, reporters, broadcasters, and writers. There were one or two Chinese artists attached to the office and a few Japanese prisoners of war (POWs). Betty quickly learned that this was the group for nonconformists. "They didn't react to authority well," she later recalled. They didn't stand when senior officers entered the room. They didn't care about protocol and didn't call the bosses "sir." They didn't salute, and their uniforms were rumpled and often quite a mess. Betty liked them immediately.

There were thousands of women serving in the OSS during World War II, but only nine hundred served overseas. Betty was determined to be one of them. Her first posting was to New Delhi, India. Her first husband Alex was in OSS training by then and would eventually be posted to Ceylon, now known as Sri Lanka. Betty had talked with the OSS about recruiting him once she was on board. Now they were in the same business but not assigned in the same location. They would grow apart during the war, and afterward the two divorced amicably. Betty and Alex remained friends for life.

Betty was just getting used to her New Delhi office colleagues and their mission when she was invited to dig through bags and boxes of papers and other items recently brought back from Japanese units destroyed in the Burma (now Myanmar) jungles. At the bottom of one moldy bag she found a surprise — a cache of clean, dry postcards. They were from young Japanese soldiers, part of a unit that had been wiped out a month earlier. The simple messages that never made it home were each written in pencil, with a censor's stamp firmly in place on every single one. They were good to go.

She had a thought. "Let's erase the original messages. Substitute our own. Then send them on. Maybe we can sow a little discord at home. Parents, wives, and girlfriends aren't going to like it when they find out that their boys are losing."

"And the government isn't supporting them either," another MO staffer added.

"That's right! Better to surrender than lose." The others nodded. They got the idea. "And," Betty added, "Those families are going to complain too. Hope they go straight to Prime Minister Tojo."

Betty and her OSS colleagues. Photo courtesy of CIA.

Her colleague Willi was first to give it a shot. He picked up one postcard and erased the words about fighting for the emperor and country and penned a new message: "Where are the supplies from home? We are starving in the jungle!" Soon others joined in, and Betty told them to hammer home the main theme — the Japanese were losing in

Burma and the home front wasn't supporting them. It took three days, but by that time Betty and her colleagues had completed 475 cards. The doctored postcards went back in their original pouches and later were slyly slipped back into the Japanese mail system and forwarded on to Japan. It was the MO office's first "black mail" project to reach the Japanese mainland. A week later, Japanese Prime Minister Tojo and his entire cabinet resigned. The tide of the war was turning, but Betty wanted to think that the propaganda postcards played a role too.

Later, the team intercepted a military order from the Japanese high command that emphasized the policy that Japanese soldiers would not surrender in battle. *What if?* she thought. It was a perfect opportunity; with a new prime minister and cabinet in place, maybe it was time for them to make a policy change. Betty decided she would help the new leadership do just that.

Allied soldiers had found that Japanese soldiers, when faced with certain defeat in battle, would fight even harder, to the death. They had been indoctrinated that surrender was dishonorable and disgraceful. Betty drafted a new policy with a twist, one much more lenient that gave soldiers a way to surrender with dignity. Betty added the direction that the order was to be distributed to all forward units. The completed forgery was passed to a local Kachin agent who killed a Japanese courier and stuffed the false order into his pack. It was psychological warfare at its finest — establishing authenticity for the document. Later reports proved that the forged order had been passed on as intended and disseminated. It had a direct impact on Japanese soldiers' willingness to fight to the death. Surrenders increased.

Following the success of the courier project, Betty finally got her wish. She was being reassigned to Japanese occupied China, arriving there early in 1945. By that time, she was an experienced MO operator, highly skilled at "persuasion through subversion." She had undertaken hundreds of disinformation and psychological operations, and she was always thinking of ways to find more opportunities to deceive, influence, and manipulate. She said, "Someday, I knew, I should have to write a straight news story again and be a civilized human being. I drifted off to sleep thinking how dull it would all be."

In typical Betty fashion, she was getting used to her new surroundings and feeling out how the new job would be. One day after lunch at the base mess hall, a friendly dog approached her, tail wagging. She played fetch with the dog for a while and then returned to her desk. The cocker spaniel accompanied her as though he worked there too, then curled up at her feet. Later that afternoon, Colonel Richard Heppner, the director of the OSS unit in China, walked by her desk. He noticed the tip of a reddish tail on the floor by her purse and stopped short. The wagging became a heavy drumbeat, and a happy cocker spaniel emerged to lick his hand.

Betty with Sammy, the matchmaking dog.
Photo courtesy of Ms. Linda McCarthy.

"So, that's why my dog Sammy defected," he said with a smile. "MO strikes again!"

"But he followed me," she protested. "All I did was throw the ball."

Colonel Heppner then officially introduced Betty to Sammy. The three became fast friends. Sammy stayed with Betty whenever the colonel traveled, and Sammy obligingly split his time with them.

One of Betty's early assignments in Kunming was more operational than usual for the MO group. The task set had Betty recalling everything she had learned in her earlier training at the Congressional Country Club. This time it didn't involve false narratives or passing on disinformation, but she did prepare instructional leaflets, teaching Chinese agents how to use dynamite to disrupt Japanese troop movements. Next, Betty was given a firsthand introduction to how the operation worked.

It was what the OSS termed a "black joe." Explosives had been formed and shaped to look like a lump of coal. One afternoon at a crowded train station, Betty pulled dynamite from her coat pocket and furtively passed it to an OSS Chinese operative. She didn't make eye contact or speak. She simply passed the item on and continued to walk, melting into the crowd of disembarking passengers. Betty didn't know what happened afterwards. She wasn't meant to. Once the war ended and she and Richard began dating, she asked him.

Later, he told her, the agent then boarded another train packed with Japanese soldiers and tossed the dynamite into the train's engine just before it reached a bridge. He jumped to safety and the entire train blew up as it crossed the bridge. Betty was horrified. She'd had no idea.

"I felt very badly," she said years later. "I felt that this one piece of coal that I was responsible for killed all these men." She tried to tell herself, "Well, not really. I was just the one who handed it to the guy who did the job."

Days after the Japanese surrender in August 1945, the Kunming Special Operations Group was given an important assignment, the last OSS operation in China before President Truman dissolved the OSS. Betty and the entire staff were involved in this final mission, Betty playing a small part as a runner, carrying messages from the command center to the communications office.

Colonel Heppner was ordered to immediately proceed with the mission of "locating, contacting, and protecting Allied prisoners of war and civilian internees at camps scattered throughout China." Kamikaze pilots were still executing missions, and there was a fear that American POWs would be executed by overzealous Japanese soldiers. In a matter of hours, eight separate operations were underway to contact Japanese-run POW camps throughout China and protect the American POWs and civilian internees. Betty continued to read the dispatches as the teams landed and proceeded to rescue Americans. One in particular caught her eye.

Seven man OSS team under Major Stanley Steiger parachuted from B-24 flying about 250 feet above internment camp at Weihsien, Shantung Province, where Japs converted former Presbyterian Mission into prison for 1,500 civilians. Internees, overwhelmed by sight of men dropping from plane with American flag on underside of wing, defied armed Jap sentries, burst through gates to greet liberators.

One of the civilian internees liberated at Weihsien was a twelve-year-old American girl, Mary Taylor. She and her brothers and sister had been separated from their parents for five years. The rescue day, when she witnessed angels dropping from the sky, would stay with her for life.

The MO group received numerous commendations on its performance from OSS

HQ. While the plaudits were welcome, Betty noted wryly that she was never recognized for the last subversive act she performed before returning to the states. She had created a set of very real-looking official travel orders for Sammy. The orders entitled him, as a military working dog, to legally travel, and Sammy flew home like any other returning soldier. The beloved Cocker Spaniel stayed with Colonel Heppner's mother in New York until the colonel and Betty could come for him. All three were reunited later and resumed their friendship. That friendship grew into love, and Betty and Richard were married in the springtime garden at Betty's grandmother's home in Connecticut in 1946. Sammy happily attended the reception.

After the excitement and challenges of psychological warfare in World War II, it was hard to adjust to the relative quiet of peacetime. Betty left the OSS just before it was disbanded. One day while at headquarters, she saw several brand-new agents enter the building. Stephanie Czech, on her way to Poland, was among the new recruits. Her adventure was just beginning. Betty found it hard to believe that her wild ride was nearly over.

While completing her out-processing

paperwork, she learned for the first time about OSS operations in Europe and was fascinated with the stories she heard about the agency's top spy, a woman named Artemis. Artemis was the code name for Virginia Hall. Betty was consumed with abject admiration. The stories of Artemis's courage were the stuff of legends. Later, as Betty was leaving the OSS headquarters for the last time, she took a final look at the OSS Honor Roll on the wall. "There were only a few who had received the Distinguished Service Cross, and Artemis's name was high on the list."

But Betty faced a tough adjustment getting back to plain old reality. Becoming a civilized human being again was as boring as she once feared. Betty took a job with *Glamour* magazine as an editor but found the work so profoundly mind-numbing, it was untenable. A bounce to a broadcast media position with Voice of America was somewhat better, but the work was still not important enough to satisfy her. Then Richard was nominated for a senior job in the Defense Department and served as deputy assistant secretary of defense for international security affairs. Betty kept searching for something comparable. She took on various assignments within the Defense and State Department and the United Nations (UN).

She was doing important work, but the new rhythm didn't last long. In 1958, when Richard died at his desk of a sudden heart attack, her friends urged her to go back to the life she loved. Betty finally agreed, and one day she sought out CIA director Alan Dulles in Washington and asked him to hire her.

"Where do you want to go?" he asked.

"Japan," Betty replied. The rules were still the same. Her conditions were the same too. It was going to be overseas or nothing.

"When do you want to go?"

Betty smiled. She was back.

The CIA wasn't the OSS, though. It was more bureaucratic and less creative, she found. Still, it was the same in other ways. Betty found herself in another male-dominated organization that treated women operators as an anomaly and not the norm. It didn't faze her. "I guess I developed something that helped me, maybe. An attitude." She'd learned another lesson too. "I learned to be covert about things and not to shoot my mouth off."

In 1947, she wrote a memoir about her wartime service, titled *Undercover Girl*. Major General Donovan, former director of the OSS, wrote the introduction, calling her a "most effective agent." His only criticism about her book, now out of print, was the fact that she described him as "penguin-shaped."

"Well, he was," she said later.

She also wrote two children's books, and later, the spy history book she was eventually best known for, *Sisterhood of Spies: The Women of the OSS,* in which she featured the careers of many of the approximately four thousand women who served with the OSS during the war. Ever the reporter, Betty was clearly fascinated with the stories of the women she featured in her book. Virginia Hall, especially, remained one of her heroes.

She recalled later, "The war meant women could do a lot more than they'd been allowed to before. Where I was there was equality and openness between the sexes. That's what made it work." They could collaborate. They respected one another, and they could brainstorm as equals. She reveled in that atmosphere. It made her better as a professional, she thought. It made them all better.

Betty had several overseas assignments with the CIA. On one of her missions in Japan, she met a handsome fighter pilot named Fred McIntosh. They were married in 1962 and stayed together for forty-two years, until he died in 2004. As for her work with the CIA — she never talked about it.

Yet Betty remained extremely interested in

the CIA's progress in continuing to provide opportunities for women to excel. She wrote extensively about the agency's progress in hiring, promoting, and encouraging women to serve, carefully tracking the promotion of many to the executive levels. She quoted from a speech by Nora Slatkin in 1996: "We cannot afford to waste the talents of women or minorities now, any more than we could in the days of Donovan and the OSS. We still need the breadth of view that only a diverse work force can provide."

She retired from the CIA in 1973, then became involved with the OSS Society and edited their newsletter. "Like siblings separated at birth, 'Donovan's Dreamers' began to find one another again." A number of them kept in contact over the years, and in 2012, several of those still in the Washington area were invited to a special event. Betty was being recognized as one of the Virginia Women in History honorees, an annual award sponsored by the Library of Virginia. Her longtime friend, CIA historian Linda McCarthy, had nominated her. Betty was in an assisted living facility at the time, but the Librarian of Virginia came to her, along with a number of OSS veterans. It was a party and a reunion to remember. Later she said that it was one of the happiest days of her life since before her husband passed away eight years earlier.

On March 1, 2015, she received an invitation to visit CIA headquarters. Director John Brennan hosted a special one-hundredth birthday celebration for her that day and said the "CIA is honored to count Betty McIntosh as one of its alumnae . . . Her many achievements and storied life are an inspiration to all women, and particularly so to those of CIA. It is fitting that Women's History Month begins each year on March 1, the birthday of Betty McIntosh."

"I'm glad I was in the OSS," she said at the celebration. "It was a wonderful experience, and I cherish it as the most exciting part of my life."

That special party was her last. Betty passed away six months later.

She had led a truly exciting life, and in many ways, her ingenious, subversive ideas helped write the book on current propaganda programs, psychological operations, and information operations directed against a specific enemy. She made a difference to the war effort in the China-Burma-India theater in many ways that few ever knew or could understand. She continued that work after the war during her time with the CIA. Betty had a sharp sense of humor and the ability to not take herself too seriously. She played as hard as she worked and got along with her colleagues — as equals. Always as equals. She wouldn't have it any other way.

Betty's one-hundredth birthday party at Central Intelligence Agency headquarters. Photo courtesy of CIA.

CHAPTER 5

THE LIMPING LADY

"I must have liberty with as large a charter as I please."
**HIGH SCHOOL YEARBOOK QUOTE,
VIRGINIA HALL (GOILLOT),
AGE EIGHTEEN**

"Over you go."

Virginia waved her hand with an elegant flourish, inviting her three American colleagues to climb over a sagging fence in the middle of a marshy field. She stayed back, a field guide she'd hired through the embassy at her side. It was a mild winter day in December 1933, and Virginia sniffed the crisp air with approval. She was out for a nice afternoon hunting snipe with friends from the U.S. embassy in nearby Smyrna (later Izmir). The weather was mild, the sun shining, and the conversation stimulating. It was a much-needed break from the inevitable yawning monotony of a clerk's dull daily life.

133

"You next," the guide said with a slight bow.

"All right," Virginia answered. She loved hunting and fishing, and the Turkish countryside was an area of abundant wildlife that boasted numerous opportunities for the dedicated sportswoman to enjoy the outdoors. She was eager to begin the hunt.

As she stepped forward and lifted her right leg to stretch it over the tangle of old fencing, her left foot angled slightly on the damp ground, slippery mud over wet grass. The grass squeaked in warning. Tucked under her arm, the 12-gauge shotgun shifted, the trigger catching on her coat pocket.

Bang! Flocks of birds burst into flight from the surrounding trees and scattered into the sky, their formation a black question mark against the clear blue background. They streamed out of sight, screaming back at the hunters as they fled.

Ten seconds. Ten short seconds, and her life changed forever. She would relive those life-changing ten seconds over and over again for the rest of her life.

Her horrified friends gathered around her.

"Oh my God, your foot!"

"Stop the bleeding."

"We've got to get her out of here."

"A tourniquet. How do you make a tourniquet?"

She was unconscious by the time they reached the car. But the improvised first aid on the part of her friends most likely saved her life. At the Istanbul American Hospital, doctors determined that an amputation of her left leg below the knee was the best chance they had to save her.

Virginia "Dindy" grew up near Baltimore, Maryland, the daughter of a wealthy family who encouraged her love of learning and relentless drive. As a high school senior, she had longed for a charter of freedom, the freedom to write her life script herself. She would be in control of what happened, wherever it might go, at whatever cost. There was nothing she couldn't handle, but she had to at least get to the starting gate first.

She went to Radcliffe and then Barnard College, but the classes there didn't challenge her. Her parents didn't consider it unusual to send their young daughter to Europe unchaperoned, so she attended university at the Sorbonne in Paris, then in Vienna, graduating in 1929. With her knowledge, background, language, and now cultural expertise, she had become more qualified than many of the men she met in the diplomatic service. With the righteousness of the young, she was certain nothing could stand in the way of her pursuing a career in the diplomatic service.

She was wrong.

Virginia applied for her first consular position at the age of twenty-three. Unfortunately, her initial applications were turned down because she was a woman. She lowered her sights from serving as a foreign service officer and focused on the clerical job listings. *That* finally worked. It took three years for her to break through, but by 1931 she had at last scored the prize of employment. It was a minor one, an entry-level job as a clerk at the U.S. embassy in Warsaw. It meant filing, typing, answering the phone, and carrying messages between offices. But she was there, finally on the inside, ready to make her mark and sure she could find a way to move up. Unfortunately, once there, she was just another invisible clerk, on a path that was another dead end.

Her first experiences in Warsaw were enough to captivate her attention, at least outside the office — a new city, new language, new people — although the novelty wore off quickly. A Polish military liaison officer named Murat offered to show her the city. Warsaw's charms were distracting from the boredom of the work. They dated, casually at first, then seriously. Two years later, when the relationship began to stall, Virginia requested a transfer and was relieved to soon find herself on the Orient Express, steaming south through Ukraine, Romania, and Bulgaria toward the border with Turkey.

Unfortunately, her new job at the American embassy in Smyrna, Turkey, was no different from the last. It was not going to feed her hunger for meaningful work. She decided she needed to prove herself if she was going to advance in her career. Virginia was no clerk. She could type and she could file, but she wasn't very good at administrative work and definitely didn't try to improve. She didn't have the patience, though at least she got to read the diplomatic correspondence and learn about the political upheaval in Europe. Things were changing fast, and she wanted to be in the center of the action, not filing papers on the sidelines. She applied for the Foreign Service and was turned down. It was the mid-1930s, and she tried to convince herself she was lucky to have gotten this far. It was a hard lesson to learn that determination and preparation were meaningless when it came to regulations and an unmovable institutional prejudice.

And now, she'd had the accident with the shotgun. Following the amputation, she spent several days in a drug-induced haze.

One night, Virginia recognized a visitor in her hospital room. Her father came to her, held her close, and asked her to fight. If not, he promised he would come back for her. She knew it was him — his voice, the smell of pipe tobacco and bay rum. He called her "Dindy," her nickname from childhood.

"Can you be strong?" he asked. She said yes. She promised her father that she would fight for herself, and he sang her to sleep.

The next day, Virginia realized that the nighttime visit was just a dream. Her father had died two years earlier. But she'd made a promise to him to fight for herself and her charter of freedom. That much was real. Once she had recovered enough to travel, she returned to the United States for months of difficult recuperation. Every step forward was forged in pain. Learning to walk again while trying to hide the constant ache from the prosthesis was all a trial. But she was nothing if not focused on the future.

The prosthetic leg and brass foot weighed seven pounds altogether, fastened to her upper thigh with a tight girdle that then attached to a belt around her waist. The buckles dug into her skin. The straps cut off her circulation. She gave the contraption a random nickname so she would have someone to blame for her troubles. "Cuthbert" was a constant companion and unpredictable trickster who always tried to hold her back, trip her up, or throw her to the ground. He was cursed loudly and often.

She took her pain and frustration and focused it on the job search. With a renewed sense of determination and resilience, she kept applying for positions overseas. In 1934, she managed to secure a position with the State Department, this time with the American embassy in Venice. As with her other roles, this position had no potential for advancement either.

Once in Venice, she applied for the Foreign Service again. By some strange chance, the oral questions never arrived at the embassy for a member of the ambassador's staff to administer to her. She would have passed the test easily, she knew. She had the language skills, was loyal to the United States, and understood how embassy staffs conducted business under the direction of the State Department. There wasn't much more to the test than that. An incomplete meant automatic failure. Was the omission somehow sabotage? It didn't matter. She'd failed a second time.

Virginia didn't give up. She checked all the requirements very carefully. This time she'd gotten everything done and submitted on time. "Third time's a charm. Third time's a charm," she whispered. Fingers crossed. One day she would be the first female ambassador for the United States. But first she had to get a foot in the door. Even if it was a prosthetic one.

When the third letter arrived, Virginia tore the envelope open. Although she expected the results, it was still a disappointment. The third time wasn't a charm. "We regret to inform you. . . ." She didn't need to read any further. Virginia was rejected this time

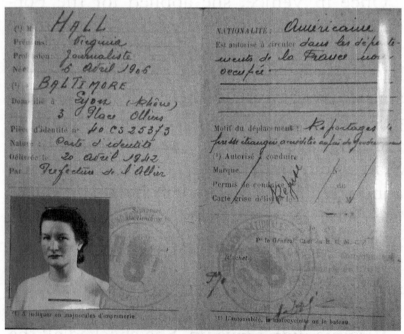

Virginia Hall's French Identity Card.
From the Lorna Catling Collection at the International
Spy Museum. Used with permission.

because she had a disability. Finally, the agency had a legitimate excuse for telling her no. The State Department didn't hire women as consular officers. Particularly women with disabilities. It didn't matter that she had the right degrees, spoke six languages, and had experience in the European theater. Her dreams seemed light-years away.

Dismissed, belittled, and ignored, Virginia couldn't get anywhere in fulfilling her dreams of adventure and making a career for herself in diplomacy. She had been fighting the system for nearly ten years. She was thirty years old. Something had to change. It was time to look for a back door.

It didn't matter that she proved her disability wouldn't get in the way. Upon learning she was to be reassigned to Estonia to yet another dead-end clerk position, Virginia resigned and made her way to Paris.

When World War II broke out in Europe, she volunteered to drive an ambulance for the French and managed to wrangle a part-time job as a stringer for a newspaper. The agreement was that she would write the occasional article describing living conditions in occupied France, and the paper would pay her by the word. It was just enough to give her press credentials without being too demanding on her time.

Soon after the country fell to the Nazis in 1940, Virginia finally had a bit of luck. She was on her way to London when she met an undercover British agent, George Bellows, at a railway ticket station in Spain. Bellows couldn't help but be impressed by the tall, elegant woman with the flaming red hair.

"May I help you?" He offered. "I'm a salesman and I've got a lot of experience with the frustrations of arranging wartime travel. Allow me to be of assistance?"

"Thank you," Virginia replied. "I'm very grateful." Once the train was underway, they began to chat. He asked about her ambulance driving during the fighting, and how she felt about France's surrender to Germany. Virginia didn't hold back. She recounted her stories of food shortages, curfews, and random shootings. While she was careful as always in what she revealed, Bellows was amazed at her courage under fire, her recall and observation of details of occupation life, and her passion for helping the French fight back.

"So, what are you going to do for a job once you reach England?" Bellows observed her closely.

"I don't know. I'm afraid I might have to

drive an ambulance again." Virginia didn't want to admit she didn't have any idea what she was going to do next. She didn't want to have to go crawling to the U.S. embassy to beg for a position. But that was possible.

"Listen, let me give you the number of a friend. Will you give him a call when you arrive? I think he can point you in the right direction." Bellows handed her a card with a phone number on it, and Virginia pocketed it absently.

Some months later, she was surprised to find herself talking with a senior officer in the British Special Operations Executive (SOE) F Section, a secret paramilitary organization. F Section was responsible for operations in France. The SOE was looking for agents who were more like special forces operators than spies. A spy would observe German forces planning to cross a bridge and report the movement to HQ. An SOE agent would simply blow up the bridge. Virginia knew which option she would choose.

Her unique experiences, language capability, and drive at last made her the ideal candidate for a job, an operational position. The British took a chance on her, and she wouldn't forget it. Virginia became the SOE's first female operator. She was prepared for the job, whatever it might entail

— recruiting other agents, helping Allied prisoners and POWs escape, or blowing up bridges. It didn't matter to her. She was going to go up against Hitler's forces. She was ready.

In the summer of 1941, Virginia Hall arrived in Vichy, France, and registered at the local police station. She used her real name and said that she was a reporter for the *New York Post*. That much was true. Then she spent weeks getting to know community leaders, doctors, police officers, black market merchants, and many others, on both sides of the law. Tall, with shining red hair and a pronounced limp, the elegant American made an unforgettable first impression. That would later prove to be a hindrance; the last thing an operative in the secret paramilitary force needed was to be memorable. She did occasionally file stories with the *Post,* writing about mundane topics like wartime shortages of butter and milk, but she always maintained her vigilance. Occasionally, she would embed coded messages in her news reports, meant for her SOE bosses in London. She began to develop a network of Resistance members and set up locations for safe houses for downed Allied pilots, spies on the run, or anyone wanted by the Nazis. She was laying the groundwork, getting the logistics support system in place, and preparing for what was sure to come.

Once America entered the war following Pearl Harbor, she was obviously too conspicuous. Virginia was forced to go underground. At one point, she had over twenty aliases and could transition her appearance, cover, and purpose as often as four times in a day. She had her wigs, glasses, extra clothing of all types, and her language skills. But she couldn't hide her gait. Her French comrades coined the nickname *la Dame Qui Boite:* the Limping Lady.

She ran safe houses and directed Resistance members through a loose network of colleagues. They established an "underground railroad," helping downed Allied pilots and former POWs escape to Britain. She filed detailed reports on the role of the weak Vichy occupation government in cooperating with German occupiers and the increasing crackdown on Jews. She was careful, always ready to move, cautious about whom she talked to. Or trusted. It bothered her that she didn't have a radio. Using the radios belonging to other agents put her at risk.

But she was creative with other means of communication. She would put a geranium on the windowsill of her flat when there was a pickup scheduled. The message itself could be hidden behind a loose brick in a certain wall or in a note left at a special café. She always had two potential escape routes and several new identities waiting. But despite her best efforts to remain in the background, she was becoming famous for her successes. Lyon Gestapo chief Klaus Barbie came to hate her, having learned of her exploits from members of the French Resistance he tortured under questioning. But he never could discover her real identity, name, or nationality, mistaking her for Canadian.

"I'd give anything to lay my hands on that Canadian bitch," Barbie complained. All his double agents were tasked with finding her and bringing her in. The order read, "The woman who limps is one of the most dangerous Allied agents in France. We must find and destroy her."

They failed. But there were wanted posters everywhere with a fairly accurate drawing of Virginia. The risk of being caught by eager Gestapo agents was becoming too great to ignore. Once the Allies invaded North Africa and Nazi troops began pouring into France, Virginia Hall, once a hunter, quickly became the hunted.

One night in November 1942, one of her contacts slipped a copy of the Gestapo wanted poster under her apartment door.

She gasped at the sight of the drawing. It was clearly her, and Virginia thought anyone else could probably see the resemblance as well. There was still so much work to be done, but if she was captured it wouldn't make any difference. Virginia had shot herself once and remembered it too well. The thought of a firing squad was too much to bear. She went on the run that night.

Days later, Virginia linked up with a few other Resistance members and a guide to lead them straight into the snow-covered Pyrenees mountains. There was no other choice. The only way to avoid capture at a border crossing was to cross undetected into Spain. Just before the final trek over the last of the mountaintops with her companions, Virginia transmitted a final message to the SOE, letting HQ know her situation.

"We're ready to make the final leg of the journey," she reported. Their guide waited impatiently. Virginia knew she couldn't rest for long. If the guide knew she had a wooden leg, he probably wouldn't even have come.

"Is everyone okay?" the SOE operator asked.

"We're fine," Virginia replied. "Cold and tired, sure. But we'll make it." She sounded more upbeat than she felt. They were at 7,500 feet. The air was thin and icy. It was snowing, and the radio battery was going dead. They couldn't stop for long.

"Roger that," he said. "We'll be watching for you. Do you need anything?"

"Well, Cuthbert is being bothersome," Virginia transmitted, blowing out a long breath. She winced, feeling blood seeping from her stump.

The radio operator on the other end was new; he didn't know Virginia's story. He assumed "Cuthbert" was an enemy agent. "If Cuthbert is giving you trouble, have him eliminated," was the response.

They all had a good laugh at Cuthbert's expense as they continued through the drifting snow, Virginia using her good leg as a snowplow, dragging the seven pounds of dead weight behind her. The cold was biting, the pain constant. Virginia could feel cold blood congealing on her upper thigh as the corset straps from the artificial leg dug into her flesh.

Once across the border, Spanish officials demanded to see their papers. Having entered the country illegally, they were tossed into jail immediately. The American embassy intervened, and within six weeks, Virginia was released and reported back to her SOE contacts in Madrid. While she was in Spain, Britain's King George VI recognized her work with the SOE, awarding her the Order of the British Empire. She asked that there be no public ceremony. It would have called too much attention to her work. She simply mailed the medal home to her mother for safekeeping.

The good life in Spain was quite different from her undercover work in France. Virginia found her time in Spain reminiscent of her earlier work with American embassies in the '30s. It chafed at her need for freedom, the liberty to make her own choices, and the satisfaction that could only come from doing important work. She wasn't being challenged enough.

After four slow, mind-numbing months, she requested a return to France. "I am living pleasantly and wasting time," she reported. "It isn't worthwhile, and after all, my neck is my own. If I am willing to get a crick in it, I think that's my prerogative."

Her superiors were reluctant to grant her request. With her cover blown, they thought it too dangerous. But Virginia persisted. She requested training as a radio operator, hoping to improve her usefulness to the cause. The SOE sent her back to London, and she began to learn how to operate the wireless and learn Morse code. At the same time, she was recruited to work for the U.S. Office of

Strategic Services (OSS). The OSS was only too happy to take on the now experienced spy, and Virginia signed up with the rank of second lieutenant. Now she was getting somewhere.

Because she was unable to parachute in, Virginia had to return to France at night, across the channel by British torpedo boat. She landed along the coast of Brittany, near the port of Brest on a dark night in March 1944. Virginia's new code name was Diane, or sometimes Artemis, and she had changed her gait, now walking with the unrecognizable shuffle of an old woman.

Assigned to the Haute-Loire region in south-central France, Virginia's new disguise was as an elderly milkmaid. She dyed her hair gray, wore multiple layers of clothing to appear stout, and moved slowly. Virginia spent time at a series of farms, appearing old and infirm. She learned to make cheese, shepherding sheep, or sometimes goats, out into the fields, scanning for potential Allied drop zones.

OSS Agent Betty McIntosh heard about Virginia's role in France in late 1945, just after returning to the states from China. Awed by the story of Virginia Hall's exploits, she said, "I preferred to think of her as a sort of Goddess of the Moon Drops, waiting for our planes, watching the skies for mushrooming parachutes with their precious supplies, tapping out a message that another bridge had been blown, sending the words from some thatched mountain *place d'armes,* or from the back of a French truck."

Reality was much less romantic. Virginia walked bent over, using a cane, shuffling like she'd been taught in order to hide her limp. Her mission was focused on intelligence support to the upcoming invasion, keeping an eye out for Nazi troop movements, battle preparations, and drop zones while she slowly roamed pastures with goats or sheep. D-Day was in the works, and she was going to hamper the Germans' ability to fight back. It was time to disrupt and destroy the enemy's lines of supply and their routes back to Germany.

After dark, she could move a bit more freely. Many nights Virginia could be seen with members of her team out in the fields, coordinating drops of supplies and arms. Using a wireless radio powered by an old car generator, she would tap out her messages while a young Resistance member would stay at her side, pedaling hard on a reconstructed bicycle, its motion recharging the radio's battery.

Supplies and weapons being dropped into France for the Resistance. Photo courtesy of CIA.

Her communications style was instantly recognizable. The OSS London office always knew when she was calling in. She reported German troop movements, bombings, and identified areas for the dropping of supplies. By early 1944, the Nazis had become adept at tracking radio signals, and they recognized their old foe's style too. Patrols crisscrossed the countryside looking for the Limping Lady.

It seemed that everyone knew D-Day was coming. Virginia and her team armed and trained three battalions of Resistance fighters. "Be ready," she told them. In her final report to OSS headquarters in London in June 1944, she stated that her team had "destroyed four bridges, derailed freight trains, severed a key rail line in multiple places, and downed telephone lines." She made things as hard for the Germans as she could, slowing their retreat, preventing escape for many, and rendering them incapable of fighting. Virginia and her team also killed over 150 enemy soldiers and captured at least 500 more.

Virginia Hall set the stage for Allied success in France. Her Resistance network was so successful that there was no support from the south of France to German forces in Normandy. The Allies continued to flow freely into northern France, and they seemed unstoppable. Virginia took great satisfaction in that knowledge.

She continued running her teams of fighters throughout that summer and fall. By early 1945, she and OSS Lieutenant Paul Goillot were given the task of building a new undercover network in Austria. They were a team by then, in a relationship forged through shared trust and the shared experiences of war. They never made it to Austria. The rapid collapse of Germany meant the mission was canceled. She and Paul returned to London in April 1945, just before the war ended. She would spend time after Victory in Europe Day writing her reports commending those who assisted her.

Following the war, President Harry Truman wanted to recognize her wartime service with a medal presentation at the White House, but she demurred. Instead, Major General Donovan presented her with the award in his office at OSS HQ at Washington's E Street complex.

In a subdued ceremony, he quietly pinned her with the Distinguished Service Cross (DSC), the sole American woman to receive this prestigious award in WWII. Her mother came along, the only witness. The citation read in part, "With utter disregard for her safety and continually at risk of capture,

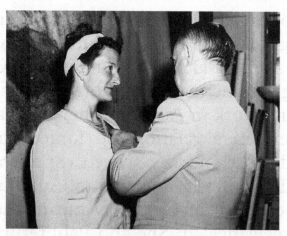

Virginia Hall receiving the Distinguished Service Cross from OSS Chief Major General Donovan in his office. Photo courtesy of CIA.

torture, and death . . . she directed Resistance Forces in extraordinary acts of sabotage and guerrilla warfare against enemy troops, installations, and communications."

The DSC is the Army's second highest award for heroism in combat. It ranks just after the Medal of Honor. The French government awarded her the Croix de Guerre avec Palme (a military award presented to those who fought with the Free French Forces during WWII).

By then, avoiding attention and declining recognition had become a way of life. It was also safer that way, she felt. "It was just six years of my life," she would say. "Subject closed." In 1950, Virginia married former Resistance fighter and OSS Lieutenant Paul Goillot. While he was eight years younger than her and six inches shorter, they were a perfect match.

After the war, it seemed as though the old barriers of discrimination she'd encountered at the State Department had been transferred wholesale to a new bureaucracy, the legacy child of the OSS, the Central Intelligence Agency. Virginia joined the CIA in 1947 as one of the first women to serve in the new agency. But it wasn't as challenging as she expected, and without an operational mission, she felt useless. Virginia resigned a year later, rather than sit behind a desk. But she couldn't stay away for long.

In 1950, at the age of forty-five, she rejoined the agency and was assigned to the French paramilitary desk where she hoped to continue to make contributions to the field of clandestine warfare. After all, the OSS had rated her performance during the war as exceptional, calling her one of the chief pioneers in the field of espionage. Maybe she could be called upon to teach? That didn't happen. Or serve overseas again? That wasn't possible either. She was still a woman, reason enough, but she was also now older and disabled. She made a few short trips to Europe with her husband Paul to do some clandestine work but, for the most part, was tethered to her desk at CIA headquarters, where her performance reports were laced with faint praise and bland commentary. Later, she became one of the first female members of the select Career Staff (permanent, with tenure), but even that small achievement took six years.

She could have complained. But that wasn't her nature.

"Why don't you ask for a new assignment?" other war veterans asked her. They understood how difficult it was to deal with the stodgy bureaucrats.

"I don't think it's right to try to capitalize on my experiences," she would reply.

"But . . ."

"No," she would answer firmly. "People I knew, knew well, died in this work. I have to respect that." She had seen some horrific scenes of murder. This kind of a conversation always brought up the memory of several of her dead agents, hanging from meat hooks, where the Gestapo had left them swinging as a warning to other members of the Resistance. She could never forget that image, and she didn't want to feel like she used her colleagues' deaths to promote herself.

In 1953, the agency undertook a study to examine the role of women in the ranks. There had been complaints by female employees that they were being sidelined and treated with less than professional respect. The CIA's Inspector General created a panel to study the issue. Dubbed the "Petticoat Panel" by its members, its report, submitted in November 1953, concluded that "although the last census reports 19 million working women in the U.S., an increase of seven million since 1940, it hasn't been too many years ago that . . . they were restricted to teaching or household services." Women were made to feel that they should be glad for what few opportunities they did have.

Basically, the report concluded that they shouldn't complain. After all, concessions to women in the workforce had been made. For example, the female employees were now permitted to use the gym one day a week.

An appendix to the report includes a fitness report for Virginia Hall during her first years with the CIA. She was given a below-average rating and rebutted it with a formal letter, stating that she found it "incredible" that her supervisor rated her so low. She included a copy of the recommendation she received for employment at the CIA that stated she was "the most qualified person for the job that I have ever interviewed." Nothing came of her rebuttal, but her objections were on record.

Her CIA career clearly wasn't what she had hoped it would be. Much like her earlier career with the State Department, both bureaucracies did nothing more than frustrate her and try her limited patience. She was too independent and self-reliant to function in a hierarchy, particularly one that didn't value her talents.

Former CIA officer E. Howard Hunt said, "She was sort of an embarrassment to the noncombat CIA types . . . Her experience and abilities were never properly utilized." She was a genuine war hero, a decorated spy in the Resistance, and had more experience than any bureaucrat ever would. It was no surprise they were embarrassed.

Virginia made it to retirement at age sixty, always enjoying time with her peers, that small group of special operators who understood each other's history, who spoke the same language, and who intimidated the bureaucrats simply by being who they were. It wasn't that she bragged. It would never even occur to her to do so. But the agency veterans agreed, "She was a presence."

Leaving the agency with little fanfare, her departure went unremarked. She enjoyed a quiet retirement, and like many who lived with security classifications surrounding their service like an electric fence and nondisclosure agreements anchoring their silence with chains, she received no further recognition. Despite the high awards and medals, she didn't receive nearly the recognition she deserved given the instrumental role she played in the war. Perhaps she wanted it that way. But her operational days were over.

Virginia Hall passed away in 1982 at the age of seventy-six. While she received little recognition in her lifetime, she was not and never will be forgotten. In 2006, on the hundredth anniversary of her birth, she was honored by both the French and British ambassadors to the United States in a ceremony. Her family was there to represent her. "Virginia Hall is a true hero of the French Resistance," wrote French President Jacques Chirac in a letter read by the French ambassador. The British ambassador presented Hall's family with a certificate to accompany the Order of the British Empire medal Hall received from King George VI in 1943.

That same year, the CIA hung a painting of her in its headquarters. It depicts Virginia in a barn in southern France, headphones on, tapping out a message on her suitcase wireless. She's just received the message from London. In 2017, the agency named its expeditionary training center building for her.

The CIA museum, located inside agency headquarters in Langley, Virginia, has only five sections that pay homage to specific agency individuals. Four are men who were also directors. The other is Virginia Hall. In 2018, when Gina Haspell became the first woman director of the CIA, she said, "I stand on the shoulders of heroines who never sought public acclaim."

Virginia Hall was an enigma. Perhaps that is why there have been at least six books written about her. Many want to know

The painting Les Marguerites Fleuriront ce Soir *hangs in one of the main corridors inside CIA headquarters, in Langley, Virginia. Sitting in an old barn loft in south-central France, Virginia Hall is communicating with London. A Resistance colleague pedals a modified bicycle to generate power for the B2 spy radio. The code phrase "les marguerites fleuriront ce soir" (the daisies will bloom tonight) alerts her to a pending air drop of supplies. Photo courtesy of Jeff Bass, artist.*

more about this secretive woman, what she thought, what motivated her, what she thought about the agency, her war service, the Cold War, and more. She didn't write a memoir or give interviews, and never spoke to a biographer. She never wanted to give anything away. Her secrets went to the grave with her.

Those who have written about her have had to rely on the meager scraps of information available from her limited quotes in reports, letters, third-party anecdotes, stories from colleagues, or her performance appraisals and official documents. Being lauded held no interest for her. To Virginia, it was all in the doing, proving to herself that she could have the life she always wanted, the freedom to write her own charter and then live that life exactly as she chose — no looking back. No regrets. In one of her field activity reports from September 1944, she answered the standard question, "Were you decorated in the field?" Her response: "No, nor any reason to be."

Virginia Hall is taking her rightful place at last. First among equals.

CHAPTER 6

FALLING ANGELS

"Some people say America has no heroes. I know their names."

MARY TAYLOR PREVITE

"It's Saturday! I'm going to win first place today!" Mary's little brother John had won the last contest. That made him king of the fly killers. There wasn't much to do for entertainment in a Japanese internment camp in China during World War II, so games had to be more creative, if somewhat odd. Bug killing was a competitive sport.

"No, you're not. *I'm* going to win. I'm faster than you!" She was determined. Saturday was Battle of the Bedbugs day, and Mary knew she could catch more bedbugs than the boys. After all, Mary had been awarded second place in the last rat-catching contest.

"Ha! We'll see." He skipped away laughing, but not before sticking out his tongue at her. "Not like you can tell on me."

That taunt made Mary more sad than angry. The four Taylor children hadn't seen their parents since just after the attack on Pearl Harbor in December 1941. That was over four years ago. Her father was British, her mother American, both Methodist ministers and third generation missionaries. They met in college in the United States and after graduation moved to Kaifeng, China, to serve at the China Inland Mission. Mary was born there and always thought of herself as a child of China. She had learned both Chinese and English, but her parents had wanted their children to have a Western education.

Later Mary recalled, "The only place to get an English education was Chefoo School, a boarding school that all the missionaries' children attended." It was an eight-hour drive from Kaifeng to Yanti, where the Chefoo School was located. The school was in the easternmost tip of Shandong province, just across the Yellow Sea from Pyongyang, Korea.

The day after Pearl Harbor was bombed, Japanese troops surrounded the school and claimed the children as their prisoners. In 1942, they closed the school, and the children were transferred 150 miles inland to a new camp. The Weihsien Civilian Assembly

Center was located in Weifang, Shandong province. It became the largest Japanese internment camp in China.

Mary Taylor was nine years old when the gates slammed shut on her life.

There were more than 1,500 prisoners, civilians mostly — businessmen, doctors, entertainers, priests, and nuns. That number included hundreds of children jammed into the confined space, and they were always hungry. All prisoners were forced to wear armbands identifying them as "A" for American or "B" for British, and so on.

Even though they were confined, the Camp Committee started a church and energized a school, crafting typical school days that included play and creative experiences for the kids, keeping as much of a sense of normalcy as possible. Academic challenges continued — spelling bees, poetry recitations, writing competitions. The school also administered aptitude tests for the teenagers to prepare them for life after the war. In the worst conditions imaginable, adults did everything they could to regularize this new life for the children.

Games were a necessary part of attempting to normalize. Mary even joined a scouting group for young girls, the Girl Guides. Their adult leaders were called the Brown

Owls. Mary recalled those wise Owls ran the camp troop like any other scouting troop. The girls earned merit badges, sang songs together, and worked on craft projects. One of the projects set the girls a goal of collecting coal shavings left behind by the camp guards. They then reformed the scraps into bricks to heat their dorms, piling them into the potbellied stoves in each hallway.

Mary found she couldn't be sad when the girls sang. It made her happy to hear their voices blend in song and prayer. One of her favorites was Psalm 91: "God is our refuge and our fortress. In Him I will trust."

At Christmas, the Girl Guides put on a special performance for the entire camp. Different groups across the camp would often put on concerts. A number of prisoners formed a mixed-nationalities Salvation Army band and were busy working on a "victory medley" of national anthems and other songs they hoped to play when the war ended. It gave hope for the future, and their buoyant playing gave hope to the other prisoners.

The schoolteachers made sure the kids didn't forget their manners either. "You could be eating boiled animal grain out of a soap dish and a teacher would come up behind you and say, 'Mary Taylor, sit up straight!' People who gave up those normal routines got sick." They slowly succumbed to the despair of imprisonment and their fears of never being released. Mary's teachers didn't let them give up; there was no time for self-pity or worry. The school stuck to as much of an ordinary life as possible, adhering to the simple things that made each day seem all right — wash your hands, no talking with your mouth full, say please and thank you.

Later Mary recalled that one teacher would remind her, "There are not two sets of manners — one set of manners for the princesses in Buckingham Palace and another set of manners for the Weihsien Concentration Camp."

Mary once described the teachers' actions as "beautiful triumphs." She added, "Our teachers set up a comforting, predictable set of rituals and traditions. Do you know how safe that makes children feel?"

Mary certainly did. And those lessons of adults working to create a safe place for children to thrive would stay with her for the rest of her life. "War and hate and violence never open the way to peace," she said. "Weihsien shaped me. I will carry Weihsien in my heart forever."

In the camp, every day was a *Groundhog Day* experience, each day a replica of the day before. To Mary, it seemed like her entire life had been spent behind a high fence. Twelve years old by the summer of 1945, she could barely remember what her parents looked like. Despite the passing years, there was no news from the outside world. No letters, no packages. And despite the teachers' best efforts, life in an internment camp was anything but normal. There was the fence, topped with barbed wire; armed guards patrolling with attack dogs, waving spotlights all night long; machine guns peeking out of watchtowers; and booby traps to stop escapees. One form of entertainment for the children was to watch the Japanese soldiers at what they called "Ya!" practice. It was the cry the soldiers made when plunging their bayonets into sandbags hanging from a pole. The bayonet drills took place weekly. "I don't think we realized at the time that they were practicing killing." Practicing to kill *them*.

From 1944 to 1945, food became increasingly scarce. Many of the children became ill. Several people died. Mary recalled the camp doctors asking any prisoners who were trading in black market eggs to save the shells for the children. They needed the calcium. "Vile," Mary pronounced the dish of crushed shells. Like eating sand. The local Chinese people risked their own safety to provide food to be smuggled in for the prisoners. Only one coolie, or day laborer, was officially allowed in. He brought eggs and other items, smiling at the guards and waving. He appeared to be slow and dull, but he also served as the courier who took out messages from one of the priests, then did his regular job, removing buckets from the toilets.

Summers in the camp were muggy, and by August 1945, Mary was miserable with the heat. It was too hot to even walk barefoot in the dirt. On August 17, Mary was lying on her bunk — an old steamer trunk — trying to ignore her grumbling belly and an impending bout of diarrhea when she heard a loud roar. Looking out the window, she saw a massive plane with a star on its underside. It was an American B-24 Liberator flying low and slow over the camp. At 400 feet, the plane spit out seven paratroopers who drifted slowly down through the steamy air to liberate the camp.

"They were angels falling from the sky," she said in wonder. Her discomfort forgotten,

Mary ran for the gates, thinking she would be the first to greet the men, but hundreds were crowding ahead of her. Outside, the men landed, rolled, and slipped off their parachutes. They didn't know what they were facing, whether the Japanese would fight them or not. They were certainly outnumbered.

Teams of Americans accompanied by both Japanese and Chinese interpreters landed at eight camps in China. They were sent by the Office of Strategic Services (OSS) Group HQ, based in Kunming. The moment the Japanese emperor offered his surrender, the Americans went into action, making certain none of the prisoners would be harmed. At Mary's camp, they didn't have to break in. The prisoners broke out.

Screaming wildly, hundreds stormed the gates and charged out towards their falling angels. Cheering loudly, they carried the soldiers into the camp like conquerors, held high on their shoulders. The children, Mary included, followed along squealing with joy. "Everyone was berserk," she said later. "I mean, out of their minds pandemonium. People laughing, weeping, dancing." Later she recalled, "I was too young to understand the miracle of seven men — against how many Japanese? — risking their lives to rescue me and 1,500 prisoners whom they didn't even know."

Up on the hillside behind the main camp building, the Salvation Army Band began to play the victory medley of national anthems they had been practicing for so long. When they reached the notes for "Oh say, does that star-spangled banner yet wave," the American horn player fell to his knees, overcome with joy and relief.

Another person entered the camp then. It was the coolie, who cleaned the toilets and smuggled in food, carrying out messages. He was actually an OSS agent who arrived just in time to support the liberators, now wearing a suit and tie. Most of the prisoners were flabbergasted to see him dressed that way. The entire day was like a scene from a movie.

The youngest paratrooper was a grinning all-American boy named Pete Orlich. The older teenage girls in camp had an immediate and breathless crush on the twenty-one-year-old soldier. Pete smiled at Mary, and her first tween crush was born. While many of the liberated prisoners were tearing up pieces of parachutes and asking the soldiers to autograph them, several wide-eyed girls embroidered a piece of parachute with scenes of the rescue at the camp and gave it to him. Mary didn't know then that she would have it back one day.

Betty Peet McIntosh, a Morale Operations (MO) officer with the OSS in Kunming, China, had been part of the OSS Planning Group that directed the mission to liberate the camps. Betty wished she could have gone along. She wanted to personally witness the liberation for at least one of the camps. Words were her forte, but she wanted to see these people too, to look in their eyes and understand what they'd been through. Her teammate, Bill Smith, was sent to Weihsien just after the rescue to report on the event as part of one of their propaganda programs. Bill spent a month in the newly liberated camp. Betty felt as though she'd been there with him once she saw his drawings of daily life in the camp. His sketches of the internees and his writings were later published in the *American Asiatic Association* magazine.

Bill reported that the 1,518 liberated prisoners represented a "League of Nations" of sorts. Besides the Americans and Brits, there were Italians, Filipinos, Norwegians, Iranians, and more. Just after the camp was liberated, planes parachuted in tons of food and clothing, including canned hams and turkeys, sugar, and even violin strings for the camp orchestra. People were amazed to see things they didn't know existed, such as powdered lemonade and canned stews. The world had moved ahead without them. Mary was thrilled to explore the new rations — no more cattle food and no more ground-up eggshells.

Delighted with their oversized GI jackets and fatigue pants, kids in flopping Army boots followed the soldiers everywhere they went. These were the first new clothes they'd had in nearly three years. Until the prisoners began to be repatriated, the paratroopers were besieged with kids every moment of the day. They wanted the men to play baseball with them and sing the songs of America. They wanted to sit on the soldiers' laps and begged them to tell stories. "That's when I learned to sing 'You Are My Sunshine,'" Mary recalled.

Mary and her siblings, John, Jamie, and Kathleen, were on the second flight out of the camp. On September 10, 1945, three days after Mary's thirteenth birthday, they boarded a military cargo plane and flew to Xi'an, China. They spent the night at a U.S. military base where the OSS had established a field unit months earlier. The soldiers brought out a cake for their dinner that evening. Whether it was to celebrate Mary's birthday or the children's freedom, it didn't matter. It was sugary sweet, and there were sprinkles. The kids had nearly forgotten what sweets were like. They all ate too much and probably too fast. Everyone sang "Happy Birthday," and Mary began to believe that freedom might actually be real.

Mary Taylor, third from right with her brothers and sister, ready to board the flight to Xi'an to be reunited with her parents. Photo courtesy of Alice Previte.

The next day, Mary and her brothers and sister were nearing the end of their nearly 800-mile journey. They had a Chinese Christian escort, and for the final leg of the long trip were riding on a mule cart with their baggage when it started to rain. Impatiently, the kids jumped down and left him behind with the cart. *Finally!* They were so close. Mary and the others started to run through the downpour and the mud to the Fenghsiang city gate up ahead. They whooped as they realized the gate had been left open. Inside, their parents were teaching at a new mission — one the children had never seen. As they drew closer, one of the mission's students recognized them as the children everyone had been praying for, for more than five years. He led them "down the block, through the round moon gate into the Bible School compound."

Mary gasped. "There, through a back window, I could see them — Daddy and Mummy — sitting in a faculty meeting." Excited beyond words, the children pushed through the bamboo screen and fell into the room, soaked and caked with mud. Mary remembered screaming as they all — laughing, shouting, and nearly hysterical with joy — fell into their parents' arms.

She was home.

By 1946, the family was back in the United States in southern Michigan. Mary's father became the pastor of the Spring Arbor Free Methodist Church. The children's parents had them tested for proficiency to see what grade they should enter in an American school. Despite the hunger and deprivation, Mary and her siblings were generally healthy, in good spirits, and two years ahead of where they would have been had they attended U.S. schools during those war years. The internment camp's makeshift education program was clearly effective at more than just establishing a routine.

A year later, Mary and her siblings were visiting a farm in Canada while their parents traveled. She was curious about a revolving saw that had been left running. She reached out and somehow bumped it — she never knew exactly how — and her left hand was shredded by the whirring blades.

The horror of that day haunted her throughout her hospital stay. Once she was fully awake, the horror multiplied as she held up her arm and realized with a sick and sinking feeling that her hand had been amputated.

Later, her younger brother commented, "It's too bad Mary can't ride her bike anymore." Mary's father answered, "I don't see why not." She rode her bike as soon as she could, and taught herself to embroider, sew, and quilt. She learned to braid her hair and later took piano lessons. There was no slack when it came to chores either. Her mother made certain she took her turn at washing the dishes. There wasn't anything she couldn't do. And because she believed it, it was true. Late in life, she would come to understand how that life-changing accident could help her relate to children in ways that she couldn't have imagined then.

As she grew up, Mary often found herself recounting the miracle of her rescue from the internment camp. She never forgot her heroes, those seven men who parachuted into the camp that stifling day in August 1945. Would she ever see them again? Did Pete Orlich still have the embroidered scrap of parachute?

Mary started college near home, attending Spring Arbor University. She then transferred to Greenville College in Illinois, a Christian school with a strict honor code and ethical stance. She met her future husband Ernest Previte there and earned her BA. They married in 1955 and later moved to New Jersey. She received her master's degree from Glassboro College (now Rowan University) in New Jersey. Both degrees were in English and education. Mary taught English at Camden High School, known as "The Castle on the Hill."

After her daughter Alice was born in 1962, she left teaching but remained active with the local board of education. Twelve years later, Mary accepted a new job, taking over as superintendent of Camden County Youth Center. She ran the center for over thirty years, from 1974 to 2005. It was the perfect spot for a woman who had spent her childhood in a detention camp. She understood the fear and loneliness of the teenagers in detention and was solidly in their corner. Bruce Stout, a policy advisor for then New Jersey Governor Christie Whitman, said, "She was a tireless advocate for the voiceless, the underrepresented. She gave kids hope."

In 1974, just after she'd taken the job as superintendent, she was called in to the youth center one Saturday evening to respond to reports of a riot. The boys were locked in their cells, banging on the doors, making as much noise as they could. The corrections officers stood silent, watching and waiting to see what she would do. Mary had been summoned from home where she'd been hosting a dinner party. She was wearing a flowered cocktail dress, and at five-feet four inches tall and 125 pounds, certainly didn't look the part of a stern and imposing superintendent

Mary recognized immediately the coiled spring of repressed violence in that situation. On one side were the detainees, on the other side the jailers. If there was a violent act on one side, it would be met with violence by the other. This was obviously a test for her, to see which side she would choose, how the new superintendent would respond. She chose another route — her firm rules, her way the only way. She talked quietly to one of the boys through the bars, asking what was going on. "It was really about listening," she said. And being open, answering questions about herself, even if they were personal. The kids were curious about her. "Were you at a party?" "How much did that dress cost?" "What were you eating?"

Mary called upon the lessons from her own childhood to establish how she would operate as superintendent. "We discovered that when boys and girls come in, one of the first messages . . . is, we will not let you hurt somebody while you are here, and we will not let anyone hurt you. So there was a sense that you were going to be safe in this place." There were standards.

She led by example, and the staff followed her lead. She also spent time in the teenagers' classrooms, helping individual youngsters and encouraging them to dream about the future. She talked about when she was incarcerated, her life during the war, the camp she was in, about her captors. And especially about her rescuers.

They would stare at her wrist, but most were hesitant asking about her missing hand. Mary found other ways to tell that

Mary Previte, Administrator of the Camden County Youth Center, watches an inmate pass her in the hallway. She turned the center into a nationally recognized program for juveniles. June 16, 1995. Photo credit: AP Photo/Allen Oliver.

story and used it to explain that actions have consequences. "Some kid will say, so-and-so just got sentenced, and he was so nice, and he was only fourteen. And I'll say, let me tell you a story. I was so nice, and I was only fourteen. And I one time bumped my hand on a revolving saw, and now . . . I'm carrying a mistake that I made when I was only fourteen. Sometimes, saying you're sorry does not make the mistake go away. So you have to be careful what you do, making a mistake, even when you're so young as fourteen, can leave you marked for the rest of your life."

In a 1993 interview with NPR, she was asked about burnout in such a high-stress job. "What keeps you going despite all the obstacles and the losses?" Mary replied, "I go home every day knowing that I get so much more than I give. There's no such thing as burnout." Her book about her life story and her journey to become superintendent at the juvenile detention center, *Hungry Ghosts,* was published in 1994.

In 1997, Mary decided to run for the New Jersey State and General Assembly. Her running mate John Adler had an invitation to speak to a group of World War II veterans at their reunion banquet. He couldn't attend and asked Mary to substitute.

"It's pretty simple," Adler said. "All you have to do is to thank them for their service and read a proclamation from the General Assembly."

"All right," Mary agreed. It wouldn't take too much time from her schedule, and the event was being held at a hotel only ten minutes from her house.

"And by the way," he added. "This is the China-Burma-India Veterans Association."

Mary felt goose bumps on the back of her neck. "That's who rescued me!" The realization stirred a piece of her heart awake. Could it be? Could her saviors be part of the veterans' group? Later, she looked in her files to make certain she had their names spelled correctly. Of course, she remembered them, all of them. Anxiously, she awaited the veterans' reunion. That night, she approached the podium with all the hope she could muster.

The veterans and their spouses looked up at her expectantly. There were 150 of them, men and women in their seventies and eighties. First, she read the proclamation as she had been asked to do. However, she had added her own message to the official language. She continued slowly, "I know it was no accident I was invited here tonight to substitute for Senator Adler." She sighed, shakily, one single note echoing through the microphone. All eyes were on her as she began to speak.

She told the story of her imprisonment at the internment camp as a child and the miracle of their rescue on August 17, 1945. When she reached the moment of their liberation, she paused for a long moment. Trembling, Mary took a deep breath.

"Let me tell you their names. Major Stanley Staiger, Ensign Jim Moore, First Lieutenant James Hannon, Sergeant Raymond Hanchulak, Specialist Five Pete Orlich,

Japanese Interpreter Tadashi Nagaki, and Chinese Interpreter Eddie Wang. Are any of them here tonight?" Her voice cracked as she asked the question. It was too much to hope for.

There was a long moment of silence while people looked around the room. No one stood up. Not one of her angels was in attendance, Mary realized sadly. Following the program, she was surrounded by appreciative veterans offering ideas, suggestions, and help on how she might find them. Many hugged her and cried with her too. One promised to do some research for her. Mary thanked him but didn't expect to hear from him or anyone else again.

In 1997, she was elected the first woman president of the New Jersey Juvenile Detention Association and ran for the General Assembly. Once elected, she served in the General Assembly until 2006. Notably, Mary served as Chair of the Family, Women, and Children Services Committee. She leveraged both of those positions to champion the rights of children in foster care, support sentencing reform, and improve prison conditions for women. She always advocated for the underrepresented and often forgotten children of the community. She sponsored legislation that established drug-free school zones and fought for a town's ability to hold alleged drunk drivers in custody until they could safely drive.

Kevin DeSimone, a former legislative aide, said she was a lawmaker who could work across the aisle with all parties. "She cared about kids in foster care, she cared about sentencing reform, about women in prison. She opened people's eyes to many of these things."

But that accidental speaking engagement when she was running for office continued to impact her future. Several days after her speech to the China-Burma-India veterans, one of the veterans from Maryland sent her a large package, a computer printout of his research. It contained phone numbers for the names of all the veterans she had listed. In addition to all the veterans with the exact names she had shared, there were many people with similar names and iterations of those names. The list was daunting. Mary decided to contact them all. She started writing letters with return envelopes enclosed. The letters asked one simple question: "Are you the Stanley Staiger who liberated the Weihsien Camp on August 17, 1945?" Many negative responses were returned, "I'm sorry, I'm not the man you're looking for," but there were also words of hope and encouragement from strangers blessing her in her search.

It took over a year, but in September 1998, Mary got her first break. A woman who lived down the street had read Mary's story in the China-Burma-India veteran's magazine and called to tell her that Raymond Hanchulak lived next door to her sister. Mary called the number for Raymond that Sunday only to learn he'd passed away the year before. She was crushed. Her crusade didn't look promising for any of the fellow vets either. She got the same result when she tracked down her young crush, Pete Orlich. He'd passed away before she could thank him as well.

Mary felt a deep sense of loss; she still remembered that scrap of parachute embroidered with scenes of the camp liberation. Now she couldn't talk with him about it and ask if he'd kept it. She told Pete's widow, Carol, that story. In response, Carol shared how important that rescue mission had been to her husband. He'd told her about it and thought of the people who were rescued often over the years. Later, she mailed Pete's special souvenir to Mary. Mary was deeply touched by the gesture and kept the cloth close. She took that precious memento with her to every one of her speaking engagements for the rest of her life.

Mary Previte in 2000 with a piece of parachute used by Pete Orlich, who rescued her from the concentration camp in 1945. Photo courtesy of Richard Bell.

Disheartened that she'd been too late to thank Raymond and Pete in person, she worried about finding any of her other heroes still living. Yet, she persisted in her search. Mary was bound and determined to find at least one of the men who had saved her life. And then suddenly, one by one, they began to surface.

The first one was Tadashi Nagaki, now a farmer in Nebraska. He answered the phone when Mary called, and startled by her first successful connection, Mary started to cry. She'd finally located one of her heroes.

Tad promised to help her find Jim Moore. He and Jim had remained friends, exchanging Christmas cards and letters for more than fifty years. When she talked with Jim, she was amazed at his story and the parallels to her own life. Like Mary, Jim was a child of missionaries and had spent his childhood in China, even attended Chefoo school. After college, he'd joined the FBI, and as a special agent was exempt from serving in the military in WWII. "But his heart said something else," Mary recalled. It was personal for him. Jim joined the Navy and then the OSS. Because he spoke Chinese, he was called on to join the mission to liberate the camps, specifically Weihsien. Mary and Jim ran up her phone bill as they reminisced about their experiences, and he offered to help with her search. With the knowledge of search protocols that he'd learned from a lifetime in intelligence work and the tenacity of a trained investigator, he quickly found Stanley and Jim Hannon.

Mary began to feel as though her mission was being fulfilled. However, she wanted to do more than simply find them. Mary felt a need to see them, to thank them in person. "My heart said it wasn't enough. So I started my pilgrimage, crisscrossing America to say thank you to each one of these heroes face-to-face. I went looking for the soul of America, and it is beautiful."

Despite her best efforts, one man she couldn't seem to locate was Eddie Wang, the Chinese interpreter. Unfortunately, the other team members also couldn't help her. He was a Chinese national, and they didn't have any more information on his whereabouts. Mary never gave up. She kept writing articles and giving interviews, hoping that somehow one might find its way to him. Perhaps someone else would recognize the name and contact her. She didn't give up . . . and eventually that is exactly what happened.

In March 2015, Wang Qian read one of Mary's articles about her quest to locate her childhood heroes. He gasped at seeing she was still looking for a Chinese man called Eddie Wang. He read the story again, then once more. He was convinced she was looking for his grandfather, Wang Chenghan. He wrote her a letter. They talked and confirmed what Mary had hoped. It was him.

"I've realized a dream that I thought would never come true. There is nothing better than that." Mary said happily. At age eighty-three, she traveled to Guiyang, Guizhou province, China to meet her rescuer, Wang Chenghan, who was ninety-one. Mary was active on a website for survivors of Weihsien, and many of them had been following her journey to locate the team who rescued them all. A number of them wrote their own thank you letters, and Mary gladly brought eighteen of them along to China.

Mary Previte with Wang Chenghan at their reunion in China in 2016. Photo credit: ImagineChina Limited/Alamy stock photo.

Throughout her life, Mary Previte remained a strong advocate for children's rights. With the lessons of her own childhood seared into memory, she would always remember what a child needed to feel safe, to feel cared for — what a child needed to thrive. Her own ordeals, from imprisonment to the shocking amputation of her hand,

189

became the stuff of which her character was formed and her ability to lead was born.

Sometimes we think accidents are just that: accidents. That they don't happen for a reason; that some hardships just occur as a twist of fate. Mary's path in life revealed the opposite. It was no accident she became a teacher and later the director of a Juvenile Center, calling on the lessons she learned in Chefoo internment camp. It was a terrible misfortune that she lost her hand, but it also helped her relate to at-risk and potentially violent teenagers. It was clearly fate that Mary was asked to speak to the China-Burma-India veterans' group. The event sparked a pilgrimage of the heart, prompting her to seek out and personally give thanks to each and every one of the men who liberated the Weihsien Camp where she'd been held for over three years.

Mary Taylor Previte's search for the "angels" on her rescue team became a fulfilling journey of discovery, gratitude, and joy. By the end of her search, her heart was full. Mary knew she could never say thank you enough to those men, but having the opportunity to try was more than she once could have imagined. Her story was one of purpose, where early suffering and loss shaped her life's mission as a teacher, advocate, and mentor. She called the liberators "heroes," but through her life's work she truly became a hero herself. "I had walked with angels and miracles all my life," she recalled. "My world was full of mystery and surprise. You sailed into this giant ocean, moving away from the safety of the shore, not knowing the destination — but knowing God was there. The world isn't flat — the way folks said. It is round, with distant shores to find."

When she passed away in 2019 from injuries sustained in a car accident weeks earlier, she left behind an incredible legacy of hope for the youth in her hometown and across the state. Her achievements had been recognized by the National Women's History Alliance, who presented her with the Woman of Achievement Award, and in numerous articles, interviews, and through the telling of her own incredible journey. Upon her death, the governor of New Jersey ordered the U.S. and New Jersey state flags to be flown at half-staff — "in recognition and mourning of a dedicated and tireless public servant, Assemblywoman Mary Taylor Previte."

Her rescuers influenced her throughout her life. "Some people say America has no heroes," she always said. "I know their names."

CHAPTER 7

INSIDE OF TIME

"I was trembling with the discovery that, from this moment on, my life would be forever bound with rescue and survival."

RUTH GRUBER

There was no moon, but the night sky was thick with the splendor of a million stars. Ruth Gruber stood on the ship's upper deck alone, gripping the brass rail tightly. The summer breeze was hot, blowing a hint of distant tropical blossoms past her loosely tied black hair.

"It's so quiet," she whispered. The troop transport ship had shut down its engines. The running lights — in fact, all lights — were off. The sea was still. More than two thousand people aboard held their breath.

"I can see every star," she craned her head back.

The trip west across the Mediterranean Sea

from Italy was particularly hazardous this late in the war. It was July 1944, and Ruth was aboard an American warship guiding a group of nearly one thousand Jewish war refugees to safety in the United States. Over one thousand wounded U.S. servicemen were aboard, too. Their ship was protected as part of a larger convoy. She looked over the rail, peering into the darkness.

"I can't see anything." There were twenty-nine warships in all with their group. Each one of them silent, blackout conditions absolute. This was their second blackout. The first had scared the refugees nearly to hysteria. Many were newly released from concentration camps. They were trauma-tized, jumpy, and the sound of Nazi war-planes made some scream in terror. Ruth had talked to them, hoping to ease their fears. They were still learning to trust her. *Mother Ruth*. The nickname made her smile. Echoing from one of the decks below, a baby's wail wafted upwards. It was quickly shushed. Silence returned.

Ruth turned her eyes back to the skies. She knew the banshee shriek of a Messerschmitt in a dive-bombing run. But tonight, there was nothing. Her thoughts drifted again.

Suddenly it came. Not an attack, but a moment of truth from her soul.

"Standing alone on the blacked-out deck, the wind blowing through my hair, I was trembling with the discovery that, from this moment on, my life would be forever bound with rescue and survival. I would use my words and image, my typewriter and my cameras as my tools. I had to live the story to write it, and not only live it — if it was a story of injustice, I had to fight it."

She knew her destiny now and understood her life's purpose. "I'm ready," she whispered to the sky.

Ruth's life had always been headed for this incredible effort. She defied expectations, convention, and oftentimes her own previously constructed goals. She finished high school at fifteen, graduated from New York University at eighteen in 1929. Next, she blew through a master's degree in American and German literature at the University of Wisconsin and paused to take a much-needed breath. Why not? She had earned it. She then applied for and received a fellowship from the Institute of International Education and traveled to Germany to continue her studies. It was 1930, and as an impressionable young woman, she was a witness to the early days of Hitler's rise in the public eye. But Ruth was never just a witness. She was always involved in the stories she wrote, the studies she undertook, and despite her parent's fears at the news coming from Germany, stayed and earned a doctorate from the University of Cologne in one year flat. At the time, she was the youngest person in the world to earn a doctorate. At last, it was time to come home. Her parents were relieved to have her back safely in America.

She was twenty years old.

Ruth was frustrated in New York. The years of academic challenge were done, and she found herself stuck at home filling out job applications. Finding work during the Depression was nearly impossible, and it was even harder for a woman, no matter how brilliant or how educated.

She started writing. It was a small piece first, an easygoing travel piece about her neighborhood in Brooklyn. But it got her noticed, and she landed a job with the *Herald Tribune.* On a special assignment with the *Tribune,* she became the first journalist to visit the Soviet Gulag in Russia to write about the plight of women under communism and fascism. She published her first book, *I Went to the Soviet Arctic,* in 1939. Ruth found that women were bearing a greater share of economic hardship in the years leading up to World War II. A first-rate observer with a gift for both interview and insight, she went beyond the Stalinist platitudes she was given and painted a portrait of life there that was heretofore unknown.

U.S. Secretary of the Interior Harold L. Ickes read it and was impressed with her reporting and her ability to build a persuasive narrative. So, he asked her to come to work for him and serve as his emissary to Alaska. He wanted a report on the conditions there, the people, and the opportunities for settlement by soldiers returning from the war. Ruth didn't know it at the time, but he was considering the possibility of proposing to the president that Alaska be made available to Jewish refugees. She completed her report on the beauty she found there, not just the stark wilderness and wonders of Alaska, but also her encounters with a broad spectrum of people. Ruth spent over nineteen months in Alaska as she crafted her assessment of the social and economic development of this relatively unknown part of the country. Ickes was impressed, and suddenly, Ruth had another book to write.

In June 1943, Ruth read about the death of a *Tribune* colleague and sent a condolence note to Helen Rogers Reid, owner of the *New York Herald Tribune*. Helen Rogers Reid was one of the most powerful women

Ruth Gruber in Alaska, 1941. This was her second book. Photo courtesy of Celia and David Michaels.

in America. She was known for hiring more women than any other newspaper owner in the country at a time when newspapers largely only employed men. She was famous for her work, including her successful merging of the *Tribune* with the *New York Herald,* creating the modern newspaper.

Helen thanked Ruth for her note and several months later sent Ruth a request to speak at her forum. Helen Rogers Reid had read Ruth's earlier book on the Russian arctic and knew that Ruth had been to Alaska as the emissary of the U.S. Department of the Interior. She knew a good story when she heard one. Once Ruth got permission to do the speaking engagement from her boss,

Secretary Harold Ickes, Helen, and Ruth began a lifelong friendship.

That fall, the *Herald Tribune*'s forum got underway, with Helen presiding. The *Tribune* owner glanced at her guest. The room quieted. Two thousand people in New York's Waldorf Astoria hotel ballroom turned towards the slight woman with short dark hair waiting beside the podium. "Our next speaker is an adventure in and of herself. She has the keen inquiring mind, the vivid aliveness, and the zest for exploration that make the perfect reporter."

Ruth's cheeks flared pink at the praise, and she smiled nervously. Previous speakers at the forum included Winston Churchill, Charles de Gaulle, and Eleanor Roosevelt. It was heady company to be in. Ruth listened as Helen continued. She knew how Mrs. Reid researched her speakers and introduced them with an incredible flair. Still, it was unnerving to hear herself described as a person in the same category as those other speakers.

Ruth walked slowly to the podium, her knees weak. She talked about what Alaska meant to her, what she learned about the people, the land, and the wilderness, and how it could be an ideal place for homesteading. She was obviously more than the average reporter. She was a woman who lived inside her story and examined it from every angle.

After that night, she began to meet more influential people in Helen Rogers Reid's circle, crafting a network as she continued to work for Secretary Ickes. Soon, Ruth was restless and looking for a major new project. Having witnessed Hitler's early days as a rising star when she was in graduate school in Cologne, she was particularly concerned about the plight of Jewish people in Germany. Word was leaking out about Nazi atrocities in Romania and Poland. The United States was restricting immigration of Jews, and Ruth was frustrated by what she saw as bureaucracy and anti-Semitism in the State Department.

In 1944, President Roosevelt created the War Refugee Board, taking responsibility for supporting the Jews in Europe away from the State Department. He made an important announcement: "I have decided that approximately one thousand refugees should be immediately brought from Italy to this country." This executive decision was a way around established policy and would provide asylum to a group of the 36,000 refugees being housed in Allied facilities in Italy. Those selected to emigrate would come to the United States as the president's personal guests.

Even though she was serving as a special assistant to the Secretary of the Interior, Ruth was still a reporter at heart. Her humanitarian instincts led her straight to Secretary Ickes's office. Ruth charged in.

"Mr. Secretary, these refugees are going to be terrified — traumatized. Someone needs to fly over there and hold their hand." Ruth was adamant.

"You're right," Ickes said. He always admired her passion. "I'm going to send you."

Ready to argue further, Ruth stopped cold. She caught her breath. Later he told her, "I know this whole thing, saving refugees, means a lot to you, as it does to me. You're going to be my eyes and ears. I'm depending on you."

"Mr. Secretary," Ruth replied in a low voice, "this is the most important assignment of my life."

Gussie Gruber was not at all pleased when Ruth broke the news of her upcoming voyage. She had been afraid for her adventurous daughter's safety when Ruth went to Germany in 1931. She disliked the thought of this trip into the European theater of war even more. Mrs. Gruber immediately made a call, requested an appointment, and traveled to Washington to confront Secretary Ickes. "How are you going to keep my daughter safe?"

He had a plan. He gave Ruth a temporary rank of Army general as insurance. It meant Ruth would receive Geneva Convention protections should her secret mission to bring a thousand Jews to the United States be discovered. Her mother (somewhat) soothed, Ruth was ready to go. Her reporter instincts were at a fever pitch, her humanitarian side even more determined to succeed. While several of her later books won awards and may have been more directly responsible for her popularity, it was this act, Ruth felt, that was the single defining moment of her life. Everything had led to this surprising voyage. Everything that came afterward was because of it.

On July 20, 1944, she arrived at the port in Naples, Italy, the same day the news broke of a botched assassination attempt on Hitler. Ruth heard the hysterical reports on the radio and thought, *If only it had succeeded, we would be saving not one thousand but tens of thousands of refugees.*

The next day, she traveled to the dock to see her ship, surprising many of the sailors. They weren't expecting to see a woman in charge of the refugees, yet they accepted her quickly. One sailor, though, noted she wasn't dressed appropriately to board a ship. Since the *Henry Gibbons* was out in the harbor, she would have to take a tender across the water, then scramble up a net onto the ship. Ruth wryly looked down at her skirt and borrowed a pair of trousers from a sailor so she could navigate the ropes with appropriate modesty, not to mention safety. It was a moment that gave everyone something to smile about.

Ruth stood on the deck looking around as small boats packed with refugees approached the transport. Further out in the bay, twenty-nine U.S. Navy ships were assembling for their convoy. Eleven were warships, armed escorts for the *Henry Gibbons*. Two ships carried German POWs. The others were cargo ships and transports for the wounded.

The refugees arrived in spurts, clambering onto the ship slowly, some fearful and others suspicious. Ruth was there to welcome them with a smile and open arms to show them they were safe. Seeing her on the deck, one man cried out, "It's Eleanor Roosevelt!" Ruth felt herself blush. There was absolutely no resemblance, she thought.

Years later, on her way to a reunion of the refugees and their families, Ruth recalled,

Ruth Gruber waving from the Henry Gibbons *in July 1944.*
Photo courtesy of Celia and David Michaels.

"I still see some of them, that first day I saw them on the ship. Some of them were still in concentration camp pajamas . . . some had no shoes, and their feet were bound with newspapers."

This was the only attempt by the U.S. to shelter Jewish refugees during the war. And there definitely weren't as many as Ruth would have liked. The *Henry Gibbons* could only accommodate about one thousand refugees. One thousand felt like a magic number somehow, even though only 982 of them actually made it on board. A few of those designated had declined at the last moment.

Others fell sick. The final number included people from eighteen countries. While the majority were Jewish, there were also Catholics, Protestants, and Greek Orthodox mixed in.

More than three thousand displaced persons applied for the slots, priority going to those who had survived concentration camps. Ruth was keenly aware that while the United States was making efforts to save these refugees, Adolph Eichmann was in Hungary, sending nearly a half million Jews to their death in Auschwitz. She always said the United States should have done more to save lives.

Those selected had a tough deal to make. The refugees all had to sign a paper stating they understood that the asylum would be temporary, and that they would have to return to their home countries following the war. They had to agree to be interned at an Army post in Oswego, New York, the Fort Ontario Emergency Refugee Shelter.

There were also wounded soldiers on the ship returning home. At first, the two groups were to be kept separate, but inevitably, there was engagement, conflict, then understanding and the development of friendships. Some of the refugees had been artists and performers in their former lives. A few knew opera and others played musical instruments. Maybe a little variety show would enable the refugees to give thanks for the Americans and expose the GIs to people they had only heard about, the ones they were fighting for. It might go a long way to helping the two groups get along. The refugees wanted to perform songs for the wounded and put on a show for them.

Ruth talked to the captain. To her it was important the soldiers "*see* the refugees, *hear* them, *sense* them." Based on her own experiences living inside the stories she wrote, she knew that to humanize the widely different groups, downplaying the differences in language, nationality, and religion, would enable real engagement. It would let them truly come to know each other for the first time.

The wounded soldiers arrived on deck in their wheelchairs, bandages, and casts. They were thrilled to see some of the beautiful young refugee women ready to perform. "Hubba, hubba! Hey, Good Lookin'!" "Check out that tomato!" The audience quieted to sing the national anthem and the refugees joined in. In that moment, they began to come together. There were jokes, songs, and even some opera. Ruth smiled, watching from behind a hatch door. The ice had finally broken.

As someone who had always been in a hurry, Ruth had learned in Alaska how to slow down and relish every available moment, as she termed it, to "live inside of time." During that thirteen-day voyage, Ruth continued to live inside time, getting to personally know the refugees, teaching them some basic English, interviewing them for her report to Secretary Ickes, and through him, to President Roosevelt. Maybe later there would be a news article, or perhaps a book. Theirs were the first stories to come out of Europe about the death camps, and she wanted to record them.

"Tell me what happened to you," she prodded gently.

At first, several of the men refused to tell her what they had been through. "We can't tell you what we went through. It's too obscene. You're a young woman!"

"Forget I'm a woman," Ruth replied. "You're the first witnesses coming to America."

Later, she recalled, "They talked. Nobody refused to talk."

As they told her their stories, she often had to stop writing because of the tears that smeared the pages of her notebook. She could only remain composed for short periods of time. Day and night, she absorbed their stories of loss and deprivation. She took thousands of photographs on the thirteen-day journey. Ruth even taught the children to sing in English "You Are My Sunshine."

In her English classes, she told the refugees, "If you are asked, you say the name of the ship is a secret. If people ask where you're from, you say the North Pole." They learned that lesson well. Even months after their arrival in the United States, the refugees would proudly tell people they met that they had sailed on a ship named Secret, and that they were all from the North Pole. Mother Ruth had told them so. She may have been given the rank of general, but the moniker "Mother Ruth" stuck.

They trusted Mother Ruth. On that fateful evening, when there was a nighttime blackout due to concerns about Nazi warplanes, Ruth realized how she was being changed by the experience and how her life would be forever different.

She was still contemplating this realization as the ship neared New York Harbor. The refugees were overcome with emotion at the sight of the Statue of Liberty, seemingly standing there just to welcome *them*. Many refugees cried. Others waved frantically at the statue as they greeted America. A rabbi offered a prayer: "As we enter America, we must speak with one voice, with one heart."

Photojournalist Ruth Gruber (center with cap) with a group of Jewish refugees upon their arrival from Europe, August 3, 1944. Photo credit: The U.S. Holocaust Memorial Museum courtesy of Michel Oliver.

Following an impromptu press conference in New York, their journey continued. Ruth and the refugees took a train from New York City to the Fort Ontario Emergency Refugee shelter in Oswego, a former Army post. While many refugees slept, others remained anxiously awake, remembering other trains, other destinations. Trains delivered them to the death camps. One trembling woman tottered up the aisle and asked Ruth if she could sit with her.

Ruth patted the seat beside her and tried her best to comfort the woman. "But you're safe now — in America."

"It's the train. Trains scare me. I know it's — it's not a cattle car, but . . ." The woman pulled her shawl tightly around her shoulders.

Ruth heard her gasp as two military policemen walked by. "The soldiers — they aren't shoving us together. They aren't pushing us into those terrible trains. . . . people died in them. Still — oh God, I'm so scared."

"This is all behind you." Ruth tried to reassure her. "Shhh." The young woman laid her head on Ruth's shoulder.

Finally, the car was quiet. But fear reasserted itself once the refugees saw the camp where they were to be interned. There was a fence. There were guards. The guards were in uniform and had guns. The refugees were terrified, many thinking they had exchanged one concentration camp for another. Ruth tried to explain that the fence was there because the camp had been an Army base. Some were not convinced. Others said they felt safer because the fence was there. Ruth understood the concern. "They were stateless, paperless, and homeless," she wrote.

But apart from fears that they had landed in yet another prison, the refugees slowly began to learn about America. In preparation for their arrival, soldiers had partitioned sections in the barracks for housing. Families had their own apartment, some for the first time. "Bedsheets!" One woman cried. "Imagine having bedsheets for the first time in years!" Her husband was more excited about the mattress. He fell onto it the moment they saw their little apartment.

A building was set aside to use as a temple. Services were held for all religions. There was food, and plenty of it.

The refugees were quarantined for their first month in the United States, and Army intelligence specialists interrogated them about their experiences. Only government officials and the press were permitted inside the fence. Once the Army interviews were complete, Ruth brought War Relocation Authority (WRA) representatives and other officials to the camp to officially welcome the refugees to America.

Ruth had her own office at the camp, though Mother Ruth didn't have any official duties. She served as a liaison, spending her days reassuring both the refugees and the townspeople, each side about the other. One afternoon, the office of Mrs. Helen

Reid called, inviting Ruth to dinner. Ruth took the train to New York City, where she mixed with Helen Reed's famous dinner guests, reporters, and correspondents, all friends of the influential publisher. Naturally, Ruth was asked to talk about her experiences escorting the refugees, and she took the opportunity to express how it seemed the townspeople of Oswego were having difficulty accepting the refugees. Many thought the newcomers were living in the camp in luxurious conditions, and they resented it. One of Helen's friends at the dinner mentioned that her mother lived in Oswego. She offered to make an introduction.

That opened the door and resulted in the formation of the Oswego Advisory Committee, a group of townspeople who came together to help the refugees assimilate. The National Council of Jewish Women provided cribs, carriages, and high chairs for the twelve babies in the camp. Two rabbis brought enough dishes so the camp could operate a kosher kitchen. The townspeople threw gifts over the fence for the children: Ping-Pong balls, cookies, candy, and even a bicycle for a little girl. When the ice cream truck came around, refugees young and old marveled at the creativity of a country that had produced that amazing invention, ice cream on a stick.

Local schools opened their doors, and the kids brought American life, language, music, and culture home with them. Soon, children started school. Some of the young men and women thought they were too old to go back. At twenty, some had been away from schools for more than five years. It didn't matter. This was America, and everyone was welcome.

Daily life began to have a rhythm and new purpose. The WRA gave them each a clothing allowance. At first, volunteers bought shoes for everyone. No one wanted to go to town barefoot. Gradually, the refugees ventured into town to buy their own clothes. Many were shy at first because they feared their English wasn't good enough. Others still were afraid to venture out. They felt safer inside the fence.

One day, Manya, one of the refugee women who was bold enough to want to see the new world, came to visit Ruth. The young woman looked anxious, twisting her hands in her lap. Ruth smiled reassuringly.

"What is it, Manya?" She asked.

"We want to get married, Ernst and I," Manya said. "Can we get out of here long enough to do it?" During the voyage, the couple had tried to have the ship's captain marry them, but he told them to wait until they arrived in America. Now they wanted to get married immediately. Ruth held up a hand. She needed to check on a few things first. Would the War Refugee Board approve? Did they need to? What about a marriage license? Blood tests? Where could they have the ceremony? Ruth quickly got the approvals she needed.

A week later, all red tape had been cut, folded, and disposed of. The paperwork was completed, and the license was stamped with the official seal of approval. Manya had one last question.

"Can we get married tomorrow?" She asked.

"I don't see why not," Ruth answered. Manya smiled, then looked shocked.

"But Ruthie, I have no dress!" It was as though the young woman just realized she'd been so busy meeting all the legal requirements, she'd forgotten to be a bride. Ruth called her mother in New York and asked her to come immediately, bringing a dress and a veil. Manya listened to their phone conversation.

"Would your mother give me away?" Ruth's mother cried a little at the sweet invitation, even as she crocheted the veil on her train trip to Oswego.

It was a beautiful wedding, the first for Holocaust survivors in America. Life was moving on. There was a death, the birth of a new baby, and some refugees began to locate long lost family members. Life began to normalize. It was time to make plans.

Before those plans could be realized, one special visitor showed up. First Lady Eleanor Roosevelt came to see the camp. The refugees were honored that she came to visit. They knew that they were in America as the president's "special guests," and they wanted to take the opportunity to thank her. She spoke to the refugees in the auditorium, toured their living areas, and was touched that so many seemed delighted to see her. She stayed for lunch with the refugees and enjoyed a performance by some of the camp's singers and musicians. On September 20, 1944, she wrote in her newspaper column, "My Day," "Somehow you feel that if there is any compensation for suffering, it must someday bring them something beautiful in return for all the horrors they have lived through."

Many of the refugees were devastated by President Franklin D. Roosevelt's death in 1945. After all, they were in the country as his guests. His death caused great concern. The same fears were heightened as the war in Europe ended in May 1945. While conditions at the camp weren't ideal, many had started to warm to American life. The majority didn't want to return to Europe. Would a new president offer them the opportunity to stay? Many had nothing to return to.

By this time, Ruth had resumed her job at the Department of the Interior, but the refugees were never far from her thoughts or her heart. She visited frequently. She persuaded Secretary Ickes to help convince President Truman to permit the refugees to stay in America after the end of the war and to grant them citizenship. On December 23, 1945, President Truman gave the refugees a Hanukkah and Christmas present. He announced on the radio they were welcome to stay and become U.S. citizens. Of the 982 who had sailed to the U.S. as refugees, 899 stayed to become Americans.

In January 1946, the *New York Post* asked Ruth to take a leave of absence from the Department of the Interior to cover a fact-finding trip by the newly established Anglo-American Committee of Inquiry on Palestine. Their mission was to develop recommended solutions to the problem of stateless and homeless victims of the war.

She went to Secretary Ickes with the request. He flatly said no: "I need you here."

A few days later, he summoned Ruth to his office. "I was wrong," he announced. "You must go. You owe it to the Jewish people." He shared with her a letter from the Committee, pleading with him to reconsider. Ruth read it, blushing harder at the flattery in that letter than she had at that speaking engagement in New York a few years earlier. The commission wanted her along as more than a reporter. She was necessary to the mission because her experiences in Europe gave her unique qualifications.

She went as quickly as she could. The delegation passed through London and Paris along the way to Germany. There they had a firsthand, in-depth look at devastation — bombed cities, huge makeshift cemeteries, abandoned death camps. Wide-eyed, Ruth and her colleagues traveled through the ashes of Germany, visiting displaced persons (DPs) and death camp survivors, from Stuttgart to Munich. Munich was "full of blasted buildings; the old landmarks were still there, but their backs were broken. The city was crippled." Hundreds of thousands of refugees were pouring out of Poland and into the American zone. In one refugee camp in Munich, newlyweds Hilda and Harry Eisen were trying to figure out their own path to the future. Many refugees chanted as committee members visited, "We want to go! We have to go! We *will* go to Palestine!"

Ruth sat in a cramped gallery, witness to a portion of testimony at the Nuremberg trials, and felt her perspectives on the war and its aftermath continue to expand. She saw the accused war criminals up close and heard the chilling evidence against them.

But what resonated the most was hearing the war's survivors express their passionate desire for a Jewish homeland. She felt that need come alive in her heart, first in Germany, then grow through her remaining time with the committee. Ruth's impassioned reporting made readers a part of the efforts to build a new Jewish state.

Secretary Harold Ickes resigned from the Department of the Interior in 1946. He'd held the job for thirteen years, the longest tenure of any secretary at Interior. Ruth left government service shortly thereafter, returning to her journalism career, and issues of Jewish injustice continued to stay front and center in her life. She covered the story of the refugee ship *Exodus* in 1947 where Holocaust survivors battled the British in their attempts to reach Israel. Her book became the basis for numerous documentaries and the movie *Exodus*.

In 1951, she married Philip Michaels, a New York attorney and social activist. They had two children, and Ruth kept reporting and writing, first and always the witness to history. She continued to serve as a special foreign correspondent to the *Herald Tribune*, covering stories of Jewish immigration to Israel until the paper folded in 1966.

In 1978, she received the National Jewish Book Award for Best Book, her bestseller *A Woman of Israel*. In total, Ruth wrote nineteen books. She received five honorary doctorates and numerous awards for her lifelong work in rescuing Jews. She was also recognized by her peers in the profession. In 1998, she received a Lifetime Achievement Award from the American Society of Journalists and Authors as "a pioneering journalist and author whose books chronicle the most important events of the twentieth century." The 2001 television movie *Haven* starring Natasha Richardson as Ruth Gruber told the story of the refugees and their journey.

Even if she had never sailed with the refugees to their American haven in 1944, Ruth Gruber's life would have been remarkable, for her writing, her witness to history, her personal involvement in the human truths of every story. More than being about work, her life's purpose crystallized during those thirteen days aboard the troop ship, and her commitment to saving Jews and exposing injustice became the hallmark of her life. Her destiny never involved stepping out of line. Her life was spent forging a new path, both for herself and for others.

On October 6, 2002, Ruth helped dedicate the Safe Haven Holocaust Refugee Shelter Museum in Oswego, New York. The museum library was named the Dr. Ruth

Ruth Gruber at the dedication of the Safe Haven Holocaust Refugee Shelter Museum and Education Center. Photo courtesy of the Safe Haven Museum, Oswego, NY.

Gruber Library and Resource Center in her honor. Speaking about the refugees two years later, she said, "Just look at them now. They're doctors and lawyers, and they've given back to America everything that we gave to them. This is one of the greatest stories there is."

Ruth Gruber continued to witness, report, and live inside her stories well into her nineties. She covered acts of humanity and inhumanity and became involved wherever she found injustice and oppression. She was emotionally engaged in the stories she told, and her passionate storytelling got results. She had been deeply affected by the terrorist attacks of 9/11. Ruth said, "In these difficult days, with heartbreaking stories of suicide terrorists and innocent victims, I find it more important than ever to live and write inside of time . . . We must keep working for peace, fighting injustice, and raising our children and grandchildren to live with decency, dignity, and hope."

She passed away in 2016 at the grand old age of 105, having personally experienced a range of twentieth-century history that few others could grasp. She lived inside of time and moved forward within it, leaving behind her testimony as reporter, advocate, and champion of humanity. She showed how a life forever bound to rescue and survival could not only bear witness to history unfolding in front of her, but through her passionate words and compelling photographs, actually change its course.

CHAPTER 8

THE TORCHBEARER OF FREEDOM

"I have never considered myself a survivor. I have always considered that what I did, that was my duty to do."
DAME MARY SIGILLO BARRACO

"Arthur!" Mary cried out as she saw her fiancé walking ahead, down a long tunnel. His footsteps echoed softly against the concrete walls. There was water on the ground. It splashed up on his trousers as he continued on. They had been walking together, hand in hand, but now he was ahead of her and hurrying away.

"Arthur! Wait for me!" She called again. And again and again. Finally, he turned and walked back, took Mary's arm, and gave her a kiss on the cheek. He placed her hands in his. "That's the last one. You have to go back," Arthur said. "I love you," he proclaimed, and dropped her hand. Then he turned and was gone.

The tunnel's light faded to gray too quickly, and the dream was over. Mary woke with a start and gasped in pain, back in the real world of a dark Gestapo prison cell. She was battered and sore from the beating she'd endured the night before. Her back was covered in scabs, just barely formed after she'd been whipped late into the evening. Her cheekbone felt broken. She could tell. They'd fractured it before. Her eyes were nearly swollen shut.

Mary Sigillo and her fiancé Arthur Libre in their engagement portrait. Photo courtesy of the Holocaust Commission, United Jewish Federation of Tidewater, Virginia.

Focusing on the pain was dizzying. She drifted; the sweet dream called her back. She closed her eyes, trying to see Arthur again. Her heart lingered at the edge of wakefulness; it had been so real. She longed to see her beloved once more. She'd seen him only once since they had been imprisoned, one quick glimpse out the high prison window. But that had been months ago. It was hard to remember what it had been like to be young and free and in love. What did the dream mean? Why was he in that tunnel? In her heart she knew the answer.

Mary started to cry. Suddenly, the cell door was flung open, the steel screeching in protest as it bounced off the cold cement wall. Two Gestapo officers entered with Sister Marie Hélène trailing behind. They had a letter for her from Arthur, his last. The Gestapo officer stood up straight and proudly announced that Arthur had been executed the night before. Unable to stop, Mary cried harder as the nun pleaded with the Gestapo men. She persuaded them to give her the letter so that she could make notes to read the letter to Mary. When she was able to see well enough, she could read it herself and maybe accept his last words.

That's how Mary received the news her fiancé was gone from the world. First in a dream, and then from his executioners. At the time, she thought her life was over.

Mary Sigillo was born in Lawrence, Massachusetts, in 1923. Her father, Fortunato

Sigillo, worked as an electrical engineer, and her mother, Leona Colpaert Sigillo, was a sometimes-hairdresser and always-housewife. The first few years of Mary's life were unremarkable. Happy, typical, gloriously average. She remembered little from that early time. Mary's younger brother Fred came along in 1927. By 1930, at the start of the Great Depression, their father had lost his job and had been unable to find another. They talked about moving in with Leona's parents, still in Belgium. Leona and Fred thought it would be best for the children. Just as the family was finalizing plans to sail for Europe, a call came. Mary's father had a job offer. But it meant moving to Canada. The couple decided he would go on ahead to the new job, and she would continue as planned, taking Mary and Fred to meet their grandparents. Mary, her mother, and her younger brother sailed to Antwerp, waving goodbye to their father from the high deck rail. Fourteen days later, her grandparents met them at the port and swept them away to their new home. They were located in Renaix, also known as Ronse, a town in the Flanders region of western Belgium.

She enjoyed a happy childhood there. She sang, studied music, learned French, and was loved and spoiled. Mary was a tough little girl, one who didn't cry when she fell and skinned a knee. She wasn't afraid of spiders, snakes, or thunder, and learned early that she was pretty good with her fists. When Fred was bullied at school, she took those boys on — beating them to avenge her little brother. Her mother was appalled; her grandfather beamed with pride. Mika (Little Mary), as she was known, was only fourteen when her grandfather called her to his side. A veteran of World War I and a former prisoner of war, he remembered Germany's occupation of Belgium in the Great War. He could see the future too clearly.

"Mika," he said, "there is going to be another war. I'm afraid Germany is going to take over Belgium. I may not be here." He didn't elaborate, but Mary knew what he meant.

"I'm going to depend on you to take care of your grandmother, your mother, and your brother. Promise me you will." Mary was the fighter in the family. Her brother was too young, her mother not strong enough. It had to be her.

Mary nodded and put her hand on her grandfather's shoulder. She could almost feel the weight of responsibility transfer to her. She promised him she would do her best and watched as he wiped his eyes once she agreed. Her grandfather passed away two weeks later.

It took another three years, but his unfortunate prediction came true. Germany invaded Belgium. The fighting lasted only eighteen days before Belgium surrendered. To the Belgian people, it felt like everything changed overnight. The Belgian flag was lowered; the swastika flew high. The German military government moved into every city and town. Mary found her freedom curtailed almost immediately. She was a foreigner, the enemy.

Mary, her mother, and brother stuck out to the Germans. They were the only Americans in Renaix. "We were required to report to Gestapo headquarters every day," Mary recalled during her testimony with the Holocaust Commission of the United Jewish Federation of Tidewater, Virginia. "Three times a day! We had to present ourselves at 8 a.m., at noon, and again at 5 p.m." It wasn't fair, but as Americans, they were considered the enemy. It grated on her; Mary hated being forced to face the smirking Gestapo soldiers. On their daily trips through town, they saw prisoners of war being paraded through the streets, bloodied and barefooted. Eventually, she decided to do something about it.

Mary went home and put on a Red Cross

armband. Then she flirted with the guards, talked her way into the POW camp, and began to bring food to the prisoners. She began to make friends. A few prisoners were released weeks later. She took them home with her to look after them. Once they were healthy and able to travel, she talked to some of her friends about how they could travel west, to France or even England. Her friends were eager to do something to get back at the occupiers. They quickly agreed. It was almost a game, stealing bicycles from the front of the German government building at night. Sometimes Mary's mother would look out the window to see bicycles in the bushes in front. She would shake her head and pull the curtains shut.

By that time, Mary was seventeen years old.

Fearless, she joined the Resistance. It was an exciting if dangerous time, and Mary relished being able to make a difference and fight back, even if at first their efforts were just nibbling at the edges of the occupiers' authority. Later, their involvement grew. She bought clocks that could be turned into bombs, helped sabotage rail lines, smuggled documents, and along with her friends, rescued downed paratroopers.

After living in Belgium for several years,

Mary's mother had begun to work as a hairdresser again. She ran a little salon in her house, giving permanent waves and haircuts to local women. She obtained her beauty products from traveling salesmen. One day, one of the deliverymen arrived with her box of salon products and two ragged children in tow. Mary and her mother quickly conferred and agreed. The salesman shook her mother's hand, then left. The children stayed. Mary's mother cut their hair differently and made both children into pretty blondes. Then Mary shepherded them to a member of the Resistance in the countryside so they could escape to the west.

Mary had a beautiful soprano voice and loved to sing. Apart from her exciting new life in fighting Nazi occupiers, she also sang in a band. Naturally, everyone in the band was with the Resistance. One night in a club, she met a handsome young man named Arthur Libre. She smiled at the irony of his last name. Libre means "free" in French. He was with the Resistance too. But unfortunately, he was also there with a young woman. Once she saw that, Mary turned away. She ignored him for the rest of the evening, but a few months later, they met again. "So, are you single now?" Mary asked.

He just grinned, and Mary was about to turn away, when he said, "Of course I'm free. My name is Libre after all." They both laughed, and when he asked her to a dance, she quickly agreed. It wasn't long before they were engaged. The two were often in different places due to the demands of their Resistance work, traveling with refugees or helping former POWs travel west — writing letters to each other when they could. When she had time, Mary began work on an underground newspaper, a task she looked at as another important Resistance duty. She typed up the stories, and other members of her group made deliveries, keeping locals informed about the actions of the Allies against the Germans.

One rainy night, Mary came home extremely late after working at the paper all evening. When she finally fell asleep, it was around 4:00 a.m. and to the sound of the birds chirping; they were already greeting the new day. Moments after she had drifted to sleep, there was a crash, jolting her awake as the Gestapo burst into their house. Mary was incensed that they could just burst in and ransack her house, taking anything they wanted. A Gestapo officer sat on the sofa in the living room while soldiers searched the attic, looking for Jewish refugees. Thankfully, there weren't any staying with them at that time.

The officer picked up several of Mary's letters from Arthur and began to read them. The personal affront stung. She had no right to keep him from doing so. Mary stood by the doorway, watching him, rubbing her arms as though to keep herself still.

"I said to him, 'What were you sent here for, to read love letters?'" Mary recalled. It was the wrong thing to say. One didn't talk back to the Gestapo. "He turned around and gave me such a smack that I fell to the floor." She'd been told earlier not to resist, not to fight back. It would only make the situation worse. Mary didn't fight back then. But she vowed she would later.

One thing was clear. It was impossible to stay in Renaix any longer — being counted three times a day, her movements restricted, and having her most personal items defiled. She had to go. Less than a week later, Mary and Arthur left for France. Mary had a false passport, and it gave her some small sense of security. Arthur didn't have one. But in France their group had Resistance connections who could help him obtain one.

They were arrested the first night after crossing the border. The Gestapo found them easily. Too easily, Mary thought.

"Who are you?" the officer asked. He had Mary's false passport in his hands.

"I'm Germaine LeFevre," she said firmly, giving the name on her false passport.

"No, you are Mary Sigillo from Lawrence, Massachusetts," he replied. "An American," he added with a sneer.

Unnerved by his knowledge, she tried again. "I'm Germaine LeFevre."

The Nazi's lips curved up in a knowing smile. "You're lying."

Mary was numb with shock. As she and Arthur were being led away in handcuffs, they exchanged a look and a question with their eyes. How? This should have never happened. How did the Gestapo know who they were? How did they know she was American? Who betrayed them? Someone from their hometown Resistance group had to be responsible. She asked who had betrayed them. Her captors refused to say but told her they'd paid 750 francs for information on Mary and Arthur's location. Their freedom was taken away for the sum of $15.00 USD.

Prison was one horrifying day after another. Mary was interrogated, tortured, beaten, and starved. The Germans sterilized her with electrodes on her stomach, ensuring she would never have children of her own. She lost track of the days because she'd

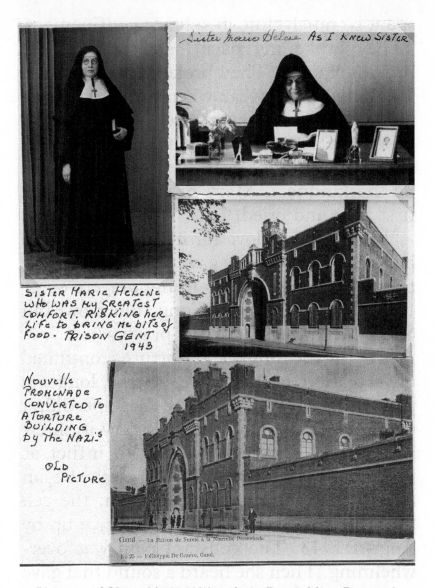

Sister Marie Helene As I Knew Sister

Sister Marie Helene who was my greatest comfort. Risking her life to bring me bits of food. Prison Gent 1943

Nouvelle Promenade converted to a torture building by the Nazis

Old Picture

Gand — La Maison de Sureté à la Nouvelle Promenade.

No 25 — Héliotypie De Graeve, Gand.

Pictures of Sister Marie Hélène from Dame Mary Barraco's wartime scrapbook. Photos courtesy of the Holocaust Commission, United Jewish Federation of Tidewater, Virginia.

spent so much time in solitary confinement. "They broke my back," she said. "They broke my nose. They broke my teeth." She was hungry and weak when transferred to a prison in Ghent, where a Belgian nun, Sister Marie Hélène, brought her bread and jelly and began to look after her. Overwhelmed by the kindness, Mary broke down for the first time and cried.

"I have such a love for her," Mary said in her testimony. "She gave me the courage to keep on going. She's in my prayers every day. She's been dead a long time now, but Sister will always be in my prayers."

Still the beatings and torture continued on a regular basis. There was no longer a point to punishing her. The Gestapo didn't even bother to ask questions or try to interrogate her. They just wanted to inflict as much pain as possible. As soon as she began to heal, they would drag her from the cell again. Mary was nearly ready to give up by August 1943. The constant pain was overwhelming. Then she heard a sound that gave her hope. "I heard the roaring of American bombers flying over the prison camp," she said. "And against all rules and regulations, I put all cautions aside and shouted through the small window of my cell, 'Viva la liberté and viva l'America!'"

Mary was released from prison on Christmas day in 1943. She had served six months of her prison sentence. There was no time to rejoice though, no time to heal. Mary would only heal through the force of her actions. She immediately rejoined the Resistance, and following the Normandy invasion in June of 1944, served as a liaison officer with two Canadian regiments. It was a brazen act of defiance to return to the Resistance and even more so to openly don a uniform and work with Allied soldiers.

Mary Sigillo, Resistance liaison officer to Canadian Forces in Belgium. Photo courtesy of the Holocaust Commission, United Jewish Federation of Tidewater, Virginia.

After the war, Mary was recognized by Prince Charles of Belgium for her service and her personal sacrifices. She moved back to Massachusetts with her family, but the memories of prison were still too fresh, her pain at losing Arthur still sharp. Mary participated in a local newspaper interview, recounting her wartime experiences. Afterward, she began to receive threatening letters from German Americans who felt that Mary's story disparaged their German brothers and sisters back home. Mary took copies of the letters and reported the threats to the FBI. Special agents watched out for her and her family until Mary and her new husband Joe Barraco moved to Virginia.

After everything she had been through, those threats didn't even faze her. They only made her more determined to speak out. Mary began to realize that she needed to do more, to continue tell the story of what happened to her, what she learned, and what a new generation could learn about how valuable their freedom was. She had to talk about it all — what she lost, but also what she gained through her fight, the meaning of patriotism, and the strength to be found in faith and resistance. She spoke at churches and synagogues, in schools, nursing homes, conferences, and in state houses, fulfilling her life mission to speak out about freedom.

"For me to live free I had to forgive. But I'm not going to let anyone forget." In 1959, Mary and her husband Joe adopted a daughter. The Tidewater area of Virginia was a beautiful area to live, and it would have been so easy to just sit back and enjoy the beach, the azaleas in springtime, and family life. But Mary felt she still had more to give. And more people needed her.

During the Vietnam War, Mary created "United We Stand," a national letter writing campaign for POW/MIA soldiers. She continued to speak about the horror of war. People listened to Mary; her story and the power of her beliefs made her unforgettable. She worked on political campaigns. Having the freedom to do so was a powerful motivator. She had a voice and a choice and relished using both.

She was beloved by many soldiers and their families. Mary spoke at the Noncommissioned Officers Association Annual Convention in San Antonio in 1982. Not only were the attendees and their families inspired by her story, many also found themselves left with a feeling of hope and "reassessing their personal feelings on the true meaning of patriotism." Once she learned that NCOA had a scholarship fund, she immediately pledged all speaking honorariums to the fund. Amazed by her generosity, NCOA's Board of Directors immediately established the NCOA Mary S. Barraco Scholarship. The scholarship has been awarded since 1983, with the recipients having submitted a winning essay on Americanism.

Mary was knighted by the King of Belgium in 2004, giving her the title of Dame. She was named a modern-day patriot by the Treasury Department. The Daughters of the American Revolution (DAR) awarded her their Medal of Honor. The United Jewish Federation of Tidewater presented her with the Righteous Gentile Award. Virginia Beach recognized her as the city's ambassador and Torchbearer of Freedom.

The more she spoke to groups, the more she reached out to young people, the more they clamored to hear her story, feel her love for others, and accept her encouragement as a bolster to their own resolve to fight for what is right. In 2009, a play about her life, *The Torchbearer of Freedom,* was performed at Bluefield College in Western Virginia. Mary had assisted in writing the script and hoped the play would help continue to educate young people about the importance of freedom. Virginia Tech undergraduate Donny Bales was part of that production, and Mary's story was etched into his consciousness. Following a white supremacist rally in Charlottesville in 2018, he said he felt powerless watching the violence unfold, yet wanted to act against hatred. He asked himself, "What can we do to speak out against hatred and bigotry?"

Donny recalled meeting Mary and how her story affected him. He said, "She was committed to sharing her story so that future generations would never forget the past. She believed that together we could make a better future."

A life touched by her was a life changed. She certainly affected many through telling the story of her life. At the end of each visit with the people she cared about, she always said "I love you." She couldn't bear to pass up the opportunity to tell them her feelings. What if she didn't have another chance?

In her later years, she suffered from numerous physical ailments. Old war injuries began to limit her movements. Pain from her broken back and broken bones had never left her, but with age, they ached constantly. She had kidney damage from her time in prison, having often been refused bathroom breaks and forced to wait for relief until she cried.

The drugs she'd been given by her captors when she was sterilized may have caused the intestinal cancer she'd beaten in the 1950s. She had numerous dental issues resulting from the broken teeth she'd sustained during repeated prison beatings.

Mary Barraco passed away on December 6, 2019, at the age of ninety-six. On her obituary page, one former high school student wrote about having met her when she spoke at his school: "She changed my life and my way of thinking forty years ago when I was but just a teen, and I'm a better person today for having met her."

Mary spent over sixteen months of her life in Gestapo prisons and concentration camps. She had been scarred, inside and out, but her tormentors could never touch her heart or soul. In prison she wrote these words on her cell wall: *C'est lorsque'on a perdu la liberté que l'on en connaît le prix* — "It is only after we have lost our freedom, we appreciate its value." Those words are now inscribed on a plaque to her memory, located on the Avenue of Veterans in Princess Anne Memorial Park, Virginia Beach.

They called her the Torchbearer of Freedom because she held up the ideal of freedom as the prism shining through the trials of her own life, bringing its brilliance to others. In learning her story, thousands were bathed in that light, finding it renewed their hope and spurred their patriotism and devotion to the cause of freedom. Mary saw it as her life's duty to hold that torch up high. It still burns brightly.

Dame Mary Barraco, then ninety-two, waves to the crowd during the 2015 Veterans Day Parade in Tidewater, Virginia. Photo credit: 2015/Vicki Cronis-Nohe/Virginian-Pilot/TCA.

CHAPTER 9

LOVE CONQUERS ALL

"I felt peace, even though I was still scared. I thought that, whatever would happen to me — I could still be killed, I didn't know — and in what I'd already been through, God was in control."

BERENDINA DIET EMAN

"Look, I already told you. The answer is no! Now go away."

The door slammed in her face, blowing back Diet's unruly blonde hair. "Goodness! I can't believe he turned us down." Furious, Diet turned to her boyfriend, Hein Sietsma. "And here I thought he was a good Christian!" She stamped her foot.

"He probably has his reasons. We just don't know them now." Hein shrugged. There were others they could talk to, others who would be willing to help.

"That's true. Come on. We don't have

time to worry about it. We have a hundred other things to do."

"Places to go." He took her hand and swung it back and forth.

"People to help," she added, smiling. The young couple hurried off. It wasn't until after the war that Diet learned from neighbors why the man at the door couldn't help her hide any Jewish people in his home. He was already sheltering an entire Jewish family in a back room. They stayed with him throughout the war. In later years, Diet co-wrote a memoir of her war activities and chose the title based on that encounter, *Things We Couldn't Say,* "because there were things we couldn't talk about, things we couldn't say," for fear of exposing both the refugees and their protectors.

Diet (pronounced Deet) was born Berendina Roelofina Hendrika Eman on April 30, 1920, in The Hague, the Netherlands. Her father ran an interior decorating business, which was successful until the Depression hit, and sales began to falter. Despite the family's struggles, even when money was scarce, the children were oblivious. Diet recalled her childhood as a happy time, riding bicycles in the countryside and playing with friends.

She met Hein in 1937 when the young man got a job in the city and needed a place to stay. The Eman family took him in as a boarder. While seventeen-year-old Diet didn't like him much at first, they later became friends. By the time she turned twenty, their relationship had turned into something more: love.

She didn't decide to join the Resistance as much as she fell into it naturally. It was just a casual conversation over coffee with her friend and colleague from the bank, Herman, in September 1942. Before the war, Herman, a wonderful violin player, would visit the Eman family in the evenings, and they would form a trio. Herman and Diet's brother would play their violins while Diet accompanied them on the piano. That day over coffee, he told her that he and his family had received a summons and were apparently being sent out of the country. As Jews, they'd been told to pack only one small suitcase each. He didn't seem afraid, just bewildered. As he wondered aloud, maybe it would all work out.

Diet knew better. She'd noticed Jews being marginalized at work and disappearing from stores and public transportation. She told Hein what was happening to Herman. They agreed it was wrong and they couldn't allow

their friend to be taken away. They decided to hide him from the Nazis. Diet found a family with a small farm outside of town who was willing to hide Herman, his fiancée, and her mother. It was only the beginning.

Diet had been watching her country change since the Germans had invaded it in 1940. She witnessed the royal family flee, the German government take over, and the flag with a swastika fly high. German troops goose-stepped through the city for all to see and fear. Gradually, the German approach to occupation had changed from one of mild oversight — the velvet glove — to one of increasingly harsh treatment of Jews and general repression — the iron fist. Now the country's 140,000 Jews were being deported. They had already been banned from public transportation, shops, parks, and certain parts of the city. Herman could no longer visit the Eman family. There were no more musical evenings.

As the situation grew ever more dire, Diet was horrified. While her German was fluent, she resolved that she would not speak the language as long as the Nazis occupied her country. She wouldn't give them an inch. Either they spoke Dutch to her or she wouldn't answer. Once Herman was safely hidden away, his older sister asked for help. Others followed. It snowballed from there. Two weeks later, Diet and Hein were coordinating shelter for more than sixty Jews.

Some of the farmers balked at hiding Jews because of the danger. If they were caught, the Germans would treat those harboring the refugees the same as Jews themselves. Many Dutch families weren't willing to risk their farms or their lives to help others.

Diet and Hein realized they needed to get new identification papers for those they were helping shelter. Jews were required to carry papers with a large black J on them. Once they were hidden away, some in other towns, others on remote farms, they couldn't afford to be found with the telltale "J" papers on them. It would be a death sentence.

Diet and Hein devised a sneaky plan. It was Diet's father's birthday, and a large number of family and friends were at the house for a celebration. Diet looked at the winter coats, purses, and bags scattered about, in the hallway and in a spare bedroom upstairs, and knew they were filled with identification. It was too good to be true. They decided to help themselves, albeit very carefully.

Diet felt guilty. "What if some of my relatives get stopped by the Gestapo?" She whispered.

Hein shrugged. "They'll have to get new papers." They could do that. The Jews in hiding couldn't.

"Should we tell them?" Diet was rifling through her aunt's purse.

"No. For their own good, we won't tell them." Hein pocketed two sets of papers from coats on the floor.

"After the war," Diet replied. "We'll tell them after the war." It eased her conscience a bit.

They tried to not take too many from one household or set of neighbors so as not to raise suspicions. But as Diet later recalled, "That night there were more than a dozen Jewish people who became my aunts and uncles."

Word of the couple's good deeds continued to spread. It wasn't long until there were sixteen young people in their little Resistance group, including Hein's brother Henk. They named their group HEIN; besides being Hein's name, it was also a Dutch acronym for "Helping Each Other In Need."

Their activities expanded beyond finding hiding places. They provided food, money, ration cards, and identification papers to those in hiding. They couldn't take any more papers from their own family members, so as their operations grew, they needed to resort to forgery or further theft. The group reported on German troop movements, and Diet typed out BBC news broadcasts, spreading news of the outside world to the people of the city.

It was a lark at first, their little gang finding ways to fight back and taking risks. It was exciting, small thrills and moments that were necessary to help those in need. But as the work grew more dangerous, they decided they might now actually need weapons. The boys stole a few from German vehicles, and Diet stowed them in her parent's rose bushes. They helped organize transports for fleeing soldiers. Suddenly, the work was not only exciting; it was dangerous and frightening.

"In the beginning you have no idea what risk you are taking," she later recalled. "Then, you're so deep in it, you can't go back."

By 1944, Diet and Hein were engaged. They were experienced at their rescue work by then, and even more careful to avoid detection. Diet began visiting an older lady named Mies Walbeim in The Hague. Mies was sheltering an incredible twenty-seven Jews in her small apartment. Diet was afraid she was taking on too much: They spoke too loudly in the small flat. The toilets flushed too often. Diet worried Mies was going to attract attention to herself.

Gradually, Diet and Hein helped find new hiding places for many of the Jews sheltering in Mies's apartment, and Diet thought she was helping Mies keep a low profile. But every time she visited to offer assistance, bring supplies, or simply check in, she was afraid she would find more guests. Often, she did.

The Germans finally caught on and raided the safe house, arresting all the occupants. Diet wasn't there, but the soldiers found a diary that talked about a Resistance fighter named Toos. It was a fictitious name, but the description was too close to Diet — her with the unruly blonde hair and a crew of young men. They were brazen about their efforts and were becoming well known to informants and getting noticed by German patrols. The Nazis guessed it could be her.

Diet became a fugitive, shuffling from group to group, always moving. She didn't go far, staying on the outskirts of the city or in some of the farms they'd previously used as safehouses. She saw Hein infrequently, and when she did, it was for only a few hours at a time. She didn't dare visit her parents.

In April 1944, Hein was stopped by the Gestapo on a train and arrested. His false papers said he was a pastor, so they were about to let him go but decided they needed to search him first. Then they found the false ration cards, IDs, and other stolen documents. He was sent immediately to a prison camp.

The Gestapo caught up with Diet a few weeks later.

She was on a train from nearby Zwijndrecht to The Hague when a Gestapo officer asked to see her papers. It was just a routine check. There were five other Gestapo officers on the train. They spread out among the cars, just hoping to catch someone or something. Diet's papers were so obviously forged that he pulled her from the train at the next stop,

Rotterdam, and held her. The other five officers joined him. It was their lucky day; they nabbed a fugitive. It was Diet's unlucky day, caught in a random check. The six officers were holding her captive, watching.

"My heart was nearly in my mouth, I had to keep swallowing so it wouldn't burst out. I was so afraid I thought I would be sick." Under Diet's blouse there was an envelope with stolen papers and ration cards in it. The thick packet was burning a hole in her skin, the paper crinkling so loudly she was sure they could hear it. "I felt as though there were flames shooting out of me, because those papers in my bra would be enough to kill me, possibly a number of others, and risk so much of our whole operation."

Fortunately, the Gestapo didn't notice. They were too busy gossiping with each other, laughing, telling stories, and taking their time before questioning her and searching her. Diet said a quick prayer: "If at all possible, grant that those six men give me half a minute so that I can get rid of this envelope." Suddenly one of the soldiers stood up.

"Is that one of the new raincoats?" one soldier asked the officer who had nabbed Diet. "Is it really waterproof?"

"It is. I was caught in a downpour this

251

morning but stayed completely dry. Look at this." He held out his arm for the soldiers to admire the material.

"That is very nice." Another soldier fingered the sleeve.

"It has so many pockets!" one exclaimed.

"You think that it has a lot of pockets on the outside? You should see the inside."

"Oh, look at that!"

"Let me see." The soldiers crowded around like bridesmaids clucking over the fine lace in a friend's white wedding dress. With their backs to her, they didn't see Diet reach into her blouse and toss the envelope away. It lay there on the ground, close by the door to the station, but it didn't matter. She would claim she'd never seen it before.

She breathed a sigh of relief and wiped sweat away from her upper lip. Then she felt almost annoyed. The Nazis were so casual. While this was just a game to them, it was her freedom they were playing with. However, despite their casual attitude, they were very efficient. On the basis of the false identity alone, the officers hustled Diet off to a prison in nearby Vught.

Later, Diet reflected on how very nearly the papers and envelope had come to discovery. "That moment to me was one of the most important miracles that happened in all those years of the Occupation — and it was waiting in the empty inside pockets of a brand-new plastic raincoat." She knew then that God was looking out for her and that she would survive.

The Herzogenbusch Concentration Camp in Vught was the only camp run by the SS outside of Germany. When Diet arrived, 31,000 prisoners were being held there. They were Jews, gypsies, political prisoners, homeless people, and others, including Resistance fighters. She met the well-known evangelist and Resistance hero Corrie Ten Boom and her sister, Betsy, there. Corrie had her own small Bible in prison, and the women often held a short, if subdued, Bible study class in the evenings.

Diet spent only a few months at the camp, but it felt like a lifetime. She was assigned to work in the prison laundry and forced to wash the bloody clothing taken from prisoners who had been shot the night before. At least 749 were killed in Vught. In her memoir, she wrote, "The men who had been executed — usually every night at sunset we could hear the machine guns — would be lying somewhere for hours before they died. I was absolutely heartbroken." That night, Diet took a bobby pin and scratched a message of hope onto the wall of her cell. It was message to herself: Matthew 28:20, "Lo, I am with you always, even unto the end." Was it the end? She didn't know.

View of the barbed wire fence and a watch tower at Vught. Photo credit: U.S. Holocaust Memorial Museum courtesy of the National Archives and Records Administration College Park.

As time wore on, Diet could feel her faith stutter, her beliefs beginning to break down. Any one of those men shot each day could have been her Hein. At the time, she didn't know what had happened to him or where he was. Following his arrest, Hein had been shuffled from camp to camp, finally arriving in Dachau, near Munich, Germany.

Like a mantra, Diet repeated one overriding thought to herself every day: "I've got to get out." Another prisoner helped her rehearse her cover story with a new fake identity. She pretended to be a simple maid named Willie Laarman. Diet was conflicted about lying but realized she needed to do it to survive. She repeated the story so many times she had no trouble telling it to the German official during her hearing. She got every detail right, her imaginary father's middle name, when her imaginary mother died, and her imaginary mother's favorite recipe. She spoke this life as though she'd lived it.

But somehow, the interrogator wasn't fooled. Hearings and interrogations were his area of expertise. He looked Diet straight in the eye and said, "I can *feel* what is true and what isn't true. I can't put a needle in your story. It fits — all the way through. But my sixth sense tells me that it's all made up." Diet gulped. Although her inner conflicts must have shown through somehow, she'd made it through.

It was summer by then, and the Allies were advancing. The Germans wanted to empty the camp. Diet heard the chattering machine guns as male prisoners were executed each evening. The widows were being released. She walked out of the camp in August 1944 and traveled home to find her parents. Then she started to search for Hein.

Hein's last letter found its way to her. He had scribbled it on a scrap of paper and tossed it from the train as he was on his way to the concentration camp at Dachau, Germany. Train tracks outside the camp gates were littered with clothing, notes, letters, and other personal items that desperate people had thrown from the train in hopes that they would reach their loved ones. Later, Diet recalled, "He addressed to me at my parents' address in The Hague. Someone, somehow, picked up that fragile, tiny piece of correspondence, and later — I don't remember exactly when — I received it." It was all remarkable — that the letter survived through the Netherlands' constant rain and fog, that someone found it, mailed it, and she received it. She kept that special letter close, knowing how blessed she was to have it.

Hein wrote, "Even if we won't see each other on earth again, we will never be sorry for what we did, and that we took this stand. And know, Diet, that of every last human being in this world, I loved you most." He ended the message with the three Latin words that were engraved on her engagement ring, *Omnia vincit amor.*

Love conquers all.

The war was over by the time the Red

Cross informed Hein's father of his death. Hein's parents summoned Diet, and they all held hands as his father gave her the news.

"No, no. Not my Hein," she sobbed. "It can't be true." Even so, she had somehow known. A small voice had tried to warn her, but she had dismissed it as simply doubt. Her knees buckled and she slowly lowered herself onto the floor. Her life was over. His parents watched, wiping their own tears away.

"Why him?" she gasped, trying to get her breath. "Why not me, instead?" She didn't understand God's purpose. *Why?*

Weeks later, she learned more of the story. Because his papers said he was a preacher, he'd been imprisoned with other religious leaders and priests. "I began to receive letters from people I'd never known — farmers, pastors, other men from the Underground: they said that they had met my fiancé in this camp or that camp, and that in the deepest misery they faced, Hein had spoken of his faith in God's promises. He was a light in their darkness, they said."

It was a small comfort. Diet still felt the light was gone from her life. She couldn't face life there in The Hague, trying to dig out a new path from the rubble of the old. She found herself imagining she could see him around every familiar corner, to think

she heard his voice in a crowd. "I wanted to forget . . . to start a new life in a country where there were no memories and never talk about that time again."

She was determined to get as far away as she could, to scrape together a new life and career that had no relation to anything or anyone she had known before. Diet studied nursing, learned Spanish, and took a job in Venezuela. It was a lifetime away from her prewar existence as a bank teller in the Netherlands. In South America, she worked in a hospital for Shell Oil Company workers, in the rural western provinces of the country. She married and had two children, remaining in Venezuela for nearly ten years before moving to New York; Diet and her husband later divorced. She moved again, settling in Grand Rapids, Michigan. There she worked as a translator at the Kelvinator Appliance Company before retiring in 1986. With her newfound time, she was able to get back to her calling and doing what she loved most: volunteer work to those in need.

For over thirty years, Diet Eman didn't want to talk about the war. She had long suffered post-traumatic stress from the horrors she'd witnessed and experienced. As a devout Christian, she leaned on her faith for

support. Her pastor was one of the first to try to convince her to speak out. He said, "If something happened in your life, and God is involved, you have to tell it." Diet thought about it and replied, "God was involved, because we wanted to obey God to help the Jewish people."

In 1978, Diet was reunited with Corrie Ten Boom, whom she had met and befriended while working in the laundry at the Vught concentration camp. Ten Boom, also a devout Christian who had aided in the Resistance prior to her arrest, had remained in the Vught prison when Diet was released and had been one of the female prisoners sent east to Ravensbrück (the men were sent to Sachsenhausen) as the Allies drove through the Netherlands in the fall of 1944. Vught was liberated in October 1944 by Canadian troops.

It was Corrie Ten Boom's autobiography, *The Hiding Place,* that first moved Diet to consider telling her own story. A combination of other factors began to nudge her too. She was concerned about the Holocaust deniers and what she saw as an alarming rise in anti-Semitism. Scripture seemed to send her messages too. "My conscience started to gnaw, and it seemed that every time I opened the Bible, something like, 'Tell the great things that I have done' was staring me in the face."

A few months later, Professor James Schaap at Dordt College in Sioux City, Iowa, was hosting a "Suffering and Survival Convention" featuring speakers who had survived the Holocaust and/or served in WWII. Many Dordt students had parents and grandparents who were Dutch, living in the Netherlands during the War. After a keynote speaker canceled, Dr. Schaap was casting about for a substitute when he got a break: A local chicken farmer had met Diet during a recent relief mission to South America and knew her story. He gave Schaap her phone number, and Schaap called to see if she would share her story with his students. Although she'd only spoken in public about the war once before, she agreed to come.

Following the passionate retelling of her story, Schaap offered to help her write her memoir. He later said Diet's story was the ultimate love story. It was about "a girl, a guy, and a God who won't allow them to tolerate the innocent deaths of His people." He wanted to help her tell that story in such a way that it would educate a new generation.

Diet didn't agree initially. She was still reticent about uncovering the painful old memories, but she believed God spoke to her, telling her she should share her story. She called Schaap back. It was as Corrie Ten

Boom had said, "Books do not age as you and I do. They will speak when you and I are gone, to generations we will never see."

Schaap's eight-part series, "The Diet Eman Story," was first published in November 1993 in *The Banner: A Weekly Publication of the Christian Reformed Church.* The complete biography, *Things We Couldn't Say,* was published the following year.

Graphic depicting Diet Eman's story of resistance and love from The Banner. *Illustration © Scott M. Holladay.*

That was the first major recognition she'd received in many years. Filed away, she had a Certificate of Appreciation from General Eisenhower, recognizing her work in helping Allied soldiers escape from the enemy. President Ronald Reagan sent her a letter in 1982 that recognized the importance of her efforts to tell her story. "In risking your safety to adhere to a higher law of decency and morality, you have set a high and fearless standard for all those who oppose totalitarianism."

Later, Diet became an American citizen and continued to receive recognition for speaking out about her work in WWII. Israel's Holocaust memorial, Yad Vashem, recognized her with the Righteous Among Nations Award in 1998. She was honored by the Red Cross in 2010, and in 2015, the Dutch King Willem-Alexander called her one of the country's "national heroes."

For Diet, it was never about the awards. It was as it always had been for her, a devotion to helping others. James Schaap described her passion well. "She was a fierce little woman who told her story in a torrent of laughter and tears." Well into her nineties, Diet continued to speak out and care for "those people who Christ described as 'the least of these my brethren.'" She volunteered with several relief societies, including the

Red Cross, making dozens of trips into Guatemala, Ecuador, Honduras, the Dominican Republic, and other locations on missions to provide medical treatment for the poor. Her Spanish language skills and nurse training were an advantage. She accompanied medical students from the University of Cincinnati to El Salvador on multiple missions.

In the postscript to her 1994 autobiography, she wrote, "When the war ended, we all said, 'This can never happen again.' But now polls show that 22 percent of the U.S. population does not believe there was a Holocaust. The story *has* to be retold so that history does not repeat itself."

Diet's views were unfortunately accurate. Today, Jewish community leaders have begun to fear that the horrors of Nazi Germany are fading from the world. By the time Diet passed away in September 2019, there were only 400,000 Holocaust survivors still alive, half that number in Israel. Today, 31 percent of Americans (41 percent of millennials) don't believe that six million Jews perished in the Holocaust. Fifty-eight percent think something like that could happen again.

Thankfully, Diet's story of faith, sacrifice, survival, and a humble willingness to serve others lives on. Following World War II, she tried to move away from her deep pain and loss in order to settle into a new life. Yet the past was always with her, along with God's love and a gentle reminder that she had a purpose to fulfill. As a nurse, a volunteer missionary, and as a woman with a story to tell, she served through her truth.

At her funeral in September 2019, her granddaughter read her favorite Bible verse, Psalm 27: "Though an army besiege me, my heart will not fear; though war break out against me, even then I will be confident."

Love conquers all.

CHAPTER 10

WE FOLLOWED OUR STARS

"We were lucky enough to see the problem in terms we could understand."

IDA COOK

"He's giving me the eye!" Louise's nose was nearly inside Ida's ear, her surprise a shrill whisper. Ida pulled back, leaving her sister's nose suspended in mid-air, mouth open, another play-by-play about to be delivered.

"I'm telling you he's checking me out!" Louise hissed. "Look over there by the front desk. He's with the others. *Them.* You know who I mean." Blinking rapidly, Louise inclined her eyes dramatically to the right, about as obvious as a klaxon at a railroad crossing.

Them over there.

"Be quiet. You're making a scene." Ida frowned, dashing over and shielding her sister from the view of the military men near the hotel concierge desk. "Look at me. Now," she commanded. "Eyes front."

Louise pulled her gaze away and gulped. She met Ida's unblinking stare. "Do we have anything to worry about?" Ida asked. She looked down meaningfully at her purse and grabbed Louise's wrist, squeezing tightly. Ida was serious. Louise let her eyes drift but not to Ida's purse.

"Oh my God! He winked at me. Ribbentrop actually winked at me. The Foreign Minister himself!"

"Mary Louise! That's enough; we're leaving." Alarm bells were ringing loudly in Ida's head. No more pretend flirting. She tugged at Louise's arm and began to pull her younger sister towards the revolving door at the front of the posh hotel.

Maybe it had been a mistake to book a room at one of Berlin's finest hotels, the Adlon. Right there beside the Brandenburg Gate, it was obvious who the clientele would be: diplomats, Nazi Party officials, SS generals, and other elites. It was 1936, and the Berlin Opera House was waiting for them.

The two certainly looked out of place: two awkward, middle-aged English sisters. In their homemade house dresses, the pair wanted to fit in with the hotel's wealthy and important guests. Unfortunately, they didn't. Their oversized fur coats and gaudy costume jewelry did nothing to hide their square features and plain looks. Perhaps they were trying to appear elegant. But they simply looked foolish. Out of place. And a little bit twitchy. Not that they had anything to hide, obviously. They wouldn't be capable of any subterfuge. Not these mousy-looking women. As they neared the door of the hotel, the cluster of men by the front desk burst into loud and raucous laughter. Cheeks hot and backs rigid, the sisters shuffled out into the night.

They waited for their taxi at the corner. The Berlin State Opera was performing *Rigoletto,* and a boorish group of government officials, generals, and Nazi party leaders weren't going to stop them from attending. Usually, they were invisible. Young lieutenants barely gave them a passing glance; maybe a sneer, but nothing more. The senior officers, Goebbels, Himmler, Streicher, Ribbentrop, and once even Hitler himself, looked right through them. One by one, they all turned away, at blitzkrieg speed, before eye contact could be made, or a shy smile sent their way. Typically, no one noticed the two middle-aged women on their way out for a big evening. The Cook sisters were on their way to the opera.

Budding opera fans Ida and Louise Cook posing in their homemade finery. © Permission (Rupert Crew Limited)/Victoria and Albert Museum, London.

But Ribbentrop . . . Tonight, he'd decided to notice Louise. Well, Ida thought, it was more likely she'd noticed him first. The former German ambassador to Britain was well known for his social awkwardness and public gaffes. The English press hated him, and now that he was Germany's Foreign Minister, there was even more reason to despise the man. After all, once he'd nearly knocked King George on his bum, flinging a stiff-armed Nazi salute at the monarch.

Next time, they would stay in another hotel, blend back into the woodwork again. It was a blessing to be taken for granted and dismissed without a second thought. With their bland, unassuming faces and gawky figures, the Cook sisters would never stand out in a crowd, much less be considered a threat. Louise had sewn the English labels into the fur coats herself. She often made their clothes from patterns she'd found in women's magazines. Ida's deep pockets and her oversized purse were typically filled with a tangled wad of expensive jewelry. They knew full well what they looked like: nothing special, nothing memorable. It was what made them so successful in a risky, illegal, and dangerous business. Years later, Ida said, "The funny thing is, we weren't the James Bond type — we were just respectable Civil Service typists."

That scene in the lobby of the Adlon wasn't a singular occurrence. The sisters typically met their "cases" nearby or at other first-class hotels. But occasionally, it became a little bit awkward, Ida explained in her understated way. One woman spent her life's savings to purchase a diamond brooch, hoping to get it out of the country and have its sale guarantee her passage. Ida agreed to smuggle the jewel out, but that was before she saw it. It was breathtaking in its ugliness, so big as to look fake. Ida thought it looked as though it had to be from the dollar store. She decided there was nothing to do but show it off. She nervously fixed it to the collar of her faded cardigan and turned to Louise. "So, how do I look?" she asked.

"Like you've just been to Woolworths," Louise said. She nearly smiled. "Quite lovely," she added, but didn't sound convinced.

"Let's hope the guards agree," Ida said nervously. "I'm going to leave my coat unbuttoned too. Let everyone get a good look. I haven't got anything to hide." She set her chin, picked up her boxy little suitcase, and the sisters set out for home. The brazen ruse worked.

In fact, they may never have ventured into the gray areas of smuggling without a nudge. They were helped and encouraged by their friends from the opera community; their first encounter was almost by chance. Orchestra conductor Clemens Krauss and his wife, the opera singer Viorica, asked a favor: would they accompany a woman traveling alone? Take her back to London with them? Naturally, they said yes, and Mitia Mayer-Lismann accompanied the sisters on their route back through Holland. It was just a favor for a friend. At the time, the sisters didn't know Mitia was fleeing Germany.

Ever helpful, the two showed Mitia around London several times after her arrival, taking her to the usual tourist spots, including Buckingham Palace, Westminster Abbey, and Saint Paul's Cathedral. In each church, Mitia asked, "Is this a Catholic or Protestant church?" The sisters exchanged a glance, *What does this mean?*

Moments later, they were seated in a tea shop and Ida pulled off her gloves. Just as their guest was about to pop a bite of fairy cake into her mouth, Ida asked, "So are you Protestant or Catholic, dear? We don't have to visit any more churches of one kind if you are the other."

Blinking, Mitia choked, took a sip of tea and blurted out, "I'm Jewish. Didn't you know?"

The sisters didn't; religion wasn't something they concerned themselves with very much. They knew about the situation in Germany, Ida said, but not firsthand. "The friend opened our eyes into the appalling situation Jewish people in Germany found themselves in. They were without any rights as human beings at all."

If anything, learning about the plight of the Jews made them even more determined to help. Louise began to study German so she could conduct interviews with potential immigrants. They examined their personal finances to see what they could afford.

Ida had a little money of her own. In the 1920s, she had begun to write love stories, serialized for magazines. Later, she wrote romance novels under the pen name of Mary Burchell. She wrote 130 romances over the next fifty years, earning a respectable £1,000 a year. That extra money had funded their travel to operas; now it could support their trips to the continent to save as many people as possible from extermination.

As Ida once exclaimed, "Oh blessed light romance that kept the money rolling in. I said I could and would willingly pay (the guarantee) myself. And two more people could live." Louise was a typist for the Department of Education and was glad for Ida's contributions. However, they soon needed more. To increase their funds, Ida traveled all over the country, giving lectures and speaking in churches to support their rescue work and find sponsors for refugees, another effort the shy woman began almost by accident.

Ida continued to save everything she earned from the sale of her magazine articles and romance novels. Later, as they honed their craft, the sisters arranged for forged documents, dealt with government deportation officials, interviewed people who needed sponsorship, and even bought a small flat in London for the refugees to live in while they began to pick up the pieces and build new lives. Mitia was one of the first residents. She'd returned to Germany to bring out her entire family.

Every few months, the two flew to Berlin or Vienna on Friday, not at all common at the time. Flying was expensive, and the German government was tightening border controls as the country began to change under Adolph Hitler's reign. Sometimes they headed for an opera in other cities, perhaps Cologne, Munich, or Frankfurt, even Salzburg, Austria. That was their story anyway. Most opera story lines they knew by heart, so it was easy to talk about them and answer questions, even if they didn't have time to actually attend.

Ida and Louise heading out on another trip, ostensibly to attend an opera. © Permission (Rupert Crew Limited)/Victoria and Albert Museum, London.

But the soldiers didn't question them often. They were typically ignored. The sisters would return to London by train and boat from the Netherlands on Sunday evening. Their pattern was to always enter Germany through one port and leave by another. On one of their longer trips, they spent a tense, eternally long half hour watching guards lounge lazily outside their railcar. They were sweating with fear, white knuckles tightly wrapped around the handles of their heavy purses. It was just a "bit awkward," as Ida drolly recalled.

Ida had a rationale she explained to herself just as often as she did to Louise. "If our jewelry were discovered and queried, we were going to do the nervous British spinster act and insist, quite simply, that we always took our valuables with us, because we didn't trust anyone with whom we could leave them at home." That story sounded like a good idea at the time. Luckily, they never had to test it.

With each trip, they smuggled out enough riches to enable Jewish families to buy their way to freedom, proving they could provide for themselves and meeting Britain's strict requirement to prove financial stability, thus earning passage. Some of the individuals Ida and Louise assisted didn't relocate to Britain, but to the United States.

Many families liquidated their savings, putting the money into tangibles — diamonds or other precious jewels. Once the sisters agreed to take on a couple, or even an entire family, they personally carried the family's nest eggs out, usually around their necks. Once the refugees arrived in London, they were reunited with their stake and could begin a new life. It wasn't an easy process, but it worked. Perhaps the most annoying constraint was limiting their opera attendance.

Forgetting about opera was unthinkable. Since the mid-1930s, the Cooks were total "opera groupies." They had been attending operas for years, standing at the stage door, hoping for an autograph or a picture, saving programs, and gossiping with other admirers about their favorite stars. They wrote innocent fan letters and sometimes were fortunate enough to meet the singers or even a member of the orchestra. They became friends with a few, particularly Berlin orchestra conductor Clemens Krauss and his wife Viorica Krauss-Ursuleac, a famous opera singer. They were the initial enablers for the sisters' mission, what Ida called "two against the Nazis."

After the Nazi party came to power in Germany in 1933, the British government had allowed very few Jewish families to emigrate. They had to provide guarantees of their financial stability, which made immigration difficult, if not impossible, for many. But following the Kristallnacht, when thousands of Jewish homes and businesses were burned and looted, average Britons were shocked and protested the policy.

In response, the government eased restrictions on immigration, but only for Jewish children, not their parents. This meant that private citizens or relief organizations had to sponsor a child or adult, paying for food, housing, and education. For the child, that meant virtually adopting them until they turned eighteen. For women, sponsorship typically meant they would face a life of domestic service. For men, it was even more difficult to buy their way out because they had no way to prove they had secured employment before applying to emigrate.

Ida looked at the problem simply. There was right and there was wrong. What Ida and Louise Cook saw happening in 1930s Germany was clearly *wrong*. Jewish people were being persecuted. They had no rights, their property was seized, and their homes and synagogues were looted, then destroyed. Detention camps were opening. But what could two older ladies actually do about it?

Ida and Louise believed they had a moral obligation to help. There was no other option. Following the war, Ida was asked again and again why they became involved in such a perilous business. What they were doing was against the law. One false move, one search of their belongings, or one arrest and they could have been shot or sent to a concentration camp. Ida dismissed those concerns with a shrug. "After all, what you are is what you do, isn't it?"

The sisters' main weapons were their guileless looks, their naiveté, and a childlike faith in the power of their British passports to ward off evil. Between 1936 and 1939, they managed to save more than two dozen families from certain death. Once they began their mission, word spread rapidly through Jewish communities, and the sisters were inundated with requests for help. The most difficult part of their mission was determining who they could save and who they could not. The fate of those who they couldn't help weighed heavily upon them.

Following one particularly harrowing trip, Ida and Louise returned home exhausted from the stress of their fear of being caught and their guilt over those left behind. They lived with their parents at the time, and it always felt a bit disconcerting to come to the comfort and safety of home from a world of risky travel and the possibility of being arrested. Louise went straight to bed. Ida sniffed the air and followed the homey scent of baking bread. She walked straight through to the kitchen where her mother was rolling out dough. Ida tried to talk about what they had seen, but her guilt and frustration won out.

Ida sunk into a chair at the kitchen table and burst into tears. Her mother didn't even look up. She just kept adding flour to the pastry. Ida cried herself out, dried her eyes, and began to watch her mother, curious by her lack of response.

"Mum?" She asked. Her mother didn't reply.

Ida wiped her nose and let the warmth and normalcy of the home settle over her like an old shawl. She was home and safe. Slowly, Ida's nerves began to settle. Her mother just went on rolling out the pastry, adding a bit of water, and then cutting it. Finally, her mother looked over and said, "It's no good tearing yourself to pieces. You're doing the best you can. Now tell me all about it."

Ida was reassured, and her mother's common sense relieved her fears. By then, it was 1939, and the war was approaching. Their very last mission nearly ended in disaster. A boy had written to the sisters from the Polish prison camp Zbaszyn. The Nazis herded German Jews there in 1938, pushed them just over the border from their home country. The boy said he knew he had no more claim to ask for help than thousands of others, but he'd heard so much about the sisters and had to try. Only a certain number were permitted to emigrate at any one time. His quota number to get to the United States was so high that it meant he would wait for at least three years to be called. He knew it was foolish to ask, but could the sisters help him?

Ida wrote him back, hoping to give him the courage to go on by promising him they would put him on their list. He was "overjoyed" the sisters had agreed to help him and wrote back that he could live on hope alone for several more months. But living on hope alone wasn't enough for the sisters. They were more determined than ever to get him out of that camp.

Ida redoubled her efforts to find him a sponsor. At her next opportunity to speak to a church congregation, she talked about the boy. Three weeks later, she had the pastor's guarantee that the church would help. His entire congregation was in support. But it wasn't as simple as that. The boy had to prepare new papers in order to be considered, and as Ida discovered, she was just three days too late to have his case considered by the bureaucracy. A new quota had been set, and he didn't meet the cut. But after a little persuading by Ida, a helpful clerk at the

British consulate backdated his application letter, and he was approved. "And on such details people's lives hung," Ida mused.

After clearing this obstacle, there were the typical delays and problems, but by August of 1940, the boy's British entry visa was granted. By then, however, every boat leaving Poland was booked. People knew that war was imminent, and they were all running for their lives. Ida had only one chance to get him on that boat, and she took it. They sent him money for his fare and hoped for the best. They waited and waited but didn't receive an answer.

The sisters were on their last visit to Germany when they learned that the boat, the final children's transport, had sailed. They didn't know if he made it on board, only that the ship was on its way. They worried about their boy while on the train home. The next day, they rushed to the receiving office in London, but no one there knew who was on board. They suggested to Ida that the only way to find out would be for her to go down to the docks and greet the ship when it arrived. Ida kept checking on the ship's progress, and her and Louise's worrying continued nonstop. They looked at maps, scanned newspapers every day for word, and prayed for him.

Finally, the day came and their ship was entering the port — not a cloud in the sky and the water sparkled brightly, little fireworks announcing the happy arrival. It seemed a morning meant for prayers to be answered and hope fulfilled. Ida and Louise stood anxiously on the dock. There weren't many others there to meet the children, just some sponsors and a sprinkling of relief workers and adoptive families. Louise spotted their clergyman in the crowd and waved, but he had turned away to face the docking ship. The gangplank was coming down.

Ida looked past him. "I see them now," she cried. There they were — a ragtag bunch, "coming slowly down the gangway, carrying their little bundles and gazing around on a strange world. None of them spoke English. None of them had a hope in the world, except to live, instead of being killed."

There were two hundred children on that boat, ranging in age from four to sixteen. Every one of them had to leave their families behind. They had to leave everything. It was unimaginable, seeing those ragged, stunned children coming towards them, their faces blank, eyes downcast in the strong sun.

"It's him! It's him! Oh, thank God, he made it!" Ida grabbed Louise's arm. They jumped up and down and waved wildly. He looked like his picture, their boy. He was the very last child in the large group, almost running down the gangplank, a huge smile on his face. With only that passport photo in hand, the sisters were able to recognize the Polish boy they had fought so hard for. And somehow, he recognized them, the women who had risked so much to save him. He ran straight into their arms where all three cried tears of relief and thankfulness. He was the last refugee they were able to save, Ida recalled.

The war had officially begun.

From then on, life in London became perilous. The blitz was on and enemy planes clustered overhead at all hours, bombing the city. Louise was evacuated to the west country with her civil service office comrades, and Ida volunteered as an air raid warden. When the sirens blared, warning of the approach of enemy bombers, Ida helped shepherd her neighbors into local shelters. It was a small job, but an important one in her neighborhood. She continued to make a difference, helping others, always in her own circumscribed way and in line with her own abilities.

Following the war, they continued to live in the small flat in Wandsworth (a southwest

London suburb) they'd originally purchased for newly arrived refugees. But for the rest of their lives, the ones left behind lived in Ida and Louise's memories and remained the subject of their daily prayers. It was one thing to do all they could, but the sisters still wished they could have done more. For years, they kept letters and photographs from many who had written to them for help and often wondered what had become of them. But they kept on.

They hoped to meet up with some of the families they'd helped once the war ended. Some they simply lost track of. Others didn't write or respond to their letters. Other reunions didn't take place for many years. But those who owed their lives to these two unassuming women never forgot what they risked and how they were determined to help. One reunion took place in an unusual way.

The sisters were invited guests on the popular British television series *This is Your Life* on March 11, 1956. The series primarily highlighted the achievements of celebrities and sports figures but also focused on average people who had done extraordinary things in their lives. Two years earlier, the international tennis star Alice Marble appeared on the American version of the program. She was introduced by her protégé Althea Gibson.

Both the British and the American programs were based on a simple premise: a surprise and a reunion. The British program host, Eamonn Andrews, would then read the story of the guest's life from a prop, "The Big Red Book," before handing it over at the end of the tribute, with the words, "This is your life."

Eamonn Andrews presents Ida Cook with her "Big Red Book."
© Permission (Rupert Crew Limited)/Victoria and Albert Museum, London.

Ida thought she and Louise had been invited because of her series of successful romance novels, written under the pen name

Mary Burchell. She'd published forty-nine of them by 1949, and her publisher considered her one of his bestselling authors. Instead, the Cook sisters were surprised by guests who talked about how Ida and Louise had saved them from the Holocaust. One was Viorica Krauss-Ursuleac, who talked about how she and her husband helped start the sisters on their path to save others. Ida's response to it all, in her typical understated manner, was, "Perfectly wonderful evening . . . still happily dazzled."

Her new status as a television star enabled Ida to gain agency representation and speak on a lecture circuit. She often gave talks about their wartime work, although opera remained her favorite subject.

Ida and Louise Cook were named "Righteous Among Nations" on July 28, 1964. For their work in helping twenty-nine Jews escape Nazi persecution, they received a medal from the World Holocaust Memorial Center and their names were added to the Wall of Honor in the Garden of the Righteous at Yad Vashem in Israel. At the time, they were two of only four Britons to receive the honor. The Israeli ambassador to the UK, Arthur Lourie, held a special ceremony recognizing them at the embassy in London. A number of the people they had rescued were on hand for the event. The title of the award, "The Righteous Among the Nations," originated in 1953 when Israel's Parliament, the Knesset, created Yad Vashem, the National Martyrs and Heroes Memorial organization.

This award honors non-Jews whose service meets four criteria: They must have been actively involved in saving Jews from threat of death or deportation, risked their own lives in the process, had no motive other than that of saving Jews from the Holocaust, and finally, there must be firsthand testimony from those rescued. Several gave testimony about the role of the Cook sisters in helping them escape the Holocaust. One was Jerzy Maliniak, a Pole who was the former assistant conductor of the Vienna Opera; the sisters also saved his wife and baby girl. The other was Friedl Orlando, a German journalist. She was rescued just as she'd lost all of hope for escape. The sisters got her out on a student permit.

They continued to receive public recognition for their efforts. The publication of Ida's memoir *We Followed Our Stars* resulted in a wide general awareness of the Cook sisters' efforts. At least three-quarters of the book focused on Ida's favorite subject, opera, and discussed the pros and cons of various singers, the operas they had seen, and the stars

Ida and Louise at the Israeli embassy in London on March 23, 1965. Photo credit: Daily Mail/Shutterstock.

they had befriended and even visited. Ida's recount of their work to help Jewish refugees was much more circumspect, describing those dramatic days in an almost casual manner. She was deliberately vague about the details. Yet people knew what they had done.

It would have been easy to get used to being celebrities. Despite the accumulating awards, the television shows, and the applause, Ida and Louise never forgot how it really felt in that dangerous time just before the war. "Even now, when I am alone," Ida said, "I sit down and think quietly over those terrible days, because I never want to forget — or get used to the fact — that we were saved by a miracle." Just before Christmas in 1986, Ida died of cancer. Her beloved sister Louise died five years later. Their sacrifice and their courage gave hope to many, and while they were unable to save every person who approached them for help, they did everything they possibly could. Some days, it wasn't enough, but Ida simply said, "We called ourselves Christians. We tried to do our best."

They continue to be remembered for their actions and their inspiration in moving others in communities across the country to support them. In 2010, the sisters were named "British Heroes of the Holocaust," a new national award given to those who helped rescue victims of the Holocaust. Twenty-five Britons were given the award posthumously, including Ida and Louise. And on January 27, 2017, Holocaust Remembrance Day, Sunderland, a coal-mining city in northeast England, erected a plaque in their honor at the site of their childhood home.

While they never married or had families of their own, the sisters lived long and fulfilling lives. They had their books and their wide circle of friends. They had opera, and in opera circles, the sisters were renowned for the parties they threw. Their rescue efforts lasted only three short years, but these two mild-mannered women, through their small achievements, gave hope, changed lives, made a great difference to many, and had a lasting impact on future generations. The sisters were everything they appeared to be on the surface: simple, middle-class public servants. But they knew God's honest truth. They didn't have to be rich to make a difference, and they often had to rely on the kindness of strangers for donations to help them save just one more refugee. Yet they didn't quit. The thought would have never occurred to them. Author Anna Sebba wrote the foreword to the 2008 reissue of Ida's autobiography, *Safe Passage*. She said, "They were born with an innate moral gauge, a spirit level in the brain that tilted as soon as they smelled evil. Courage they learned along the way."

They weren't dashing or charming like James Bond. They were just themselves and did things as they always had. It was simply that sometimes, as they traveled to attend the opera in Germany or Austria, they would come home in different clothing, wearing furs and more jewels. Or traveling with a new friend.

Not all acts of humanity have to be large or sweeping to have an impact. Every life saved matters. More than twenty-nine families lived because of these modest heroines. Two unassuming women stepped out of line and broke the law to serve and save others.

CHAPTER 11

POWER MAPS

"I can't recall a time when your gender mattered more than your ability to contribute."

MARION ARMSTRONG FRIESWYK

Splat! Pile after pile of goopy white plaster splashed onto the floor below, coating a jumble of broken chairs and tables, narrowly missing the booth where President Abraham Lincoln had been assassinated in 1865, seventy-eight years earlier. Piles of the stuff dotted the floor of the once proud Ford's Theatre, looking like a lineup of sticky little meringue mountains.

"Oops!" Marion Armstrong laughed at the mess they were making. She felt a tiny bit guilty, but it had to be done. They had to get rid of the bad batch of the plaster and fast. It just wasn't setting; something was off with how they'd mixed it. It was too soft.

Each plop echoed loudly in the empty

theater. "Come on, Henry, help me with this," Marion said. Henry Frieswyk picked up the half-full bucket of the defective plaster.

"One, two, three!" Together they heaved the bucket over the balcony. Marion scraped out the dregs with her hands. She was covered in wet plaster. She looked around at the other members of the team. Instead of helping, they were still studying the topographic map they'd worked on all night. What were meant to be sharp peaks of volcanic mountains in Sicily now looked like rounded blobs of melting ice cream. One of them poked at a ridge. It slid off the side of the map altogether. The project couldn't be salvaged.

"Hey!" shouted Marion, getting their attention. "Come on! Let's get rid of it all. We're running out of time!"

She got her teammates lined up by the railing, and together, they finished scraping the soft, dough-like plaster off the topographic map. It was huge — a forty-pound monster map, three feet long and two feet high. Over the rail the sagging mountains went, sliding two stories down, splashing all over the auditorium of the abandoned Ford's Theatre.

Except that it wasn't entirely abandoned. The third floor of the historic building now housed the studio office for a team of cartographers, working to build one of the first topographic maps to support the War Department's operational planning. The assignment: build a three-dimensional map illustrating the rugged terrain of Italy. They had to meet the deadline. The Joint Chiefs needed this visual aid to inform their planning for an upcoming invasion.

Now they had to get the jigsaws working again to fix earlier mistakes and mix up a new batch of plaster. It was just after 3:00 a.m. one muggy spring night in 1943 when the plaster disaster took place. The team started over. By the time the new topographic map was complete, it was nearly dawn. They all went home for a few hours of sleep and then were back at it. The map still had to be painted and painstakingly smoothed, sanded, and touched up. Finally, they had it ready to be presented to the Joint Chiefs. It was delivered right on time, and the entire team took a deep breath.

Following their late nights spent at Ford's Theatre, Marion and Henry, friends since their days at Clark University, had been dating. "We made a good team," she recalled. They were married by the summer of 1943, in the parlor of the Washington, DC, rooming house where Henry was staying. The wedding guests were all work colleagues, as their families didn't have the money to travel to DC. It was still an unforgettable ceremony. "Henry gave me a simple gold band, and I gave him my high school class ring, which he wore as a wedding ring for sixty-four years."

Marion's official OSS photo.
Photo courtesy of Marion Frieswyk.

That topographic map was the first visual aid of its kind made for General Eisenhower and his staff to use in determining troop movements and planning supply routes of approach. As Marion and Henry were celebrating their wedding, U.S. Fifth Army troops were landing in Sicily. The soldiers were well prepared for the rugged terrain they were going to encounter as they fought their way east towards Rome, thanks to the map that Marion and her colleagues created for the campaign planners.

Marion Armstrong was twenty-two years old.

Customized mapping was a new concept developed in World War II. The art and science of cartography began with one geographer, Arthur Robinson, specially recruited to the Office of the Coordinator of Information. The office director then was Colonel (later Major General) William Donovan, who later ran the newly created Office of Special Services (OSS). Robinson's department was absorbed into the new organization, and the process of custom-designed maps to inform intelligence concepts to policymakers took off. Both leaders and policy experts quickly realized the significance of the maps — they helped convey strategic concepts that words alone could not.

As demand for the OSS map products grew, Robinson began to recruit members for his team. Marion was one of the first to be interviewed for the cartography team in 1942. She had just graduated from Potsdam State Teachers College in New York. She recalled, "I was a twenty-one-year-old country girl with a knack for numbers." Marion Armstrong grew up in Hamilton, a small town in upstate New York. "My parents had lost our pea farm in the Depression, and my mother worked as a cook in a fraternity house at Colgate University."

"Finishing school? That wasn't for me," Marion declared. "I always had my nose in a book." She thought of Colgate as being "high class" and definitely not for her. Marion went to Potsdam State Teachers College instead.

Marion originally planned to teach elementary school and even had a contract offer, but a little push from a mentor from a part-time job set her on a different path. Just to earn a little money, Marion had been doing work in computing averages for her former geography professor at Potsdam when he recommended her for a summer school course in the graduate school at Clark University. The course was called War Service Training and included classes in geography, economic geography, climatology, and cartography. Marion hoped it could help qualify her for a wartime job. After all, that teaching contract wasn't going to pay more than $1,000 a year. She took the leap. "I moved to Worcester [Massachusetts] and spent six weeks learning economic geography, weather, and all sorts of related skills that might benefit the government."

By the time Arthur Robinson came calling, Marion was ready. She'd heard of the OSS but thought the initials stood for "Oh So Secret."

"What do you think, Marion?" Robinson asked at the conclusion of the interview. "You have good grades and your professors at Clark and Potsdam say you're a hard worker with a creative bent. Plus, you have an analytical mind. You're just the type of person we're looking for. The whole package."

"What would I be doing exactly, Mr. Robinson?" she asked.

"Call me Robby. Well, we're doing war work for the government. But I can't really tell you anything more. Not right now."

"Oh, because it's 'Oh. So. Secret.'" Marion added, her lip twitching. "The OSS."

"That's right," he smiled. "But, we're going to pay you $1,800 a year. How does that sound?" Marion gasped. That was nearly twice as much as she could make as a teacher. To a child of the Depression, it sounded like a real fortune.

"I said yes quicker than I could find DC on a map," she later recalled.

As Marion left the interview room, her head spinning, another candidate was approaching. Marion recognized him from their geography class. Henry Frieswyk said hello and squeezed past her. Marion watched him go in.

By the fall of 1942, both young graduate students from Clark University were working for the OSS along with a full complement of twenty-eight more brand-new cartographers. These pioneers didn't start out to be cartographers. The career field didn't even exist yet. They'd been geographers, professors, and mathematicians. The new agency provided on-the-job training at its best, not to mention professional development, both for them and for the profession.

Marion's team was collegial and collaborative. There wasn't a glass ceiling for her to

Marion to the far right, with several of her fellow cartographers in front of the National Archives. Photo courtesy of Marion Frieswyk.

break. One didn't even exist yet. They were all "firsts" in their field, and they all worked well together. She said, "I can't recall a time when your gender mattered more than your ability to contribute." It was an ideal workplace, one where respect for each other's capabilities came first.

Marion thrived as a cartographer. At the outset, maps were made by hand, using pen on large sheets of translucent acetate paper, mounted on Strathmore illustration boards. Typically, Marion and her team created the maps larger than needed, on a 4:1 scale. Later, the approved product would be reduced for printing and distribution. They also began to experiment with 3-D mapping, like the Sicily map project that made a mess on the stage floor at Ford's Theatre. That effort was one of the team's best-kept secrets. No one ever knew that they had to pull an "all-nighter" to fix their plaster-mixing mistake.

Creativity and experimentation made the team successful, and each of the cartography teams got better and better at honing their craft. By 1943, there were three sections in the Map Division of the OSS: Cartography — where Marion was assigned — then Map Information, and finally a new section, Topographic Models. All three teams complemented each other.

The Map Information Team began to procure commercial maps for the cartographers to use as a starting point. Working together, the teams began to develop a process for their map building that helped to standardize the appearance of their products and speed up the construction. They standardized the symbols used for their products and affixed preprinted labels to cellophane sheets with adhesive. These "stick-ups" were applied to all of the OSS map products for uniformity. It also meant their products were immediately recognizable and were in high demand by planners at the War Department and Naval Intelligence. They were also used at Allied planning conferences. There were three major conferences, involving Allied leaders of the U.S., Britain, and the Soviet Union. The final conference took place at Yalta with Roosevelt, Stalin, and Churchill leading the process. It was the most contentious as it involved the division of conquered lands among the three great powers following the war and numerous compromises and promises in the give-and-take of dividing the spoils. Maps were critical to all parties in understanding the implications of every decision and greatly influenced the course of the negotiations.

By the end of the war, the OSS Map

Division had made 8,200 new maps, including two huge fifty-inch globes. One of the massive war planning tools was given to President Roosevelt, the other to Britain's prime minister, Winston Churchill. Marion recalled that in 1945, they couldn't fit the massive globe onto the plane for the Yalta Conference, so it had to be sawed in half and packed up for delivery. By the time her team was preparing maps to support the Yalta conference, they had answered fifty thousand requests for map information and provided cartography support to four major Roosevelt and Churchill planning conferences.

The Map Division had, in effect, created an entirely new field for the intelligence cartographer. Where once maps had been a tool of propaganda, the maps produced by the Map Division established a new standard. Maps as propaganda had been used since the Middle Ages in Europe, to justify colonization, assert national unity, and even to denigrate other countries' relative importance in the world. The new standard was different. These maps were clear, efficient, factual, and effective at transmitting critical intelligence information. The cartographer had become an indispensable tool of modern warfare. One historian said that World War II was "the best thing to happen to geography since the birth of Strabo," a Greek geographer born in 63 BCE.

That mission critical role was realized after the war. In October 1945, after the war had ended, a presidential executive order disbanded the OSS but retained the Map Division and transferred the cartography mission to the State Department. Marion and her colleagues packed up their desks and remained with State until the establishment of the CIA in 1947.

The role of cartography was about to reach maturity. Prior to World War II, the role of geography was largely academic, small scale, and domestically focused. Following the war, geography and the role of mapmaking had been operationalized, grown in scope, and was clearly focused on international relations, trends, and politics.

Maps in the postwar world told the stories of the reconstruction of Europe, the spread of the Iron Curtain, the Suez crisis in 1956, the Cuban Missile Crisis in 1962, and many other major events of the twentieth century. Marion stayed with the CIA until 1952. She'd been part of the core from the OSS days that helped the office make the transition to State and then the bounce to the new agency. She resigned so that Henry could take an assignment with the agency in its

London office. Marion and their three children enjoyed their time overseas.

Henry stayed on with the CIA, serving as chief of the Cartography Division. For his twenty-fifth anniversary of government service, the Division presented him with an unusual gift. Marion's eyes widened when he staggered out of the building carrying it. She recognized that map immediately. It was their first topographic map, the monster map of Sicily that had to have its first layers of sloppy plaster scraped off back in 1943. Somehow, they had managed to squeeze it into the back of their Volkswagen bug and got it home. Together, Marion and Henry dragged the heavy map into their TV room.

"What is this thing, Mom?" the kids asked. The map had obviously spent many years in a closet. It was a bit dusty and more than a little banged up. A few mountaintops were missing their peaks.

"Oh, it's a project your dad and I worked on during the war," Marion explained. She and Henry exchanged a look. She smiled, thinking about the plaster splattered all over the stage at the historic Ford's Theatre. She wondered what the workers thought when they entered the building in the 1960s to begin renovations. The theater didn't open again for stage plays until 1968.

The first OSS topographic map — from Marion's plaster disaster at Ford's Theatre. The legend reads "Prepared in the R&A Branch, OSS, April 1943." Photo courtesy of Marion Frieswyk.

"Do you know where this is?" Henry asked, tapping the map frame. The family had a lot of conversations about geography and maps.

"Italy," they answered in unison and began to point out recognizable landmarks.

Marion recalled Operation Husky, the Allied invasion of Sicily in 1943 that marked the beginning of the Italian Campaign. It had all started with that map. The planners congratulated her and her team, telling them how useful it had been in planning locations for amphibious landings, airborne operations, and the initial assaults. They had also prepared maps that were critical in planning for the North African Campaign. Her work had saved lives. Now that giant piece of memorabilia had a place in their home. It was definitely a conversation piece.

"The kids named it Etna, after Sicily's well-known volcano," she recalled.

About the time Henry's bosses presented him with the Sicily map, the CIA was considering disposing of the nearly sixty topographic maps remaining from the OSS days. But Henry knew what a treasure they were. The maps were spared their execution and now cover the walls of a conference room in the CIA HQ. Henry retired from the CIA in 1980, having earned the agency's Career Intelligence Medal in recognition of a career of exceptional achievements in the intelligence field. Following retirement, he taught cartography in the Department of Urban Studies at the University of Maryland.

Henry passed away in 1997 following a stroke. When Marion was cleaning out their Maryland home of over thirty years, she made a surprising discovery. "We rolled up the TV room rug and discovered a collection of declassified CIA maps that Henry had stashed there." Her daughter was surprised, but Marion just smiled. "Cartographers know that maps stay nice and flat underneath carpets. It was a reminder of the lifetime we spent together and how it all began."

Marion's contributions during World War II receded into the background. It wasn't until the CIA's Cartography Center celebrated its seventy-fifth anniversary that she was "discovered." A friend of a friend talked to someone in the Cartography Center, and they called Marion. She was the only living veteran of the OSS Cartography team they could find. Marion was invited to the CIA for the anniversary celebration. Stories were written about her, and she surprisingly found herself in the limelight. On June 16, 2017, the OSS Society celebrated the seventy-fifth anniversary of the founding of the agency. Society President Charles Pinck recognized the OSS veterans in attendance, Marion among them. In his remarks, he quoted Major General Donovan at the final gathering of OSS personnel on September 28, 1945: "Only by decisions of national policy based upon accurate information do we have a chance of a peace that will endure."

One year later, there was another ceremony, this one to publicly acknowledge the work of the OSS. On March 21, 2018, the OSS was recognized for its wartime service in a ceremony at the U.S. Capitol with a presentation of the Congressional Gold Medal. About twenty surviving members of the wartime organization were on hand, including ninety-six-year-old Marion Frieswyk. Asked about her work with the service, she said, "It was a very hush-hush time. My children didn't even know where we worked."

Marion Frieswyk at her home in February 2020 during filming of an OSS Society documentary. Photo courtesy of Marion Frieswyk.

Her story is known now. She was featured in the Special Operations Command magazine *Tip of the Spear* in 2019 and in the book *Women in American Cartography: An Invisible Social History,* published in 2020.

Today, what began as the OSS Cartography Section is now known as the CIA's Cartography Center. Much like when Marion was recruited, the agency still recruits at universities, such as Mary Washington University in Fredericksburg, Virginia, to find top talent. A recent piece on CIA recruitment for cartographers was posted on the Mary Washington University website. It explained, "Cartographers research, design, and produce thematic and reference maps to support intelligence through delivery via mobile devices, web, and print." The CIA's mapmaking feed on Twitter includes a long discussion thread on how the intellectual challenges associated with mapmaking to tell complex intelligence stories has a great appeal for new graduates. The field has come a long way from paint, jigsaws, and wet plaster, replaced by technology's many gifts: computer animation, lasers, 3-D printers, and more.

Marion Frieswyk, more than most, understood how critical her wartime role had been. She felt lucky to have been offered a position with the OSS, and like many who started out in life with very little, she never took anything for granted. She worked hard, but it was her talent for numbers and attention to detail that meant she was perfectly poised to pave the way in pioneering a new field. The OSS counted on her to get it right. During World War II, when women struggled against the cultural norms and never-ending arguments of what women could do, or should do, she simply did her job. She built maps that conveyed accurate intelligence information on a scale hitherto unseen. She was part of a team that created an entirely new career field, inventing it as they went along. There was nothing to compare it to. Marion was a "first," in an office that itself was a "first." She was a pioneer, an innovator, and a role model. The CIA's 2019 tribute to her read, "Marion Frieswyk . . . embodies the diligence, determination, and innovative spirit that we valued at CIA." For Marion, it was never a question of who would give her permission to use her talents to the fullest. No one had to tell her she could or couldn't do anything. She didn't know that what she was choosing was unusual. No one told her she couldn't succeed. So, she did. It was that simple.

CHAPTER 12

CODE SECRETS

"The work that we did shortened the war by a year and half to two years. That's a good feeling . . . Our generation . . . only did what we had to do to be free."

ELIZABETH BEMIS ROBARTS

"Oh my God! I didn't know," Betty exclaimed. She couldn't wrap her head around the truth. All those years and she didn't know a thing.

"No idea. I had *no* idea!" Someone else shouted.

"Why didn't anyone ever tell us?" a whole chorus of voices rose up. Someone in the back of the room fainted.

Then the room exploded with cacophony of sound, exclamations of shock, surprise, questions, and bursting pride. Arms waved in the air, trying to get the speaker to notice.

There were hundreds of questions. And not a few tears.

Betty Bemis Robarts was in Dayton, Ohio, for the first reunion in fifty years with her Navy colleagues from World War II. On September 15, 1995, these eighty-seven women finally learned what their war contributions had meant. They built the Bombe (pronounced bomb), the two-ton machine that broke the coded Enigma messages the Nazis government used in classified communication with its armed forces.

"We had no idea what the actual machine did," Betty recalled. "We just had to build it. It was mind-boggling to find out the truth." Betty was part of Ultra, a highly compartmented, top-secret program run by Joseph R. Desch, director of research at the National Cash Register (NCR) Electrical Research Laboratory in Dayton, Ohio. The women worked behind locked doors guarded by armed Marines. Inside, they connected wires and rotors for the behemoth Bombe. Betty was one of six hundred Navy women whose work, she learned at the reunion, saved thousands of lives.

Betty Bemis was born December 6, 1922, to Elwin and Lorraine Bemis in Nashwauk, Minnesota. She and her sister Loraine discovered swimming as youngsters, and both liked competing. Betty captured four state swimming championships while still in high school, winning in the backstroke, freestyle, and relay events. In 1939, she went to the Junior Nationals meet in Missouri and the Senior Nationals meet in Iowa. Her father drove her to meets across the country during her high school years.

While attending Butler College in Indianapolis, Betty swam for the Riviera Club AAU team. She won her first national title in 1941 at High Point, North Carolina, in the freestyle. Her relay team that year set a new world record. In 1942, at the Wisconsin meet, Betty took first in the 400 and 800 freestyle events and second in the individual relay. The Riviera team won the meet, and Betty took the individual High Point award, an especially sweet moment because her parents were there to see her win it all.

She made the women's All-American swimming team three times, fueling her hopes to try out for the Olympics. Unfortunately, the 1944 games were canceled, and Betty felt she'd be too old to compete by 1948. Plus, the constant practice it took to maintain her swimming at a competitive level was beginning to wear on her. She said, "I was sick of college . . . I was sick of swimming."

Betty decided to follow in her dad's footsteps. He had served in World War I and was delighted his daughter chose the U.S. Army. He went with her to the recruiting station, but the Army turned her down flat. Betty was only twenty years old. The recruiter told her to come back in a year.

So, she took her dad by the arm and they went next door to the Navy recruiter. He signed the papers giving his permission, and she was off. While her dad was pleased she wanted to serve, he wasn't happy she'd quit college and quit swimming. His last bit of advice was some cutting words, perhaps an attempt at tough love, that she certainly took to heart: "You know, Betty, you've never finished anything you started. You won't have that option in the service." She'd nodded, determined to make him proud.

It was all a great adventure, until she actually had to leave home for it to begin. "I think I cried my first two nights in the Navy. I was so homesick." But once at the reception center in New York, she got all the shots the Navy could hand out and then traveled to nearby Hunter College in the Bronx for six weeks of boot camp. The U.S. Navy Training School, USS Hunter, took up the entire college campus. The Navy rented it all.

Betty found the training easy enough. She

could recognize types of aircraft and ships, write reports and correspondence in Navy style, recognize ranks, and observe proper protocol. She could talk the lingo too. She learned to say *deck* instead of *floor, overhead* instead of *ceiling,* and *bulkhead* instead of *wall.* The language was the easiest part of Navy culture to absorb. Her salute probably could have used a little work, though. And she learned the one facet of military life that all new recruits came to appreciate. She learned how to march, how to take orders, and then how to give orders. Marching was easy enough, and Betty learned how to make her bed "shipshape."

"We are learning the Navy way here," the girls wrote home. "We hurry up and wait." Upon graduation, Betty was officially a WAVE — the Navy's acronym for Women Accepted for Volunteer Emergency Service.

The WAVES were established on July 21, 1942. While Congress and the president were reluctant to open the service to women, they recognized the need. Women in the naval reserve were to be assigned to shore duty, freeing up men to go to sea. More than 86,000 WAVES were assigned to 900 stations in the United States, and while it was a mostly white organization, eventually seventy-two African American women served.

Betty's first Navy rank was Able Seaman (E-1), and her job classification was Spec Q (Communications). She still had no idea what that entailed. But before her training could progress any further, there was a two-week pause. She was sent to the Naval Communications Annex in Washington, DC.

Able seaman Betty Bemis. Photo courtesy of the Women in Military Service to America Memorial Foundation.

Betty got off the train at Union Station and took a bus straight to the Nebraska Avenue complex. The U.S. Navy's Communications Annex, in Northwest Washington, DC, was located across the street from American University, one sprawling campus facing the other. In March 1943, the Nation's

Capital was still cool and rainy, but to a girl from northern Minnesota, it felt positively spring-like.

Betty dropped her duffel at the reception office and had her picture taken for her access badge. A petty officer then escorted her and several other new arrivals to the Navy Chapel for what Betty understood to be a "Welcome to Washington" briefing. Then there would be a few more classes of some kind, more forms to sign, and in just a few days, she could be on her way. Betty hoped she'd be assigned somewhere near a beach. Maybe San Diego or somewhere else in California.

There were women in uniform everywhere on the campus, Betty noticed. More than four thousand of them, she would later discover. The Navy's cryptanalysis center was 80 percent female. Women outnumbered men in every working unit at the center. In the Pacific decryption unit, there were 254 male sailors and 1,252 WAVES, plus 33 civilians. But Betty never saw the interior of those units. All she would see in her two weeks in Washington was the inside of the Navy chapel.

That first day's welcome ceremony in Washington wasn't like any of the typical Navy lectures Betty had grown used to.

The escort dropped the new sailors at the chapel door and told them to wait. She and a dozen others sat silently in the long pews, growing sleepy as the afternoon sun poured through the stained glass windows. It was hurry up and wait all over again. Finally, a serious-looking Navy lieutenant showed up. He gave each of them a long stare before starting his talk. There were no boring explanations of Navy protocol and no foot stomping for the important points. There wasn't even a blackboard or a pointer. Just preaching.

This was a pure fire-and-brimstone sermon, a speech on operational security that went beyond the typical mantra of "loose lips sink ships." Betty and the other newly arrived WAVES straightened up, suddenly wide-eyed and attentive. They blurted out "Yes, sir" or "No, sir" as required. When the lecture was over, the newcomers filed out silently, all duly impressed by the warning that they would be shot if they ever revealed what they did for the U.S. Navy.

In the following days, there were more lectures in the same vein, all concerning the necessity of protecting the secret work they would be doing, being wary of potential spies, and in particular, just keeping their mouths shut. In between the lectures, there was a raft of aptitude tests, tests for coding ability, mechanical skills, and mathematics. There was a lot of repetition, Betty recalled. But the main points stuck with her. She could never discuss her military work with anyone. Period.

After a few days, the finger wagging was getting old. During one security lecture, one of the young WAVES sitting near Betty giggled at the thought of being shot at dawn. It just seemed melodramatic. The instructor came over and stood by Betty, looking down at the other girl. "Don't think we won't shoot you just because you're a woman," he said. "Because we will." Everyone was quiet after that.

What she didn't know then was that her transfer to her first duty assignment was on hold until the Navy could complete her background checks. While she was waiting, Betty asked for a seventy-two-hour pass and used it to visit some college friends back in Indianapolis. While she was there, two FBI agents came calling. They didn't want to speak with her. They were just checking on her whereabouts. Betty had no doubts that the Navy was serious regarding security.

The personnel staff at the Annex asked her if she wanted to go out west. Betty yelped an excited "Yes, ma'am," picturing herself on that beach in California, an umbrella drink in hand.

In April, the first group of pioneering WAVES left Washington at midnight, their train heading due west. Betty didn't know where they were going, the destination was secret too. Hours later, the train stopped at another Union Station. This one was in Dayton, Ohio. In the middle of the night, Betty and her fellow WAVES stumbled onto a Navy bus and left downtown Dayton behind, heading out into the countryside. The area looked peaceful, all green rolling hills and lush pastures. "If they didn't know better they'd think the U.S. Navy was taking them to a Girl Scout camp," one veteran recalled.

Sugar Camp was a thirty-one-acre spread the National Cash Register (NCR) company used to train its sales force on their new machines while they also learned sales techniques, management, and their specific regional territories. Sugar Camp was a bucolic setting, the sugar maples dominating the green landscape. The young WAVES settled into Adirondack-like cabins, four to six per cabin, ogling the resort-like facilities the campus had to offer: a recreation center, social hall, dining hall, and even a baseball diamond. Betty had her eye on the large outdoor swimming pool, just waiting for her to come practice her winning backstroke.

There was time for recreation even though the WAVES worked seven days a week in shifts around the clock. Every day, Betty and her colleagues marched to work at NCR's main campus, about a mile from Sugar Camp. The cover story was that they were learning to operate adding machines, a pretty thin story, some thought. After all, you had to be stupid if it took months to figure out how to work an adding machine.

Later, Betty recalled their first day in the top secret Building 26. "One of the Navy officers asked if any of us knew how to solder." Betty raised her hand, "'I know how to solder.' I'd watched my Dad solder [join two wires together by melting a filler material with the soldering iron]. He taught me how to solder when I was fourteen. A lot of the girls didn't know what a solder was so they had lessons. It is a very delicate point. You have to attach the wires just right to the rotor or the rotor won't work properly. Every single one was tested."

She soldered twenty-six wires onto rotors every day during her shift. "I got pretty good at soldering," she recalled with a smile. Betty and 10–12 colleagues sat at long tables each day, each with her work waiting for her to arrive. Betty would sit down in front of a wheel made of copper, brass, and Bakelite. Hanging from a cord over each table was a soldering iron. There was a diagram that showed the proper connections, but after enough hours with the wires and rotors, Betty and the others didn't need to consult it.

The Navy found that the delicate touch necessary to expertly craft the Bombe rotor wheels was better done by women than by men with large, clumsy hands. "Their ability to produce finely crafted, yet rugged components was essential in the production of working systems."

The Polish military built the first Bombe, breaking the German Enigma code before the war. They later provided the technology to the British, but in 1942, the Germans changed the number of rotors from three to four. The new American Bombe was built to match that change.

The first two Bombes built at Sugar Camp were named Adam and Eve. After they were tested and found to be workable, production increased. When Betty and her colleagues were finished soldering, completed rotors were taken downstairs to the floor below where male sailors assembled the Bombes. Each Bombe contained sixty-four rotors.

These definitely weren't lightweight machines. Each Bombe was seven feet high, ten feet long, and weighed five thousand pounds. Once assembled, these early computers were loaded onto trains bound for the Naval Communications Annex in Washington. Betty and her colleagues built two hundred Bombes during their stay at Sugar Camp.

WAVE at the Naval Communications Annex operating the Bombe machine. Photo courtesy of the National Cryptologic Museum.

More WAVES were working in shifts at the Annex, manning the codebreaking machines. There, the Bombes, in imitating the German Enigma coding machine, did the initial work of decoding enemy messages.

Every time a transmission was fed into the Bombe, the rotors began to turn. A light would come on when a letter from the transmission was picked up. It took twenty minutes for a run on a Bombe to decode a message. Once the results were verified by a supervisor, they were sent to Building 2, where the cryptanalysts were waiting to review and analyze the results.

But Betty knew none of that at the time. In many ways, her work, and that of her WAVE counterparts, whether at Sugar Camp or in Washington, made them just another cog in the Navy's efficient codebreaking machine. In nearby Virginia, at the Army's Arlington Hall Station, there were another thousand women codebreakers, either in uniform with the Women's Army Corps (WACs) or working as civilians. The Army and Navy centers worked on some of the same challenging German codes, Japanese codes, and diplomatic traffic.

Betty knew their work was essential to the war effort. They all knew that much, and some even guessed what the machines were all about. After all, there were twenty-six letters in the alphabet, and twenty-six rotors in each machine. But no one dared talk about it.

They had many opportunities for recreation in their off-duty hours. Some played ping-pong or cards in the rec center. Others put together pick-up softball games or read their mail. Betty spent much of her spare time swimming. Because she'd won a national title in 1942, she was invited to attend the national meet in 1943, all expenses paid. Her supervisor gave her leave to attend. While she didn't win in the individual events, her relay team did win. After returning to Sugar Camp, the famous aviator Orville Wright read about her swimming prowess in a local paper and came to visit. That was an exciting moment. Another came when a group of WAVES traveled to nearby Wright-Patterson Air Force Base to see a USO show featuring Bob Hope. Betty even had time to take a class in Spanish.

Betty with her Spanish class colleagues at Sugar Camp. Betty is second from left in the back row. Photo courtesy of the National Cryptologic Museum.

While the young women couldn't talk about work, they talked about everything else. Boyfriends, fiancés, and romance were at the top of the list. One of the WAVES in Betty's cabin was constantly writing to her Army Air Corps boyfriend overseas. The boyfriend asked if one of her WAVE friends would write to his copilot, Ed "Shorty" Robarts. Ed's parents had passed away, and he wasn't getting many letters. Helen asked her roommates, and soon all eight girls in the cabin started to write to Ed. Gradually, the others moved on to more lucrative prospects, but Betty and Ed kept on writing. There was definitely a spark there, she thought.

Ed Robarts was a B-24 bomber pilot who flew thirty-five missions in the war over Italy and England. He returned home in December 1944 and was reassigned to the Ferry Division, Air Transportation Command. Just as he arrived, the pioneering WASP program ended and over 1,000 women pilots were out of a job. Ed and other male pilots took over the missions women like Millie Rexroat had once flown, towing targets and delivering newly built planes to their destinations.

One day, Betty was summoned from her worktable to the hallway phone. She picked it up and Ed said, "Hello Betty. I'm home."

They had never met in person. Betty was just thrilled to finally hear his voice. Ed invited her to come to Easter dinner with him and his aunt and uncle in Miami. Betty didn't hesitate. She hitched a ride on a military transport and in March 1945 flew to meet the man she'd been writing to for over a year.

On Valentine's Day, 2020, she recalled meeting Ed Robarts for the first time. "We met in Miami on April first and he gave me flowers," she recalled. "It was just like I had known him all the time." Her first impression stuck with her. "He was so cute. He had the softest lips and the bluest eyes," she said. Then just three days later, "He asked me to marry him and I said yes."

Their wedding was held that June. By fall she had been discharged from the Navy and moved to Memphis to join Ed. Betty didn't leave the Navy with any awards or medals. Later, she recalled that typically most WAVES at least received a citation from Secretary of the Navy Forrestal. But because of the classified work her cohort did, they got nothing. Not even a thank you. The Navy promoted Betty five times during her short stay at Sugar Camp. She left the Navy as a Communications Specialist First Class (E-6).

Betty was one of twenty-four WAVES who got married while still in the service. There were a lot of weddings at the end of the war, she recalled. Hers was a marriage that lasted sixty-four years.

By 1948, Betty was back in college, this time at Auburn University in Alabama. She majored in physical education and played on the volleyball and basketball teams. She also swam in exhibitions. With Ed still in the Air Force, they moved every few years and lived in twelve states. Betty taught swimming at many of their locations. They went on to have three children, and during the summers they traveled the U.S. with their kids in an RV.

They retired to a farm in Sylvania, Georgia, near where Ed was born. They also volunteered at the National Museum of the Mighty Eighth Air Force. Ed was a guide there for fourteen years until he passed away in 2009. Betty continued to volunteer until well into her nineties, driving eighty-five plus miles round-trip every Tuesday to volunteer. They'd watched the museum being built and were there for the grand opening. Now, "it's more for me because Ed's ashes are there," she said. They are located in a columbarium near the chapel. "When I get there, I feel close to him."

When Betty was discharged from active duty, she had to sign another nondisclosure agreement, stating that she would never reveal what she had done during the war. To anyone. The secrecy oath was binding — for life.

In October 1945, the U.S. Congress lauded the work of the codebreakers. Speaking on the floor of the House of Representatives, Rep. Clarence Hancock said, "I believe our cryptographers . . . in the war with Japan did as much to bring that war to a successful and early conclusion as any other group of men."

The women were never mentioned. It was as though they had never served. They were never publicly thanked or even acknowledged. And they were unable to complain because they took an oath. Betty didn't even tell her husband what she did in the war. She never told her parents or her children. Not until many years later, when their story was declassified. In fact, the program she worked in may have been the only classified program not compromised during the war.

No one broke that oath of silence. Like Betty, most of the 10,000 women codebreakers in World War II kept their secrets from friends and family. Some of the WAVES did remain close and kept in contact for years following the war, but they typically didn't participate in veteran's groups or organizations. Betty didn't give speeches or talk to school groups. She didn't participate in Veterans Day events. Bound by their code of silence, Betty and her veteran peers were invisible. Quietly, the women codebreakers were forgotten.

In America, of the 20,000 people working as codebreakers in World War II, more than 11,000 were women. It was no different for other codebreaking operations, whether those of the U.S. Army at Arlington Hall Station or at Bletchley Park in the UK. At Bletchley, incoming staff were required to sign the Official Secrets Act. Most never spoke about their wartime service after the war. It was more than fifty years later when stories about the Nazi Enigma codes, Bombe machine, and the important role of codebreaking began to leak out.

The Sugar Camp reunion in 1995 was the first time many of the veterans had seen each other in fifty years. The event was organized by Deborah Anderson, daughter of Joe Desch, the Dayton Project director. Anderson described the WAVES. "You talk about women in STEM — those women were incredible. They were independent, they were intelligent, they were motivated, they were very moral, very patriotic and funny. . . . I didn't realize how much it would mean to them to get some recognition. . . . Some got letters thanking them for their service but most didn't."

For fifty years, the women had been unable to talk about their wartime service. They still wouldn't talk until a Navy representative spoke to the assembled group and told them it was all right to reveal they'd served at Sugar Camp, building the Bombe. "They were so moved and grateful," she recalled.

The women were recognized at last. At the Reunion's farewell banquet, the WAVES received an Exceptional Service Award from the National Security Agency for "Exceptional service on Project Ultra in the breaking of German and Japanese codes during World War II."

Betty found the entire reunion to be three days of revelations, one after another. She was thankful for the opportunity to spend time with old friends, the recognition and thanks they all received at last, and finally the ability to be able to speak about what she did during the war. But the single most important piece for her was learning that what she did *mattered.*

Vice Admiral Tunnel from the Naval

Security Group Command told the WAVE veterans, "Their contributions building the Bombe and running them . . . were estimated to have reduced the length of the war by one to two years." The words spoken in that moment were like an earthquake rattling Betty's heart — old memories fell off the shelf and shattered. She had to piece back together her recollections of her years at Sugar Camp and solder them into a new and complete narrative of her wartime service. All of those long shifts, the endless soldering, the speculation over the program's purpose — it wasn't just busy work. Now everything fit together.

For years, she had wondered if her time in uniform had truly been meaningful, what purpose it had served. For many years, she felt like nothing more than a tiny rotor cog in the massive codebreaking Ultra program, just a small part of a huge endeavor and probably not a particularly important one either. The reunion changed all that. Betty and the other women did more than free up men to fight. They made a difference. The mobilization of women and their participation in the war effort was significant to the Allied victory.

"I cried for three months," she recalled. "We were quite . . . well, we were shocked, really." Then she thought about her mom and dad. "I only wish I could have told my parents," she recalled. "We did a great thing."

Betty Robarts at the National Cryptologic Museum in March 2019 with the Bombe machine she helped build. Photo courtesy of the National Cryptologic Museum.

Twenty-four years later, on March 22, 2019, nearly seventy-four years after the end of World War II, the Library of Congress sponsored a reunion for all women code-breakers, Navy and Army. Five veterans were on hand, all in their mid-nineties, and they were honored by the Veterans History Project at the Library of Congress. Betty Robarts was there for the event. A day earlier, she had the opportunity to tour the National Security Agency's Cryptologic

Museum at Fort Meade, Maryland. It had been sixty-four years since she had worked on the Bombe, and this was her first view of the completed machine.

Ever humble, she said later, "It's hard for me to take any honor. I'd rather give the honor to the ones that were in the thick of it."

CHAPTER 13

WIND AND SAND

"Worry about being killed? I never gave it a thought. You couldn't worry about things like that . . . You can't live forever."

OLA MILDRED REXROAT MCDONALD

"Hey, can I fly out here?" Millie asked. It was windy on the airfield as she pushed her long, dark hair out of her eyes. Located at Gravelly Point, just a half mile south of the District of Columbia, Washington National Airport had been under construction since 1941. It wouldn't open officially until 1944, but today its sole hangar was bustling with activity. There were two planes on the ground and another in the air, circling. A tight circle of men in jumpsuits saw her approach. Three peeled off, leaving two older men in bomber jackets and khakis. One tossed a toothpick on the ground when she walked up. One put his hand behind his ear as though he couldn't hear her. Or maybe he didn't believe what he heard.

"I said, can I fly out here?" Millie asked again. She'd had some lessons back in Texas and wanted to keep flying. It was part of her plan.

The two pilots looked at each other and then back to her. The senior guy shook his head. "Nope."

"Why not?" Millie put her hands on her hips. It was 1943, and Millie had been looking for a way to serve her country. Now she knew what she wanted and was determined she was going to get it. Millie was a college graduate working a secretarial job at the U.S. Army War College. Located at the historic Washington Arsenal (later renamed Fort McNair) in southeast Washington, the college was housed in an immense brick and granite hall that squatted on a slender spit of land jutting out from Washington's waterfront. It was right at the confluence of the Anacostia River and the Washington Channel, where both fed into the dark blue waters of the Potomac. Roosevelt Hall faced north, staring straight at the U.S. Capitol with its stern military facade. Millie liked the southern view better. At lunchtime each day, she would perch on the steps at the back of the building and munch on an apple while she looked out over the broad Potomac River. She loved the play of sun on water and the quiet; it was good to just have a moment away from all the demands for typing and filing. Boring stuff. Just ahead, she could see the new airport. Millie thrilled to watch the few military and civilian flights navigate their way over the water as they landed. Depending on the wind, they sometimes took off to the north, roaring over Roosevelt Hall. She liked both approaches, but what she liked best was watching the "touch and go" when pilots barely landed before they immediately took off again and circled back for another try. All too soon, she had to head back to her desk.

Surrounded by military officers, Millie felt like all conversations started with war-story bragging, then followed a typical pattern. First, there was criticism of what the other services were doing to help America win, followed by rampant guesswork about Hitler's next moves in Europe or the outcomes of Naval battles in the Pacific. The conversation then segued into gossip about who was going to be promoted and who wasn't, and much frustrated speculation about where each of them would most likely be assigned next. Millie had heard it all. Even as she typed a letter for one of the professors, buzzing planes overhead found their way through an open window into her imagination with their song — *Come fly.*

Millie already had her private pilot license. She'd taken lessons a year earlier while working in El Paso. She had worked for a group of engineers there, building airfields. She loved flying and needed to find a way to continue to build her new skills.

Millie was going to find a way to keep flying. She had already decided.

"Why not?" she asked again.

The pilot held up three fingers. "In the first place, you're a woman. In the second place, you're not in the Civil Air Patrol. And in the third place, unless you're going to be a WASP, you just can't do it."

Millie didn't know what the Civil Air Patrol was. "That's what I'm going to be," she told them. "A WASP." She had already applied to join the Women Airforce Service Pilots (WASP), a military training program. Millie wrote to the WASP, and they sent her an application. She looked at the requirements and learned that she needed thirty-five hours of flight time before her application could be accepted. She had the hours, but she wanted more time in the sky. She had to be ready.

The instructor tried again. "Look, it's

going to cost six dollars an hour for solo flight and eight dollars an hour for general instruction." He smiled, smug. Eight dollars an hour was a lot of money in those days. Maybe that would stop her.

"All right. Fine. When can I start?" Millie had a day and a half off each week from her job at the Army War College. She made an appointment and began to fly again the next Saturday afternoon. Millie didn't tell them she already had a license. It wouldn't have mattered anyway.

In order to attend these lessons, she had to take the bus from southeast Washington to the airport. It wasn't just that Millie didn't have a car. Millie had in fact never even driven a car. But to be able to fly a plane? The thought of driving up into the sky made her heart flutter.

From the very first moment in the cockpit back in El Paso, she knew it was where she belonged. While in Washington, Millie spent every free hour and every extra penny she could muster flying. Saturday became her favorite day of the week. Other days, she still sat on the back steps of the War College and dreamed about her future.

"My mother always said I was bull-headed. And maybe I was," she shrugged. Being bullheaded gave her the strength and determination to fulfill her dream. Ola Mildred "Millie" Rexroat lived a life of no regrets. If the next step was to improve on those initial thirty-five hours, then she would work to get better. Millie was pushing at the dream, meeting every gate until the goal was right in front of her. She was going to be an Army pilot.

Millie also had to complete a physical exam and take a written cadet exam. She was thrilled when the telegram arrived, telling her she'd been accepted into the program. It stated that upon graduation from flight school, she would be commissioned as a second lieutenant in the Army Air Corps.

WASP Pilot Millie Rexroat. Photo from her WASP class yearbook. Photo courtesy of the Women in Military Service to America Memorial Foundation.

The WASP program itself was born from another dream. Jackie Cochran had been a famous pilot in the 1930s, winning air races and competing against the likes of Amelia Earhart. In 1939, she wrote a letter to First Lady Eleanor Roosevelt, presenting her case for making women pilots eligible for military service.

Eleanor Roosevelt had taken flying lessons herself, and she immediately grasped the significance of Jackie's proposal. The First Lady used her platform to become an outspoken supporter of the WASP. She wrote in her newspaper column, My Day, "This is not a time when women should be patient. We are in war and we need to fight it with all our ability and every weapon possible. Women pilots, in this particular case, are a weapon waiting to be used." The President and First Lady invited Jackie to lunch at the White House, and afterward she was encouraged to find out how other American women could handle military aircraft.

It wasn't an entirely new idea. Women had already been flying in the UK for two years when the WASP program was just getting started. The Air Transport Auxiliary (women pilots) was founded in 1940 to

341

augment the Royal Air Force (RAF). Eight women signed up right away. At first, the women pilots were restricted to flying trainers and communications aircraft, ferrying planes to different bases, equipped with only a compass, stopwatch, and map. As casualties rose and the shortage of qualified male pilots worsened, women began to fly fighters and bomber aircraft in 1941. There were 168 women pilots with the ATA in the war. They were also the first women in the UK to earn pay equal to the men, beginning in 1943.

When Jackie petitioned Army Air Corps General Henry H. "Hap" Arnold with her idea for a women's auxiliary service, he turned her down. But he suggested that she take some women pilots to Great Britain to work with their women pilots. If they did a good job, it might influence the U.S. Army to try it.

This was all before Pearl Harbor and the U.S. entry into the war. It took the advent of mobilization and a severe pilot shortage to finally persuade the Army to begin to train women as pilots. Another female pilot, Nancy Love, had also been pursuing building a woman pilot training program. Both plans were put into action and then merged in 1942 to become the WASP. The program was going strong by the time Millie put her completed application into the mail in 1944.

By then Millie was twenty-three years old.

Ola Mildred Rexroat, or Millie as she preferred to be known, was born in Ogden, Kansas, in 1917. Her father was white, her mother a full-blooded Oglala Sioux Indian. The family moved to South Dakota when Millie was young, and she spent a part of her childhood on the Pine Ridge Reservation visiting her grandmother. Pine Ridge was home to the Oglala Lakota, one of three tribes of the Great Sioux Nation. Located at the southern end of the Badlands, the sprawling reservation was larger than the states of Delaware and Rhode Island combined.

Millie attended both public school and Indian School, and after high school she worked for the Bureau of Indian Affairs in Nebraska and New Mexico. She went to college, earning a degree in art from the University of New Mexico. Millie tried a few jobs after graduation, but nothing seemed to stick. She took flying lessons and thought about the WASP program. Once she found the job at the Army War College, it opened a door to move to Washington. Then flying called out to her every day.

Millie could barely contain her excitement

when she reported for WASP training at the Avenger Field Flight School in Sweetwater, Texas. It was the only training base in the country for female pilots. She was giddy that first day, flying high with the excitement of actually starting up a military airplane. Then reality brought Millie back to earth with a rude, full-blown realization that before she could be a pilot, she had to become a soldier. And before she could be a soldier, she was just a trainee. The glamour wore off the moment she saw the uniform and the boots. She quickly learned that flying was just a small part of her new role in the military. And there was definitely nothing glamorous about those other parts.

Her Army days began with reveille, a much-hated bugle call that meant getting out of bed before the sun was up. Millie had heard bugle calls at the Army War College, but she'd certainly never been at work or even awake to hear any warbling bugle at 6:00 a.m. Following reveille, the student pilots stumbled outside to stand at attention for some unknown reason. It made no sense to Millie why they had to be "all present or accounted for." Where else was anyone going to go in the middle of the night? The only things waiting outside in the darkness were scorpions and snakes.

Dress right, dress. Millie could do it with ease. It didn't mean she had to actually be awake. She just had to be there. They all needed Army coffee for that. Following formation, the cadets marched at double time to the chow hall for breakfast. Next came more drill, classes on recognizing Army ranks, learning how to salute, physical training, an entire day on how to wear and care for the uniform, cleaning the barracks, and the other daily mind-numbing drudgeries typical of Army life. But she could tolerate that because school itself was challenging. Ground school was in the morning, flight school in the afternoon. She loved it all. Classes included navigation, weather, basic maintenance, visual and instrument flying, and finally Millie's favorite part of the course, actual flight time.

The pilot trainee uniform was surplus mechanic's overalls, which the women termed a "zoot suit." As they often joked, there were three sizes: Large, Extra Large, and Gigantic. Many struggled with the zoot suit, trying to tame it and bring it down to size. It was like wearing a set of king-sized sheets, the pant legs swished and swayed when they walked and could trip up the unwary. The drooping sleeves were so large the students rolled their sleeves and pants legs, finding belts to cinch up the ballooning material around their waists. Some more resourceful girls even cut off excess material in the sleeves, then rolled them up to hide their forbidden desecration of the uniform. They were not built for a Texas summer, but Millie never found it difficult to concentrate in class.

Having grown up in the southwestern corner of Oklahoma, Millie was unfazed by the Texas summer heat. Many of her classmates found it difficult to deal with. They would drag their Army cots into the space between the barracks buildings for a little relief on those stifling summer nights and sleep outside. Millie was invited to join them, but she knew better: better to deal with the heat than gamble with nature.

Some of the girls woke up covered with crickets. But Millie considered them lucky. After all, there were scorpions, too, and the occasional rattlesnake looking for someone to curl up with. One of Millie's colleagues found a rattlesnake on the wing of her trainer one afternoon just after take-off. While the student pilots all watched in amusement from the ground, she shook and wiggled that little plane in midair until she shook the snake off. Those on the ground suddenly stopped laughing. They screamed and scattered as the snake hurtled down towards them. Luckily, no one was hurt by the snake bomber.

During the first phase of flight school, Millie learned how to fly a BT basic training aircraft and a Luscombe, which she later likened to today's low-powered Cessna. During advanced training, she flew the North American T-6 Texan aircraft. Millie preferred the T-6 for one reason: the plane had a roof that could slide over the cockpit so the ride was a lot less breezy. And after the snake incident, Millie was doubly glad that she could slam that roof shut.

Despite its challenges, flight school had its lighthearted moments. The budding pilots played gags and tricks on each other; one class even put on a play about their challenges as trainees. And whenever a trainee took her first solo flight, she was tossed into the "wishing well" by her classmates. It was a "way to cool off a hot pilot," one WASP said.

On September 7, 1944, eight months after beginning her training journey, Millie graduated from flight school in the class of 44-W-7 (the seventh WASP class in 1944) and earned the coveted silver wings. Her class yearbook had Millie's favorite saying posted beside her name and photo. "What could be

Millie and her classmates in WASP Class 44-W-7, marching around the Wishing Well. Photo courtesy of WASP Archive, The TWU Libraries' Woman's Collection, Texas Woman's University, Denton, Texas.

better?" After all, nothing could be better than flying.

Every WASP also received a commercial pilot's license and the equivalent of a college aeronautical degree. The WASP motto was, "We live in the wind and sand . . . and our eyes are on the stars." Of special pride was the WASP emblem, a winged cartoon sprite named Fifinella. Fifinella was a female gremlin who emanated from a children's story by Roald Dahl on the dangers of combat flying. Dahl, a former RAF pilot, hoped the story would become a Disney film. Unfortunately, the film project was abandoned due to competition from other studios interested in gremlin pictures. But "Fifi," as she became known, continued her reign with the WASP.

Disney Studios created some 1,200 insignia for World War II military units. A special five-man crew of artists worked feverishly to meet the demand for posters, match covers, and cartoons for all types of units, from aviation to ships and submarines. Dahl's gremlins could only be seen, he said, by "pilots and navigators and air gunners and people who fly." Walt Disney saw the military requests for a mascot as a major morale booster. Fifi was honored to become a WASP and featured on leather patches that the WASPs had sewn onto their flight jackets. Fifi was a good gremlin, and many felt she was a helpful little sprite. She got the pilots to their destinations and safely back again.

But while they took pride in Fifi's support along with pride in their service, there was pride's ever-present partner, disappointment. One of those disappointments came at the hands of the U.S. Congress, which voted to not grant the WASPs military status. Instead of being commissioned a second lieutenant on graduation, Millie was going to serve as a civilian pilot. The WASPs were treated for the most part like officers. They were billeted in officer quarters on the bases where they were assigned. They ate in the officer's mess. But the perks were few and definitely didn't include the officer pay. Or the benefits. Or the glory, as she was about to learn.

Still, Millie loved being a WASP. There were a little more than a thousand of them, paid as low-level civil servants, not as Army officers. The WASPs were originally formed to haul cargo and personnel in order to free up male pilots to fly in combat. Graduates from earlier classes mostly ferried new planes to their designated locations. But in later classes, like Millie's, they were encouraged to take on a variety of missions. WASP Director Jackie Cochran, herself a hotshot pilot, was planning to petition Congress to move the WASP program into the Air Force. She was building the case for making them Army Air Corps pilots. The WASPs flew over 60 million miles in the war and seventy-eight different types of aircraft. In training, they flew simulated strafing runs and towed targets for live antiaircraft gun practice.

While the WASP was a small and mostly white organization, it wasn't totally so. Millie was the only Native American woman to serve in the WASP. Hazel Ying Lee and Maggie Gee were the first Chinese American women to serve as WASP pilots. Two

Hispanic women, Verneda Rodriguez and Frances Dias, also earned their silver wings with the WASP.

Several African American women applied and made it to the final interview stage, only to have their applications rejected. One woman faced *two* acts of discrimination. First, despite having earned an aviation certification at age nineteen, Mildred Hemmons Carter was asked to withdraw from the WASP application process because of her race. Then, the Tuskegee Airmen, the first group of Black male pilots to serve in the war, also rejected her — because of her gender. Seventy years later, though, she finally received redemption from both slights and was retroactively named a WASP, taking her final flight at age ninety.

Millie's first job after flight school was at Eagle Pass Army Airfield in west Texas, a pilot training facility with three 5,500-foot runways. She liked her job there, flying the T-6, towing targets for live fire training, and working with the flight instructors. When one of the male trainee pilots asked her if she was afraid, she said, "You don't have time to be frightened or scared or anything like that. I'm usually more concerned with my landings."

"Well you're a target up there yourself,

Rexy. What if one of those student gunners gets you?"

She rolled her eyes. Millie got that question over and over again. "Worry about being killed? I never gave it a thought . . . You can't live forever." It was a matter-of-fact view. And indeed thirty-eight WASPs did lose their lives during World War II.

Towing targets was a risky job but important work. The male pilot trainees and gunners used real ammunition on Millie's towed target. The antiaircraft ground troops practiced combat conditions every day in training. It was about as close to being in combat as a woman pilot could get. While women were not permitted to serve in combat, they did the jobs given to them, and they did them well. By 1944, there were about 300 WASPs training antiaircraft troops.

One blistering day at Eagle Pass, after a particularly tough training run, Millie touched down to find that one of the training targets was no longer attached to the tail of her aircraft. One of the senior officers walked over to Millie and pointed at the frayed rope.

"Great flying today, Rexy," he said. "But you lost something along the way. The boys actually shot down your target."

Millie nodded; she'd felt a little tug on the

352

tail as it broke off and sailed away. After landing, the instructors always checked the target to see how well the gunners did. But first they'd have to find this one. Typically, a strong metal wire attached the cloth target to the plane. The gunners were supposed to shoot at the sleeve, although they occasionally shot up the planes as well. Every fourth or fifth round was a "tracer," a shot that fizzled like a bright red firecracker to let the gunners know if they were hitting the target or not. From the cockpit, Millie could see little puffs of smoke from the tracers as they zinged by. She would increase speed, one way to help gunners hit the target — and definitely not the pilot.

"Of course, it was to our credit if it (the target) had lots of holes in it," Millie recalled. "That meant we had been maintaining our altitude and heading." But Millie had nothing to show for this run. Some lucky gunner had managed to sever the wire.

He pointed. "I still need to see your target, Millie. Look over yonder. You can go get it. See that? That little bit of white flapping in the wind? It's in the field over there." He pointed.

Millie shaded her eyes and looked and looked off into the distance. She thought she saw a bit of waving white cloth. The downed target was probably at least a mile away. Flat ground, sure, but still a distance.

"Here." He flipped her the keys to a jeep. "Go get it."

"Yes, sir." Millie walked slowly over to the jeep. That was an order. She had to go get her target. By herself. She slid into the driver's seat and turned the key, just like she'd seen others do. Millie still had never driven a car. She'd been too busy learning to fly.

But driving couldn't be that difficult. It sure couldn't be any harder than flying a plane. She popped the clutch and the jeep hopped into second gear. The transmission strained and moaned as Millie zigzagged the vehicle across the road, over rocks, and through little gullies, rocking back and forth until she got close to the target. Then she got out and walked over to retrieve it in the brush. Now for the tough part. She still had to turn around and drive back.

"This was a big problem for me," she recalled. "I didn't know how to drive. I'd never learned how to drive a car. I don't think anybody trusted me with a car." Thankfully, she wasn't asked to drive again.

She was asked once if she faced discrimination from the male pilots. "There was prejudice against women, definitely, but I just didn't let it worry me." Millie knew what was important and what to ignore. Sometimes they called her "Sexy Rexy." But that didn't faze her. She was making a difference through her service. That's what mattered.

Other women faced more direct prejudice every day. As women, they simply weren't valued soldiers compared to the men. At one base the commander told them, "These planes are dispensable [easy to replace] and you're dispensable." Some women actually had their planes sabotaged or not repaired correctly. At bases where the commanders were supportive about their role, the women found that the culture was more positive and accepting. The WASPs learned a lot about what good leadership was like — they'd seen both good and bad.

While Millie was pulling targets and helping train gunners for combat, another fight was going on in Washington. Jackie had begun her push to make the WASP a permanent part of the Army Air Corps. A proposal went before Congress in February 1944. It should have been easy. The women had performed well, met every expectation, and handled all the missions they were given with aplomb.

However, by the time Millie was well into her WASP training, the fight had gotten ugly. The majority of male pilot instructors were civilians. With the war beginning to wind down, they had to look out for themselves. There wasn't going to be such a high a demand for flight training following the war, and they sure didn't want to have to compete with women for jobs. The men fought back. It was a campaign of propaganda and disinformation, complete with claims that the women were harder to train, had more accidents than male pilots, and even that their uniforms were more expensive for the service to buy. None of it was true, but it didn't matter. While at the time, Millie and her fellow trainee pilots were unaware of the fight back in Washington, it was soon going to break their dreams in half.

In June 1944, just weeks after the D-Day invasion of Europe, Congress defeated the WASP bill. General Arnold was focused on the air war in Europe and decided that the fight with Congress was one he didn't want to engage in. He didn't have the time. Instead, he decided to simply end the program. In the meantime, Millie completed her training. She was flying. Her dream had come true. But the clock was ticking.

In December 1944, General Arnold spoke to the final graduating WASP class. He said, "On this last graduation day I salute you and all WASP." Jackie Cochran also spoke

WASP trainees with their instructor pilot. U.S. Air Force photo.

eloquently to the new pilots whose wings were clipped before they even pinned them on. They would never fly.

She predicted, "I'm very happy that we've trained a thousand women to fly the Army way . . . It think it's going to mean more to aviation than anyone realizes."

Days later, Arnold wrote in a letter to every member of the WASP, "When we needed you, you came through and have served most commendably in very difficult circumstances, but now the war situation has changed and the time has come when your volunteer services are no longer needed . . . I want you to know that I appreciate your war service and the AAF will miss you." It just didn't seem fair.

"We were devastated," Millie said. "I think all of us . . . No matter what kind of duty we had, we liked it . . . it's just like someone stuck a pin in a balloon when they said they were going to discontinue the program."

Millie knew she would miss flying more than it would miss her. Civilian aviation jobs for women simply didn't exist. And jobs for women pilots in the military were a generation away. Millie made the painful transition back to civilian life along with all the other WASPs. She never flew again.

The American Campaign Medal was presented to those who had served for at least a year. Millie wasn't one of them. The war wasn't even over yet, but the WASPs weren't needed. It felt like defeat. Some returned home while others, like Millie, determined they would stay involved. She took a job as an air traffic controller and remained with the Army Air Corps in a reserve status, then the Air Force Reserve. Her time with the WASP counted towards rank, and she finally received that military commission she'd been promised, pinning on the silver bars of a first lieutenant. But the new Air Force policy was that women didn't fly. Period.

She may not have been flying, but she was never far from a plane or an airport. She spent ten years with the Air Force Reserve as an air traffic controller, was promoted to captain, and served on active duty during the Korean war. In a civilian capacity, she worked with the Civil Aeronautics Administration in the Kirtland Air Force Base in New Mexico.

She continued her career in aviation as an air traffic controller for thirty-three years with the Federal Aviation Administration (FAA), at airports in Texas, and in Albuquerque and Santa Fe, New Mexico. It was a good job to have, but her time as a WASP would always be the highlight of her life. Many of the WASPs kept in close contact with one another.

They wrote, visited with classmates, and began to hold annual reunions. Millie was always eager to see her former comrades. For while her dream was gone, broken by politics and a culture that refused to accept the women's performance and their contributions, there was also something important that was gained. Millie had found a family in the young women she met in the WASP program, all with dreams and determination, like her. Through the years, their mutual support, care, and friendship continued to sustain her. They didn't just talk pilots and planes. It was now about kids and grandkids, weddings and funerals, and sharing their lives with each other. Their shared experiences and their friendships sustained them all, even as they faded from public view. Through their service, the WASPs had stepped, not out of line, but ahead, into a totally new arena, one of their own making. They forged a fraternity, then after the war a community, and finally they built a legacy. It took decades.

Like other records from the war, WASP records were sealed for thirty years after 1945, locked away from researchers, academics, and investigators. The story of these groundbreaking pilots was little known until the 1970s. Then the middle-aged veterans came under a surprise attack. In 1976, the Air Force announced they would begin to accept women for pilot training, claiming, "It's the first time the Air Force has permitted women to fly their aircraft."

That was a major insult to the women who had worn the WASP silver wings. WASP veterans rose up, buzzing in stinging protest. They were the first women pilots, and they weren't about to let the U.S. Air Force forget it. Stories were written, letters to editors were sent, and news stories about the WASPS followed. Public awareness grew, as did understanding and gratitude. Many

Americans were amazed to learn about their role and their contributions in WWII. Millie and her comrades found themselves suddenly popular; people wanted to hear her story.

A campaign for legitimacy and recognition followed. In 1977, President Jimmy Carter signed a bill making the WASP part of the Air Force. Those pioneers, every one of them a volunteer, were recognized at last. The GI Bill Improvement Act also provided the WASP with VA benefits, including health care and the right to be buried in a military cemetery if they chose. Millie was inducted into the South Dakota Aviation Hall of Fame that same year.

Each WASP received an honorable discharge certificate in 1979, and more accolades followed. In 1984, each WASP was awarded the World War II Victory Medal, along with any other military awards they were due. For many, it was too late. Family members accepted some of the awards on behalf of those WASPs who had already passed away. In 2009, the WASPs were inducted into the International Air and Space Hall of Fame at the San Diego Air and Space Museum. On July 1, 2009, President Barack Obama signed into law a bill awarding the Congressional Gold Medal to the

WASPs. The back of the medal reads, "The first women in history to fly American military aircraft."

Ola Mildred Rexroat at the 2010 Independence Day Celebration at Mount Rushmore. U.S. Air Force Photo by Airman First Class Cory Hook.

The WASP Museum was dedicated in Sweetwater in 2005. Along with the museum and the walk of honor, there is also a WASP statue, plaque, and Wishing Well at the site.

At the age of ninety-one, Millie was asked what it was like to be one of the first female military pilots in the United States. She said, "Our service, what we did, proved to the military and the civilians that women could do that. Of course, I knew that I could do it. We knew that we could do it."

In 2016, Georgia Pedro, President of the North American Indian Women's Association (NAIWA), described Millie as a "loving, caring person with a wonderful sense of humor," and emphasized that, as a WASP, she truly carried on the Native American tradition of women warriors. Millie served two terms as president of the NAIWA.

Ola Mildred Rexroat passed away in 2017, at the age of ninety-nine, just two months short of her one-hundredth birthday. She wanted to be buried at Arlington National Cemetery, a last battleground for the WASP. When WASP Elaine Harmon passed away in 2014, her request to be buried at Arlington was denied. Seventeen months and yet another Congressional battle later, the first WASP was laid to rest at Arlington, a right she, and they, had more than earned. Senator Martha McSally led that fight. She had come to know some WASP women as a young Air Force pilot and was filled with respect for their service. "I counted on our times together for comradery, advice, and inspiration."

Since then, many women pilots have become not only fans of, but also advocates for these incredible trailblazers. Millie received every honor due to her, a funeral service with full military honors, the three volley gun salute executed by the U.S. Air Force honor guard, taps played by a military bugler, and an American flag — carefully folded and creased and then reverently presented to her son, Forest. Her ashes were interred in Arlington National Cemetery's columbarium.

That fall, the Air Force dedicated a command building to her memorable legacy at Edwards Air Force Base in southern California. At the ceremony, her son Forest recalled, "Everything my mother did . . . sent a message to me when I was very young. If you really want to do something, don't let anyone tell you that you can't just because of who or what you are. It wasn't something she ever said to me, it's just who she was."

Flying for the United States of America in wartime was an honor and a privilege. For many WASPs, it was the best time of their lives. Millie would have agreed. "If I had to do it all over again, I'd do the same thing."

Jackie Cochran had predicted the WASP program would go down in history. As she said, "I'm sure it's going to do something that is so vital and has been so badly needed in aviation for so many years." She was never more right. Millie Rexroat's service and that of her fellow WASPs occurred at a time when

women had to fight for the right to fly. They had to prove their worth to contribute and to serve. That tenacity has inspired generations of civilian and military women, pilots, air traffic controllers, flight crew members, astronauts, and thousands of others who respect the guts, tenacity, and work it takes to make dreams come true.

Millie's final resting place is less than a mile from Washington National Airport, where her dream began. Having come full circle, she rests under a sky where there are often military aircraft flyovers to honor the warriors who rest there in honored glory. Ola Millie Rexroat is one of them.

CHAPTER 14

THE GOLDEN HOUR

"It felt like I waited all my life to meet just one of my former patients and know that he made it all the way home."

KATHERINE FLYNN NOLAN

"Help! It's too deep!" Kate swallowed a mouthful of saltwater and spit it out. "Help!" She went under again. *Welcome to Normandy,* she thought.

"No, dearie. It's not that deep. You're just shorter than everyone else. Here, let me give you a hand." Kate felt a tight grip on her back lifting the straps of her sodden haversack, and the load got lighter. One of the other nurses, a tall drink of water from Texas, was holding her up. Kate felt herself being pulled forward, treading water, and barely touching the sand beneath the rough waves.

"Thanks," Kate muttered, then spit out more water as a wave sloshed up over her

nose. Second Lieutenant Kate Flynn continued to sputter as she was dragged forward. The Fifty-Third Field Hospital had arrived. They had originally been scheduled to arrive by light aircraft, silent little planes with no engines, on D-Day. However, those first gliders had crashed, delaying their unit's arrival by a month.

Kate wasn't too sure the delay had been for the best. Barely five feet, three inches, Kate was the shortest of the six nurses in her platoon. With her blonde hair and freckles, she was often confused for a kid. She craned her neck trying to look over the other nurses, past them, around them. She caught bright, steely images of the beach ahead, a massive trash heap of wrecked vehicles, twisted metal, broken weapons, and smoldering ruins. The smell of death was choking her, coating her with its darkness. The deep ruts gouged into the hillsides had ripped the earth open, gaping dinosaur-sized wounds, the result of U.S. Naval gunfire, fired from fourteen miles offshore. There was a new horror in every direction. The entire beach was a cemetery, she realized. As the tide began to rise higher and slammed into the bluffs above the beach in front of them, the war became more than something they'd heard about, trained for, and prayed over.

It was July 15, 1944. And this wasn't just any beach. This was Utah Beach in Normandy, a few short weeks after the D-Day landings. Code-named Operation Overlord, the invasion at Normandy kicked off the biggest Allied offensive of the war, and Kate Flynn and her fellow nurses were neck deep in it. Kate was a brand-new second lieutenant in the U.S. Army Nurse Corps. Her unit, the Fifty-Third Field Hospital (Heavy Casualty) was assigned to support the troops there on the beach, and onward to wherever they went to pursue the retreating Nazis. Kate, like nearly 60,000 other Army nurses, was mobilized "for the duration," the orders said, plus six months, for good measure. That meant she would be in the Army for as long as it took for America and her allies to win the war.

The year 1943 had been an important one for Kate. Katherine M. Flynn graduated from Hahnemann Hospital in Worcester, Massachusetts, as a registered nurse in April. Nurse's cap in hand, she traveled south to MacDill Army Airfield in Tampa, Florida, in August. There she pinned on her second lieutenant bars in the Army Nurse Corps and hoped to specialize her skills. She applied for the flight nurse program. That meant additional training to prepare to travel on medical evacuation flights, sometimes over enemy territory. Flight nurses routinely cared for up to twenty sick or wounded soldiers per flight. They all knew the danger involved, and Kate believed she was up for the challenge. But the program was full, and the Army wasn't accepting any more applicants. Kate was disappointed, but her efforts hadn't been for nothing. She still had her commission, and she was still going to serve as an Army nurse. Just not in the air. She also met a nice young man at MacDill, her future husband Air Force Lieutenant James Nolan. Their time together before deployment was brief but, like many wartime romances, intense. They were engaged after a few short weeks, just before she reported for the Army's basic nurse course. "We didn't have time to even get to know one another before we shipped out. We wrote letters back and forth for the next two years."

She was twenty-one years old.

At the time, the Army was building new hospital units: organizing, staffing, manning, and equipping them to be ready to support the troops in the planned coming surge of Operation Overlord, the D-Day invasion. The preparation had been years in the making. In July 1943, basic training

Second Lieutenant Kate Flynn.
Photo courtesy of the Nolan family.

centers for nurses began to open. The basic course for new lieutenants was only four weeks long. But it covered all the important stuff: military customs and courtesies, marching, saluting, physical training, and the critical things the junior officers would need to know in a combat zone — map reading, camouflage, how and when to wear a gas mask, plus the essentials of military hospital setup and teardown, field sanitation, and ward management. Then the wide-eyed graduates were sent off to join their new units.

It wasn't long before the Fifty-Third unit unfurled its flag at Fort Bragg, North Carolina. Then the unit training began — moving up from the individual tasks that Kate had learned in basic to team drills and unit efficiency. The nurses had to be ready when the call came. And it came *fast*. Soon they were sent to England to wait at the staging area until they were called forward. Kate didn't know the term at first; she envisioned it as though all the units were lined up to go to France. Then, one by one, they were called forward to board a ship. That was a gross oversimplification of how the Army movement planning process worked and didn't include all the particulars of packing and loading equipment, but her own definition helped Kate understand what was happening.

Every day in this new world brought a dizzying array of new experiences. Her uniform was stiff, scratchy, and smelled like mothballs. The Army boots were new and too tight. She kept forgetting the hat. Who wore a hat outside all the time? And every day, just like in the basic nursing course, the terms were new too. Army talk was like another language. Just as Kate mastered a few Army terms, the instructors would throw more at them. And now the training got tougher too. "It was a lot of physical training, ten-mile hikes with full packs three times a week, aircraft identification, and all that." Kate didn't know how much she would need all that. But she definitely knew friendly aircraft. She'd seen and heard hundreds of planes take off and land at MacDill's airfield. Kate could identify the British aircraft too. "They had Rolls-Royce engines," she recalled. "They sounded very smooth."

Three months later, in June of 1944, their call came. It was time.

Kate Flynn with her fellow nurses at Fort Bragg as they prepared for deployment to Europe. Kate is in the front row, center. Photo courtesy of the Nolan family.

If she'd thought 1943 was a year of big changes, Kate Flynn hadn't seen anything yet. The next year was transformative — frightening, rewarding, confidence building, and packed with danger, grief, and sometimes, unexpected joy. It was twelve long months of being forged in the fire of battle. If Kate had been disappointed in not having the opportunity to use her education and training up until then, those qualms were quickly quashed.

The sight of wounded being evacuated off the beachhead and up the bluffs made it all real. Kate stood shaking in the cold sand, soaked through, her head down — hands on knees, spitting salt water. Just ahead, a few soldiers were trying to push a Jeep with a flat tire out of the mud.

"Keep moving," one of the sergeants said. "We need to get off the beach. More traffic coming in. Hurry up!" The beaches were flooded with more units arriving every day. The Fifty-Third Field Hospital was just one of them.

Kate's platoon quickly moved off the beachhead and regrouped. Everyone had made it ashore just fine, but their vehicles and equipment didn't show up. By nightfall, the soggy surgical teams and nurses were pitching their tiny pup tents. The Fifty-Third spent nearly a month near the beaches, two nurses to a tent. But they stayed busy by being loaned out to other field hospitals in the area.

When their equipment eventually arrived, the Fifty-Third was attached to General George Patton's Third Army. They typically traveled along in the wake of an infantry or armored division as the Army fought its way to the east. Kate and her colleagues never found out what caused the delay, but they were glad to see their own unit vehicles and the larger tents. If nothing else, it was a relief to be able to stand up again while getting dressed.

"We were with Patton when he broke out of Normandy and went racing across the peninsula. We were with the Third Armored Division and went from there to Northern France."

It seemed like they were always on the move. Field hospitals were supposed to stay five miles behind the battlefront, but that typically didn't happen. Sometimes the boom of artillery was too close for comfort. IV poles rattled, and medicines shook off the shelves and onto the dirt floor of the tents. Wounded soldiers moaned in their sleep. They were shelled constantly. "We weren't bombed but other hospitals were."

The first time it happened, the young nurses had to fight the instinct to run. "What do we do?" one of the newcomers asked.

"We can't leave them," Kate pointed at the patients lying in their cots. Most couldn't walk or move. Others were still unconscious.

"Here. Let's get them under the cots," Kate and her fellow nurses moved their patients under cots and got down on the ground with them. Later Kate recalled, "We got hit a couple of times, and one time they set a tent on fire. Fortunately, there were no patients in it." Kate learned quickly to keep herself focused and trained on the practical. No one got a break until all the incoming wounded were treated and cared for.

The Army called its field treatment process "The Chain of Evacuation," a series of steps and actions that proved to be tremendously effective. Kate got into the routine with her fellow nurses, and they worked together like a pro team. When the fighting was fierce, litter bearers and ambulances brought in the wounded. On average, the eighteen nurses in a field hospital could handle seventy-five to one hundred patients a day. The wounded were taken directly to the receiving tent where doctors and nurses would conduct triage. Those strong enough to travel were sent to the rear, to an evacuation hospital. The more seriously wounded were stabilized with blood, plasma, dressings, and medications before being sent on.

The most seriously wounded, who needed immediate care, went straight to the surgical tent. If they were considered too weak to survive surgery, they were sent to the shock unit.

Kate said, "You have to get to (the wounded) and start treating them for shock and stabilize them within an hour. We had to get to them in that 'golden hour.'" The death rate in field hospitals was incredibly low; less than four percent of those treated in field hospitals during the war perished. The organization and speed of the Chain of Evacuation process saved innumerable lives. Kate always credited the surgical teams too. She claimed they were the best of the best.

Usually the Fifty-Third remained in one location for about ten days. Once all the patients were evacuated to the rear, Kate and the other nursing staff would begin packing up equipment and supplies, taking down the tents, and getting personal gear in order. "We had done it over and over until it was routine," she recalled. "When the outfit we supported went back for a rest period we would be reassigned to a new outfit, just going into action." As the action was unrelenting, they didn't get to rest. With the unit moving every one to two weeks on average, they worked their way through France,

Holland, and Belgium that summer and into fall.

At one point, they were on a hillside in plain sight of a main travel route. "Of course, we had red crosses on top of the tents, with a big tarp between them and the ground, so the aircraft could see the big cross. One day we heard tanks coming . . . everybody thought they sounded like German tanks, bigger and heavier. They came down the road, but when they got to where we were, they kept going. I'm sure they knew we had some of their soldiers as our patients."

They often treated German POWs along with Allied soldiers. They were cooperative once they saw they were getting the same treatment as the GIs, Kate recalled. "I think they were happy to be in our field hospital and out of the war." She recalled only one POW who had been a problem patient, a German lieutenant. "He spoke perfect English and had been educated in England. He was very obnoxious." When he saw Kate coming with an injection of penicillin, he refused it at first, arms waving, accusing her of trying to poison him. Kate turned away and used that same needle on a GI. Only then did the prisoner realize he was getting care equal to that of the Americans.

"He started bossing me around, or trying

to," Kate said with a smile. "He wanted to be treated first, have his dressings changed first, get his injections before all the other soldiers." Kate wasn't having it. Oh, no. "He waited his turn . . . He didn't get away with it," she recalled. "He was the only one that we ever had any problem with, the only prisoner."

That fall, the field hospital continued to leapfrog behind fighting troops as they pushed to the east. Quickly, the weather began to change. The snow started in November, then came the bitter cold. On the move again, Kate and a few of her fellow shivering nurses huddled together in the back of one of the trucks. When the trucks finally stopped moving, the unit was still in Holland near the border with Germany. By that time, they had jumped forward at least twelve times since July. Kate and her buddies noticed a few of the villagers standing nearby, carefully watching them. The nurses peered out from the truck bed's leaky canvas top, scratchy wool blankets pulled tight around them. What Kate didn't know was that the townspeople thought the nurses were prostitutes because they were wearing pants. That's what the camp followers wore.

The nurses felt self-conscious and thought the townspeople were staring because they looked unkempt. "I can't imagine what they are thinking of us. We really are a mess," said Marie, the platoon's chief nurse. They all looked at each other and sniffed. It had been a long time since any of them had a bath. Or eaten anything other than cold field rations.

"What I wouldn't give for a hot shower," one of the other nurses chimed in. "And a hot meal." She moaned softly, licking her lips at the thought of turkey and mashed potatoes.

"Hot showers? Who are you kidding?" Kate pulled off her steel pot and ran her fingers through her tangled locks. The last time she'd washed her hair, that helmet had served as her sink. "We were dirty, weary, and chilled to the point of numbness," she recalled.

Thankfully, the long day ended with an invitation to set up operations in an empty school nearby. The building was located beside a Catholic church and a convent. It was the first time Kate and her colleagues had been able to work inside a building since landing on Utah Beach in July. "Quickly the cots were lined up, IV paraphernalia in place, receiving wards, surgery, and post-op made ready for patients." They had the checklist down.

*Fellow nurse Lauren Ball washes Kate Nolan's hair
outside the field hospital tent in September 1944.
Photo courtesy of the Nolan family.*

And it was just in time. For the next fourteen hours, the casualties kept on coming. Heads down, the teams kept working to triage, move, react, fix. When the worst of the rush finally let up, the nuns from the convent next door invited the nurses to stay with them, where they would be able to sleep in an actual bed. Kate saw her assigned bed and thought it was the most beautiful thing she'd seen in months. It felt like years since they'd been deployed. Sleeping in a real bed was such a luxury that the nurses felt pampered. It was like staying in a classy hotel, except for the rain, sleet, and snow continuing outside and the echoes of gunfire in the distance.

The nuns and twenty-eight war orphans in their charge were living in the convent's basement and thought it would be safer for the nurses to stay down there with them. But exposed or not, those upstairs beds were calling. Kate and the others stayed above ground with their precious beds. And one by one they each got a hot bath.

Ten days passed, and the nurses began to organize their supplies. It felt like they would be told to move soon. But the orders didn't come. Then another day. Nothing. As Christmas approached, they began to relax a little. "For the first time we had convalescent men taking food by mouth, growing stronger and getting into the holiday spirit."

A Dutch neighbor cut down a little Christmas tree for the hospital staff and their patients. Kate recalled, "The patients made silver stars from K-ration cans. The Red Cross gave out cartons of Life Savers. We used bandages to string them to add to the trees. Everyone had the Christmas Spirit." The nurses sang carols with the wounded and actually had time to think about the future. What they wanted the most was to hear from their loved ones. Maybe staying in place a bit longer would mean the mail, perhaps including some holiday packages, could catch up to them.

Kate looked forward to hearing from James. It had been months since she'd had a letter from him. She tried not to worry. No one else had gotten any mail either. They'd heard a rumor that all the mail was backed up, stuck somewhere in England. Some general had made the decision the fighting was too heavy to permit the mail to flow to fighting units. Whoever made that dumb decision, Kate thought, didn't understand how important mail would be to troop morale.

Absent news and information, there was time to daydream a little. Maybe it was safe to make some plans. The nuns were baking treats from flour and sugar that the hospital cooks scrounged up for them. They brewed tea and planned for a holiday meal celebration following Christmas mass in the convent chapel.

But it was too good to be true. On December 23, the order came to be prepared to evacuate all the patients to the rear. That meant they were finally getting ready to move out, although no one knew when. This was the part Kate found most frustrating. It was like hearing, "Get ready. Get set." Then there was a pause before they could

actually *go*. Sometimes it was hours, sometimes days. She thought it a waste of time
to hold her breath in anticipation. Kate just
hoped they wouldn't have to leave until they
enjoyed Christmas, one day of peace, prayer,
and good food with friends, old and new.

To be ready, the nurses made certain their
patients had warm clothes and blankets,
preparing them for their trip to the general
hospital in the rear area. They packed up the
hospital tents too, everything but the essentials so that they could be ready to go when
the call came. The next day was Christmas
Eve. The guns in the distance were silent. A
grateful hospital staff, doctors, nurses, and
patients gathered together for the midnight
services. After the services ended and the
nurses and their new friends all gathered in
the convent's dining room, the finest linen,
china, and crystal greeted them all. It was
rather wonderful and strange, Kate recalled,
with the nuns speaking no English and the
doctors and nurses speaking no Dutch.

"But we understood one another and that
too was beautiful."

The nurses had just plopped sugar cubes
into their hot tea when they heard the sound
of idling engines. While they tried to ignore
it and enjoy their last few minutes of holiday
cheer, one of the drivers burst through the

door and announced importantly, "It's time. Report at once."

Marie, the chief nurse replied, "Please tell the colonel to give us a few more minutes." She sipped at her steaming cup, pinkie finger up. Kate crossed her fingers under the table. Maybe this would buy them a little more time. But she was worried.

The soldier wasn't about to argue with a lieutenant. "Yes, ma'am," he said, eyebrows raised. He saluted and left.

It seemed like only a moment had passed before the driver returned. This time he didn't even knock. "You're holding up the convoy," he blurted out, taking a step back. Then all the trucks began to blow their horns. The reluctant nurses ran out into the night.

Down the street, the famous Red Ball Express was waiting. This was the supply truck convoy that rushed important supplies to the front lines throughout the war. The name "Red Ball" was meant to show the logistics and resupply effort was critical to success on the battlefield. Those trucks had top priority all along Allied supply routes. Kate looked up and down the street. A lineup of rumbling trucks stretched out as far as she could see. "Headlights blazing, horns blowing, and the colonel shouting, 'Those damn women are holding up the war.' It was quite a sight."

The nurses ran, clambered into their unit's trucks, waved goodbye to their Dutch friends, and rode off into the night with the supply convoy. They'd made it through the Battle of the Bulge. Ahead lay the German border and the final chapter of their war service. Christmas Day, their dinner wasn't turkey and all the fixings. It was the cardboard K rations. They were once again cold and exposed. But that Christmas Eve, with those precious moments leading up to departing with the convoy, was one Kate would never forget.

Kate and her fellow nurses went the whole way, from the beaches of Normandy through France right into the heart of the Third Reich. When all was said and done, Kate had served in six countries: the U.S., England, France, Belgium, Holland, and Germany. Incredibly, she participated in five major campaigns and earned five battle stars for Normandy, Northern France, Ardennes, Central Europe, Rhineland, and the Battle of the Bulge. Many male soldiers couldn't say that.

By Victory in Europe (VE) day, May 8, 1945, Kate and the staff of the Fifty-Third Field Hospital were in Germany, in the small town of Kirn, about ninety miles southwest of Frankfurt. They were still treating newly released POWs and survivors of Hitler's concentration camps. Kate was promoted to first lieutenant, having served her time as a second lieutenant honorably and with unwavering dedication to her patients. Several of her colleagues were also promoted, but there wasn't time to celebrate. From May through August, the Fifty-Third Field Hospital was "on hold." Depending on how the war unfolded in Japan, they could still be needed there. Kate didn't want to complain, but all around them, infantry and armored divisions were moving into vacated German military barracks. They had roofs, walls, and most importantly, showers. Kate and her envious colleagues were still in tents. When the war in Japan ended in August, they would all breathe a sigh of relief. Now everyone could go home.

Her unit sailed back to the States that fall; she arrived in New York in November. Captain James Nolan arrived back in San Francisco at the end of December. They met in the middle, at Kate's hometown back in Worcester, Massachusetts, and married there in January 1946. James became a career Air Force officer, retiring as a colonel. At first, they planned to retire near Philadelphia where he'd grown up, but then Kate discovered the warmth of a Florida winter. The memory of those bitter nights in a tent with nothing but a potbellied stove for heat when it was snowing and 40 below never left her. She never wanted to be that cold again.

It took Kate a bit to persuade him, but after one more Pennsylvania winter, they relocated to Naples, Florida, with their seven children. The couple were married for sixty years before James passed away in 2005. "Theirs was a real love story," their son Steve said.

Kate wasn't involved in veterans' organizations or activities until her children were grown. In the 1980s, she began to rediscover how America valued her Army service. She was proud to be recognized as a veteran. She became a charter member of the Women in Military Service for America (WIMSA) Memorial Foundation and volunteered to serve as their field representative in Naples, helping to raise money to build the imposing Women's Memorial at the gates of Arlington National Cemetery. She proudly attended the groundbreaking, the memorial dedication ceremony in 1997, the fifth anniversary event, and, at eighty-six years old, the tenth anniversary celebration.

Kate was also active with the Veterans of

the Battle of the Bulge (VBOB). She was attending a Battle of the Bulge reunion in 2000 when another veteran walked up to her and gave her a hug. Kate was startled. She didn't know him.

"I remember you," he said. "You saved my life. You look just the same, too. Freckles and all." He grinned.

Kate was overcome with joy so intense it blurred her vision. There were tears and a jumble of words that tripped over each other in her haste to thank him. She was so grateful to have met this man again, thirty-six years after treating him for shock and stabilizing him for surgery. "It felt like I waited all my life to meet *just one* of my former patients and know that he made it all the way home."

In 2001, she returned to Normandy and visited Utah Beach for the first time since she landed there, in 1944. Almost immediately, she began having flashbacks and nightmares about that July landing in 1944. Later diagnosed with post-traumatic stress disorder (PTSD), she joined a support group. She was the only woman veteran in the group, among veterans from World War II, Korea, Vietnam, Iraq, and Afghanistan. She felt at home with her soldiers.

Her story was profiled by NPR for the 2004 dedication of the World War II memorial in

Washington, DC. On that occasion, she told the story of that 1944 Christmas Eve dinner that never was. Kate was also recognized in the *American Legion* magazine and told her story and that of her fellow nurses at every opportunity. "We had the best patients," she recalled. "They never complained. One was a famous war correspondent named Ham Greene. I could tell he was in a lot of pain when he first arrived, but he helped me take care of the other patients." When Greene returned home in 1944, the *American Legion* magazine published a profile on him. The article mentioned his nurse at the field hospital. It was Kate. Her uncle had saved a copy for her although she didn't get to see it until two years later.

On June 6, 2007, Kate Nolan received the highest military award the French government could present, the Legion of Honor. Thirty-two World War II veterans were recognized that day in a special ceremony in Naples. Kate was the only female veteran in the group, surrounded by her children and grandchildren. She received the medal wearing her World War II uniform jacket. It still fit.

A number of those recognized that day spoke about how they were accepting the honor on behalf of others. Kate understood.

Lieutenant Kate Nolan with French Consul General Philippe Vinogradoff after receiving the Legion of Honor in Naples, Florida, June 6, 2007. Photo courtesy of United Sound and Video, Naples, FL.

"I know exactly what they're talking about. You know you made it back because you were lucky and others weren't." She was quick to point out that from her nursing class at Hahnemann in 1943, over half served with distinction during the war.

Kate Nolan passed away on March 13, 2019, leaving behind a legacy of duty, honor, and true devotion to serving her country when it needed her. Her two oldest sons served in Vietnam. Her youngest son is a veteran of the war in Afghanistan, and one of her granddaughters served in Iraq. Another grandson became a nurse who helped battle the COVID-19 pandemic early in 2020. Without Kate and those 59,000 nurses in World War II, the death toll would have been significantly higher, the suffering greater, and the loss nearly incalculable. Because of her, soldiers made it home. And for all of them, their children and grandchildren were able to live, flourish, and create their own legacies of service.

CHAPTER 15

HIGH MORALE

"I have opened a few doors, broken a few barriers, and, I hope, smoothed the way to some degree for the next generation."

CHARITY ADAMS EARLEY

Major Charity Adams raised her hand. "Sir, I have a question." She stood.

"Who will be the commanding officer of this new unit?" Charity asked. Having just pinned on her gold major's leaf, she was one of only two field grade officers in the Women's Army Corps (WAC) at the First WAC Training Center at Fort Des Moines, Iowa. It was September 1944.

"You're the ranking Black officer here. You will."

She shook her head no.

"I will not command such an outfit." There, she said it straight out.

There was a collective gasp and a long

pause. The room was silent. How could Major Adams be refusing such a wonderful opportunity? That was exactly what the Army was proposing, a new Black training regiment, one parallel to the white regiment, in order to create promotional opportunities for Black officers. It looked like a good idea on the surface, especially to the young lieutenants in the room, but the career path broke off right there, and Charity knew it. All higher-grade promotions would be reserved for white officers. It wasn't an opportunity. It was a sham.

"Would you disobey a direct order?" The white briefing officer from HQ was incredulous. Major Adams couldn't refuse selection for command. Could she?

"I want to make it as a WAC officer and not as a Black WAC officer. I guess this is the end because I will *not* be the regimental commander. No sir. I will not do it."

"I will not do it," she said again. No compromise. Charity looked around the packed room. Not one of the other Black officers would meet her gaze. She sat down. Crossed her arms.

Charity said later, "I was raised in the southern United States and I knew there was no such thing as separate but equal."

The room was silent. The briefer weakly

Lieutenant Colonel Charity Adams. U.S. Army photo.

concluded his remarks with the comment that there would be another update soon. As the meeting ended, all the attendees shuffled out, eyes averted, edging past her and stepping over her. Charity sat there, her guts twisting in knots, shifting back and forth across that sick gap between shock and anger. Not one of them spoke to Charity. Not one stood up with her. Or for her.

Major Charity Adams walked alone across the post to her office, head down. She'd stood her ground, and now she knew with certainty that she could only rely on herself. "I had learned one of life's greatest and hardest lessons: do not depend on the support of others for causes."

■ ■ ■ ■

Charity was born in 1919, at a time when the U.S. was celebrating victory in World War I. The next year, the Nineteenth Amendment was passed, and women were given the right to vote. It was a time of change in the country. A feeling of optimism was in the air, and it felt like new possibilities were open for women — unless you were Black. Then it was still a fight, all the way.

Charity grew up in Columbia, South Carolina, the oldest of four children. Her father was a minister and her mother a teacher, professionals with high standards and hopes for their children. She'd been first in many things in her life, including being first in her high school class, valedictorian. And since she'd started school in the second grade, she was sixteen when she graduated, the youngest in the class. In 1938, she graduated from Wilberforce College in Ohio with degrees in physics, math, Latin, and a minor in history. After college, Charity taught school in Columbia while working on a master's degree at Ohio State in the summers.

By 1942, she learned the Dean at her alma mater had recommended her for the first officer class of the Women's Army Auxiliary Corps (WAAC) in 1942 (later simply WAC).

Against her parents' and friends' wishes, she signed up. It didn't take long for the discrimination to kick in. By the time Charity reached Fort Des Moines, Iowa, for basic officer training, she'd already gotten her first taste of racism in the Army. A white lieutenant had insisted and made certain that Black recruits didn't sit with the white women on the bus headed for the camp.

In that first officer class, there were four hundred white women. Stephanie Czech was one of them, newly arrived from New York City. There were also forty Black women — the "ten percenters." While their training was integrated, their living conditions were not.

Charity held a variety of jobs while at Fort Des Moines, steadily impressing her superiors, handling every challenge, and rapidly moving up in rank. At first, she served as a training officer, indoctrinating new troops and modeling what was called "military bearing." Charity, known as "Edna" to her friends, was a charismatic leader. The young women were drawn to her, wanting to please her and gain her approval.

Charity also gained experience in administering good order and discipline as a summary court officer. She accounted for missing or stolen property as a survey officer, and continued to seek out leadership positions, building the skill set she would need as a commander. She also ran convoys, traveled with the WAC band, and conducted bond drives. Through it all, Charity focused on honing her leadership — which she found was not just an impressive skill set of hers, but a true passion. She excelled as a company commander, and by September 1944, she'd been promoted to major, making her the highest-ranking woman at Fort Des Moines. Yet despite achieving such an accomplished rank, Charity thought it was time for a new challenge.

It was hard to think about leaving Fort Des Moines. Charity had become so settled at the training center that she had begun to feel like a mother figure to all the fresh young privates arriving there, earning her the nickname "Big Ma." But she wanted to do more and challenge herself.

In November 1944, Charity learned that the U.S. Army's Command and General Staff School at Fort Leavenworth, Kansas, would accept its first WAC officers as students in 1945. Attending this important school was setting a jewel in the crown of an officer's career. It meant an officer was considered to have great promise and potential for greater responsibilities in the future.

Only the best and brightest were selected to learn how to serve in command and general staff positions at the highest levels. The selection process was extremely competitive.

Charity and the other chosen officers were excited; but they were all worried too. Would they be able to keep up with the combat veterans in the course? Charity was taking some remedial courses in important topics like map reading when she learned she would receive a different set of orders. That meant her orders to Fort Leavenworth were canceled.

Charity was disappointed but hoped there might be another opportunity to be selected for the school. Unfortunately, the timing was never right. Later she said, "I think that the only regret I have had about my years in the service was that I never got to attend Command and General Staff School."

By the time Charity was on her way to the European theater in January 1945, she'd broken so many glass ceilings it felt like she could see blue sky above. Once seated on the cramped cargo plane on the way to London, Charity finally had a moment to think about what was happening. With the overseas deployment training happening so fast, she'd been too busy to worry. Now she looked down at the sealed envelope on her lap. It was time to find out where she was going. She tore open the sealed orders and gasped. It was the job every officer coveted: command, troop time, and being in charge. Charity had commanded a training company, which was a good experience, but to be selected to command a battalion — a brand-new unit — overseas during wartime was a tremendous vote of confidence in her abilities. It was every opportunity she could have hoped for.

The Army had scrambled to assemble this new unit, the 6888th Central Postal Battalion. By 1944, there was a two-year backlog of mail for troops, members of the Red Cross, and civilians serving in Europe. There simply weren't enough postal units. Charity was headed for a postal disaster of major proportions, and the Army had picked her to fix it.

The all-Black WAC unit, known as the "Six Triple Eight," was the only Black WAC unit to be deployed — another first, with an impossible mission. The Six Triple Eight's 855 women were sent to Birmingham, England. When the first contingent arrived, Charity was there in Glasgow, Scotland, to meet their ship. Many had been seasick on the trip over. After being chased by submarines, others were glad to be on land. Their arrival came with a message about the danger of their work — a German V1 rocket, the "Buzz Bomb," came screaming in just as the women were heading down the ramp. They ran for cover as it hit the dock close to where they were disembarking. No one was injured, but it was a definite reminder that they had arrived in a war zone.

After everyone calmed down, Charity had to break the news to them. She'd met the senior commander in the Communications Zone (CommZ) a few weeks earlier in Paris while making some introductory office calls. Lieutenant General John C. H. Lee took her out for a nice welcome dinner where he asked with feigned innocence, "Can your troops march?"

It was a challenge. Charity knew what he meant. As the regional commander, he was asking if her troops could march in a parade. A military tradition, troops on parade was an expression of military might. General Lee was going to put on a show for the city of Birmingham.

Charity later recalled, "There's only one answer when a general asks you a question like that. So, I said, 'General, you've never seen better marching troops in your life.'"

Later, though, she worried. "Too late. I either had to prove my words or eat them later." After all, she'd never even seen her entire unit together in one place. She didn't have any idea if they could march or not.

Two days later, General Lee was the reviewing officer for the Six Triple Eight on parade in downtown Birmingham. The townspeople turned out in droves for the event, and to Charity's great relief, her soldiers looked spectacular. No one appeared exhausted or still suffering from seasickness. There was not a step out of place. Now it was time to get to work.

Major Charity Adams inspects her troops on parade in Birmingham, England. U.S. Army photo.

It was the first time some of the young women were away from home. They'd been sick at sea for months, bombed, and now had to work in a strange new country. The troops moved into accommodations within a former school building and marched to their work location the next day. It was cold and dreary outside, and the dark warehouse in front of them that would serve as their workspace was unheated. The windows were blacked out for safety from air raids. Reluctantly, the women filed inside to see their new place of business.

They'd all heard the rumors — there were millions of pieces of mail piled up in the dingy, overcrowded warehouse. It turned out the rumors were true: a mess of monumental proportions was just lying there in the dark waiting for them. A few of the women shrieked when they saw rat eyes glaring at them in the semidarkness. They could hear other rats racing away into the gloom, climbing the swaying towers of mail bags. Other women curled their lips at the smell of mold, spoiling food, and the sight of torn packages leaking mysterious slimy substances onto the concrete floor.

Major Adams looked unmoved. The troops watched her carefully to see if she would flinch. By god if she ran, they would run too. She didn't run. She wouldn't. Charity never backed down from a challenge.

She turned to her senior enlisted soldier. "Sergeant Major. Formation," was all she said.

"Yes, ma'am." The sergeant major formed up the battalion in the narrow space in front of the mountains of mail, and Charity marched to the front.

"At ease." The WACs relaxed their stance, hands twitching behind their backs. They stared at the mountains of mail stacked up behind their commander, 17 million pieces, they'd heard. In that moment, the stacks appeared piled up to eternity.

"I know how this looks, ladies. And I know what you're probably thinking. But we have a job to do and we're going to get it done. Now let's get organized."

She dismissed her troops and called the company leadership to her shabby makeshift office. Charity had five companies in her battalion, and she divided up the workload. Three shifts worked twenty-four hours a day, seven days a week. Under Charity's rotation system, about 65,000 letters were processed by each shift. They got the mail moving. A second contingent of troops arrived in April, and the unit manning roster was complete. Now at full strength, unit operations became routine. The women functioned together like a well-trained team.

By then it was April 1945. Charity's first priority was to get the long-overdue Christmas packages on their way. Due to the intense fighting in the Battle of the Bulge (December 1944–January 1945), all holiday mail for frontline units had been held in England. Nothing made its way to the continent. Charity established priorities and made certain those important letters and gifts got on their way first.

Once Charity directed a system for dealing with the backlog, she turned to face the other issues. Some of the letters were addressed only to soldiers by their first name, or nickname. For example, letters could be addressed only to "Junior, U.S. Army" or "Buster, U.S. Army" with no unit noted, or just "Robby." There were seven million Americans in Europe at the time. At least 7,500 soldiers were named Robert Smith.

It was a mess crying out for a system to tame it. Under Charity's direction, they set up a filing system of over seven million index cards. It was tedious, but because the battalion was also tasked with censoring troop mail being sent back to the states, it was necessary. Some packages were damaged or opened. The soldiers repacked them.

Word was spreading about what the Six Triple Eight was accomplishing. There were a number of visitors "from HQ." Some were curious about how the WACs were working their magic. Others wanted to express their gratitude for getting mail to their troops. Charity made certain her soldiers always looked polished and that their uniforms were "squared away" for each shift.

One visiting general was dismayed when not all of the battalion's soldiers were turned out for his inspection. Only the headquarters soldiers and off-duty personnel were in the formation. Of the 824 enlisted soldiers and thirty-one officers assigned to the Six Triple Eight, he was seeing only twenty-five troops standing before him. The general seemed to think the small turnout was a personal affront.

"Adams, where are the other personnel of this unit? It certainly doesn't look like a battalion to me," he said.

"Yes, sir. But we work three, eight-hour shifts so some of the women are working."

"Where are the others?"

"But sir . . ." It went on from there. He didn't care that the midnight shift soldiers were sleeping while others were having personal time.

The more Charity tried to explain, the more enraged he became. The confrontation continued in her office.

"I'm going to send a white first lieutenant down here to show you how to run this unit," he threatened.

Charity didn't back down. "Over my dead body, sir." Charity stood her ground. She was the unit commander. He wasn't in her supervisory chain at all. She knew she was right in her management of her soldiers. She wasn't going to make them change their schedules just to satisfy his ego for an inspection with every last one of them standing in a line. No sir.

"You'll be hearing from me," he leaned over Charity's desk and sputtered, inches from her face.

"And I'll file charges against you, sir, for using segregationist language. That's a violation of Allied directives."

The general backed down. He left Charity's office without another word. Several soldiers had heard the loud exchange. The warehouse walls may have been thick, but there was little more than cardboard holding up Charity's makeshift office. They nodded to each other. Big Ma had their back. They elbowed each other and spread the word.

Charity absolutely would not stand for any racist attitudes, discrimination, or attempts at segregation. She later recalled the British people were curious about them at first, but not initially friendly. "White GIs had told the locals stories about us. Tall tales. The locals quickly realized the truth. The Red

Cross tried to segregate us. The British just wanted to visit us." The white WACs used a recreational hotel in London for their leave and vacation time. They wanted a separate hotel established for the Black women. Charity just said no. The Red Cross opened a recreational club for Black women only. Charity's troops boycotted it. The Red Cross didn't try again.

Many of the women found their time in Birmingham to be socially liberating. The Six Triple Eight women were often treated better by the locals than they had been at home. Many made friends and enjoyed visiting with local families. A few dated English men.

One morning, one of the local women and her daughter visited Charity at her office. Many local housewives would come to call, some curious, others eager to talk about their wartime struggles — missing their husbands, food shortages, and other hardships. Charity felt that it might cheer up these two if she invited them to have a nice lunch. They walked together to the dining hall.

"I'm so sorry I don't have anything better to offer you," Charity said, sitting down at the small wooden table. "Today's lunch meat is Spam."

"Oh," her guest replied in surprise, hand

over her mouth. "You mean you have to eat that too? I thought that was something you Americans made only for the British to eat during the war." After those words slipped out, she blushed. Charity laughed and her guest joined in. The woman said her whole attitude about Spam changed after that.

It was like Charity always said, "People are people, regardless of race."

As more than three million soldiers were finally beginning to get their delayed mail, morale was improving in units across Europe. Meanwhile, Charity endeavored to look out for her own soldiers and their needs. The Six Triple Eight was a "self-contained" unit. That meant they had everything necessary to be self-sustaining — Charity commanded the postal operations, but she was also responsible for a motor pool, a supply room, a chapel, a military police detachment, and even a battalion newsletter, *Special Delivery*. The Six Triple Eight built a complete community life for themselves, even hosting sports teams and sponsoring dances. Charity also made certain her soldiers had access to their very own beauty salon, a major morale booster. Big Ma certainly knew how to take care of her troops.

Seventeen million pieces of mail later, Charity received a new set of orders. The

Six Triple Eight had been so successful in England that they were ordered to undertake the same mission in France. The unit arrived at the port of Le Havre on May 20, 1945, barely a month after the end of the war, and took part in a VE day parade in nearby Rouen, marching right past the square where Joan of Arc was burned at the stake. Charity barely gave the historical marker a second glance. Joan of Arc was another woman who had stepped out of line to exert leadership and stand up for her principles. Her reward was to be reviled and executed.

That was centuries ago, Charity told herself. Her reward was the knowledge that she stood up for what she believed in and took pride in her work and her troops. She got her soldiers right to work. The mission was the same. In France, Charity's orders were to fix a two-year backup of mail in six months. Again, the Six Triple Eight did it in three.

Experts now, they were next sent to Paris to straighten out the backlog of civilian mail there. That wasn't a problem either. By December 1945, Charity learned she had earned another promotion, now to lieutenant colonel. When that silver oak leaf was pinned to her collar, another first, she became the highest ranking African American woman in the Army, one step below the

Soldiers from the Six Triple Eight and French civilians sort mail in June 1945. U.S. Army photo.

director of the Women's Army Corps, a full colonel. And she reached that rank in only four years. Yet another first.

By the fall of 1945, many units were packing up to go home. Some would return to their home bases; many were being disbanded. Charity's postal unit was one of those that would stand down. As was true in many units, soldiers who had accumulated a certain number of points were permitted to return first. It kept the flow of personnel steady and did not put a strain on the transportation system. As her unit was being downsized in preparation for inactivation, Charity returned to the U.S. weeks after her promotion and learned the Army had a new challenge for her. She was being reassigned to the Pentagon.

"I'd been to the Pentagon before, twice. I had a couple of 30-day assignments there and kept getting lost," she said good naturedly. "I decided I didn't want to go back." At this point, she had done it all — met every challenge, exceeded every expectation, and proved everything she needed to prove. Plus, she'd been promoted as high as she could possibly go. Charity decided she would return to graduate school and continue her studies that were interrupted by the war.

She had done everything she set out to do. She'd proved herself — not only to others but to herself as well. Most importantly, she'd never compromised her ethics or her principles. She'd held the line in a divisive culture that "fought the greatest racist in history with a segregated Army."

By March 1946, Charity was out of uniform, and the Six Triple Eight was deactivated. The National Council of Negro Women named her Woman of the Year. She used her GI Bill to earn a master's degree in psychology at Ohio State. Next, she tried different career paths on for size, working at the Veterans Administration and later at a music academy. Eventually, she moved to

Nashville where she was the director of student personnel at Tennessee Agricultural & Industrial College (now Tennessee State University). She also had a brief stint at a university in Savannah as director of student personnel and as an assistant professor of education.

In 1949, Charity met and married a medical student named Stanley Earley. While he was completing his studies in Switzerland, Charity continued hers, too, working on her PhD. Following his residency, they moved back to Dayton, Ohio, and began their life together, raising two children.

Charity was extremely involved in her community, serving with the United Way and Dayton's Black Leadership Development program. She was a board director for a number of companies, ranging from Dayton Power and Light to the Dayton Opera Company, and was a member of the Board of Governors with the American Red Cross. She served on several other prestigious boards as well and was a volunteer with several groups, including the YWCA and the United Negro College Fund. In every instance, she broke down stereotypes and old prejudices.

Charity was focused on building opportunities for young people. She looked to the future and didn't hold on to the past. Two of her alma maters, Wilberforce University and the University of Dayton, granted her honorary doctorate degrees.

It took about twenty years, but gradually the WAC unit began to hold reunions. Charity's first Six Triple Eight reunion was the sixth annual event, held in 1988. The group continued to get together annually for several years thereafter. Many members continued to visit and write to one another for more than fifty years. They knew what they had accomplished, and they knew how special their service was.

"The women of the 6888th were under an incredible spotlight," Beth Ann Koelsch, curator of the Betty H. Carter Women Veterans Historical Project at the University of North Carolina at Greensboro, commented. Their greatest legacy "was in changing the perception of the capabilities of women of color. Their success challenged the stereotype of African-American women." The unit was so successful in great part due to the leadership of their commander. Charity Adams was a woman of principles and high standards. She never relaxed those standards or allowed herself to give in when faced with situations that were unfair or prejudicial. She brought her soldiers and their unit reputation into line by setting the highest goals for performance and professionalism and by striving for achievement herself.

In 1995, Charity Adams Earley returned to the Pentagon for a special ceremony during Black History Month, honoring the veterans of World War II. She remarked to the commander in chief and assembled dignitaries with her typical candor, "It certainly has taken a long time for us to be remembered." The following year she was honored at the Smithsonian National Postal Museum. She said, "When I talk to students they say, 'how did it feel to know you were making history?' But you don't know you're making history when it's happening. I just wanted to do my job."

Charity passed away in 2002, long before she and her unit began to receive the full measure of respect and recognition they were due. On November 30, 2018, the Army dedicated a memorial to the Six Triple Eight in the Buffalo Soldier Area at Fort Leavenworth, Kansas. The monument includes the names of 500 members of the battalion and a bust of Lieutenant Colonel Charity Adams. Charity's son Stanley was on hand for the ceremony, along with a handful of unit veterans. He said, "My mother was always enormously proud of the Six Triple

Eight. This monument is a statement of responsibility, determination, and honor, and it is gift from the recent past to the future."

In 2019, the Secretary of the Army awarded the Meritorious Unit Citation to the Six Triple Eight. This was their only military award for their wartime service. Announcing the award, Kansas Senator Jerry Moran said, "The legacy of the 6888th will continue to inspire soldiers today and for many more years to come as they take their rightful place in history." Lincoln Penny films released an award-winning documentary on the Six Triple Eight in 2019. The film continued to win awards and is still being screened in selected locations.

The quote, "Crisis doesn't build character, it reveals it," is well known in the Army. That simple statement epitomized the tenor of Charity Adams Earley's entire military career. She was tested often — through institutional gender and racial discrimination, bullying, and a lack of opportunity. Not once did she bend. Not once did she even consider making an exception to her principles, values, or morals. She was always uncompromising and fair. Charity Adams Earley knew what right looked like, and that was what she would do. Each and every time.

At Fort Leavenworth, the Six Triple Eight

memorial stands proudly on the grounds facing the Army's Command and General Staff College, the one school Charity regretted not being able to attend during her time in the service. Now, future generations of Army leaders can meet her there and learn about unwavering values and true strength of character from a remarkable trailblazer.

Retired Master Sergeant Elizabeth Helm-Frazier touches the likeness of Lieutenant Colonel Charity Adams Earley on the monument honoring the all-female, all African American 6888th Central Postal Directory Battalion, November 29, 2018. U.S. Army photo.

CHAPTER 16

RETURN TO NORMAL

"Many of us are hoping that the very suffering which women of all nationalities have been through, will bring about a greater kinship among them than has ever existed before . . . They will surely determine to work together in order to ensure that the forces of the world are used for constructive purposes."
FORMER FIRST LADY ELEANOR ROOSEVELT, V-J DAY, AUGUST 18, 1945

The Army didn't waste any time. The Women Airforce Service Pilots (WASP) program slammed its doors shut in December 1944, just when the first whiff of victory in Europe began to give hope to senior commanders that they would prevail. Thank God. The Army Air Forces wouldn't have to depend on women pilots anymore. The Battle of the Bulge was ongoing, but victory felt imminent. Maybe the war would end in the spring.

It did. VE Day in Europe was celebrated on May 8, 1945. Victory over Japan occurred just a few months later, on August 18. By the fall of 1945, troop ships were packed with soldiers returning home. Women who served in World War II did everything the men did, except fight in combat. By the war's end, they were serving in every branch, doing every job but those on the front lines. General Eisenhower felt he couldn't have won the war without them. Yet, the men they served with often showed them little respect or gave them little support. And once the conflict ended, it was time to get them out of uniform.

A tidal wave of culture change followed close behind. It was time "to return to normal." For men, that meant putting the war behind them, getting married, and starting a family and a career. It was time to enjoy life. For women, it meant taking a step back, leaving the factories, quitting professional careers, and ending the dream of education. It meant returning home, too, but to stay put, raising the children, tending to their husbands, and keeping the house clean. As the tumult of the 1940s gave way to the 1950s, it seemed that the nuclear family was, on the surface at least, a happy and safe place to be.

Not everyone felt that way, of course. For

those who struggled to survive the war, it was difficult enough to sort through the deep trauma in their hearts, the nightmares that haunted their dreams, and the struggle to adapt to newfound freedom. Finding a way to simply move forward — to decide what life and home and family could mean in a new and vastly different world — was even more difficult.

Many chose to not look back. Hilda Eisen, the Polish Resistance fighter, lived with relatives in Munich, Germany, until 1948. Only then could she and her husband Harry emigrate to the U.S. and start their lives anew. There was nothing left for her in Poland. There was no one. She shut off the past; it was done. She looked ahead to see what each day would bring.

Broken in body and shaken in spirit, Mary Barraco, a survivor of Gestapo torture in Belgium, had moved back to Massachusetts with her family, but they still lived in fear. The FBI watched out for her as Nazi threats of vengeance continued.

Mary Taylor Previte was just entering her teenage years and adjusting to school, family life with her parents, completing daily tasks with only one hand, and learning what it meant to live in postwar America following five years in an internment camp in China.

In 1946, when Nazi officials stood trial at Nuremberg, some of the evidence concerning financial crime and the theft of Jewish assets had come from tennis star Alice Marble's detailed notes on her undercover work in Switzerland. Reporter Ruth Gruber was on hand to observe a portion of the trial. She left her job at the Department of the Interior a few months later and traveled to Palestine to report on the British interception of the ship *Exodus*. Her life was still tied closely to rescue and survival; she would continue as a journalist and witness to history for the rest of her life.

Ida and Louise Cook, the British sisters who personally saved more than two dozen Jews, had never sought attention. Once the war ended, they were pleased to resume the comfort of a quiet life, to continue on as they had before, still ensconced in their flat in southwest London. Ida went back to writing her romance novels, and Louise continued working as a civil servant. They settled happily back into relative obscurity and began to attend their beloved opera once again.

Diet Eman, Dutch Resistance fighter, was deeply scarred. Unsettled and restless, she could not reconcile her survival with the loss of her beloved fiancé, Hein. She left the Netherlands, emigrated to Venezuela, and became a nurse, trying hard to overcome her loss. In time, the years would round the sharp edges of her pain and lead her back to a life of service to others. For many, recognition of their remarkable contributions would come nearly half a century later.

Those who served in the military had the option to stay or to leave. Millie Rexroat, pioneering WASP pilot, joined the Air Force Reserve when she was invited to apply, but she never flew again. There were no jobs for women as pilots in the military or civilian sector following the war. Civilian airlines turned them away, stating, "Public opinion wouldn't stand for it." She felt lucky to have had the experiences that she did and remained close to the proud memories of her brief career in the sky through communing with her WASP colleagues over the years.

Field hospital nurse Katie Flynn Nolan and her husband created a large family and an even larger legacy, their seven children imbued with a passion to serve. Three of her sons later served in the military, as did her granddaughter. Following her groundbreaking command tour, Lieutenant Colonel Charity Adams Earley was offered the opportunity to stay in the Army, but the notion of a tour in the Pentagon wasn't appealing in the least. She left active duty as the second highest ranking woman in the Women's Army Corps and went back to school to continue her master's degree program in psychology.

The women who had worked at making and keeping secrets had a different and strangely convoluted transition. Virginia Hall chafed at the bureaucracy of the fledgling CIA. She was used to three things she could not find there: independence, freedom of movement, and professional courtesy and respect. Major Stephanie Czech Rader felt lucky to have survived her time as an undercover agent. She was still operational in Warsaw just after the war ended and narrowly escaped being caught and imprisoned by the Soviets. She returned to the U.S. in 1947 and didn't speak about her time in uniform for another fifty years.

Alice Marble was another remarkable individual. Like Ruth Gruber, she would have succeeded no matter the circumstances or opportunity. Ever a true trailblazer, Alice continued to make her mark following the war. She coached tennis, appeared on TV shows, starred in a movie with Katherine Hepburn, and fought a very public battle against the tennis establishment, becoming a strong advocate for the desegregation of professional tennis.

*Tennis great Alice Marble is greeted by the
Duke and Duchess of Kent at Wimbledon in 1984.
Seventeen of the twenty living women's singles champions
were on hand to be recognized for their contributions to the
game. © The International Tennis Hall of Fame.*

For those who dealt in protecting information, signals codebreaking, and distributing propaganda, the postwar years presented a different challenge. They couldn't talk about what they had done. Many who had served in the military or the OSS married service members.

Betty Bemis Robarts married her pilot and left the Navy at the end of the war. They both went back to college at Auburn. The relationship that began as pen pals lasted for sixty-three years and produced three children and nine grandchildren, several of whom served in the Army, Navy, and Air Force.

Marion Frieswyk went from the role of mapmaker to that of homemaker, but in later years she remained active with the OSS Society. Like many of her colleagues, she didn't speak about her contributions to the war effort for years. Betty McIntosh continued to work in information operations and secret information programs. She spent years with the CIA in Japan working on projects that remain classified today.

Stephanie Czech Rader with her new husband Colonel William S. Rader, September 1945. Photo courtesy of CIA.

Just as many migrated from the OSS to the CIA following the war, many in signals intelligence likewise made the deliberate journey from Northwest Washington, DC, to Fort Meade, Maryland, joining the newly established National Security Agency. Former Director of National Intelligence (DNI) James R. Clapper said in his recent biography, "Many of the prominent code crackers of World War II had been women who'd stayed with the agency after the war, and the NSA in the 1960s was appreciative of their contributions and more open to having them in leadership positions than the rest of government or corporate America. My dad worked for . . . Juanita Moody, and Ann Caracristi, who in 1980 would shatter the glass ceiling as deputy director of NSA." He emphasized, "Hearing him (dad) talk about these individuals as smart, capable leaders, without his making a big deal about their gender" made a big impression on Clapper's view of women in intelligence work.

The world was different. The postwar transition was hard for all of society, but arguably more so for women who had abandoned prewar traditional roles and taken on greater challenges. They had been productive; their work was important. Then that self-worth and sense of pride were snatched away. Their new normal seemed like a return to the days of their own mothers, in the 1930s or even earlier. And these members of the "Greatest Generation" were beginning to give birth to the baby boomers.

The girls who stepped out of line were now far from those front lines where they once fought to survive, flew high in spite of all doubts and resentments, broke codes, built information programs, helped others escape, saved lives, and defied expectations. They broke all the rules, including some not even written yet. They invented, they advanced, and they persisted. Now, moving ahead into the 1960s and '70s, many of them were settling down and raising families.

In Britain as in the U.S., "Mothers told their daughters what they had done during the war, and how their horizons had been limited afterwards. The '60s and '70s saw the emergence of feminist groups and heightened awareness of gender inequality — campaigning for more rights and greater opportunities saw very many more women aware of their potential and the need for change."

Those daughters were part of what became known as the "Me Generation," the problem children. They were the first generation to be convinced their lives would be better than those of their parents, that they were special. They were the baby boomers, the cohort born after World War II. These children, boys and girls, represented a "celebration of life" following the war, and their large numbers meant their influence on consumerism, culture, and virtually every aspect of society continued throughout their lives. The first wave arrived from 1946 to 1954 and still make up more than 20 percent of the world's population. The second wave arrived during the next ten years, just as the social fabric of American life was beginning to fray. Gen X followed them, children born during the heady years of the turbulent 1970s and '80s.

By the 1970s, young Boomers were living in a sea of social change. There was a revolution in music, arts, and entertainment. Politics was explosive and divisive, in part because Vietnam was perceived very differently from the total mobilization that enabled an entire nation to become involved with supporting victory in WWII. Society experienced a series of earthquakes in terms of change in social norms and values. It was a time of exciting change, frightening world events, and perhaps real opportunity. The veterans looked on, some encouraging, others doubtful.

There was upheaval in the White House. A president had been assassinated. Another resigned. The Civil Rights Movement roiled across the nation. The Women's Movement challenged convention and social norms. The Equal Rights Amendment passed through Congress in 1972, stating, "Equality of rights under the law shall not be denied or abridged by the United States or by any State on account of sex." But there it stalled. By the 1979 deadline, only thirty-five of the required thirty-eight states had ratified the amendment.

The women veterans of World War II were experiencing their own reawakening. Charity Adams Earley, now a successful businesswoman in Ohio, began to attend reunions of the Six Triple Eight Central Postal Directory Battalion. Kate Nolan found veterans groups to join in Florida, where she was often the only woman vet. Millie Rexroat met up with old friends at WASP reunions in Texas. Many of those who had served in uniform now found just how much they had missed each other, the companionship, and the shared experiences. Each reunion was filled with stories of remembered adventures and always a brief memorial to those who passed. But in terms of change, it didn't look like young women choosing to serve in the 1960s and 1970s would find life in uniform to be any easier.

For those youngsters who thought about the military as a way to start a career, maybe gain a little experience, or get money to pay for school, times had finally changed. The Women's Army Corps was abolished in 1978, and women were fully integrated into all the armed services. But only certain jobs were open to them — the traditional ones. Women remained an exceedingly small part of the force and still found their aspirations were rigidly compartmented. Those positions that were solidly classified as women's work — personnel management, administration, nursing — also meant limited potential for advancement or promotion. Those who tried to step out of line and pursue nontraditional career paths, whether as military police or even as mechanics, were roughly put back into place — their "proper" place, as women.

Nontraditional career success still required the unique individual, one exceptionally ambitious, driven, and with a thick hide to slough off criticism. But social conventions, pounded back into place following the war, made it even harder for women to get a foot in the door, much less move inside. For most women, it was simply too difficult. Only the unconventional trailblazers continued forward, mostly alone.

Mary Barraco and her husband left Massachusetts and moved to Virginia. She felt her calling grow to speak out about her trials and the importance of safeguarding freedom. She met with schoolchildren, church groups, Army gatherings, and veterans' organizations — anyone who would listen. Diet Eman moved as far from her old life as possible, married and divorced, returned from South America, and was living in Grand Rapids, Michigan. In 1978, she was reunited with Corrie Ten Boom, whom she met in an internment camp in the Netherlands. She began then to think about sharing her own story. It was a wrenching decision to make. For in the retelling, she would inevitably be forced to relive each painful moment of those long war years. She knew it was the right thing to do and prayed for the catharsis she hoped would ensue.

They didn't call it PTSD then. It was known as "shell shock," or even "soldier's heart." For those who had experienced personal horrors and great trauma during the war years, the memories were often too difficult to approach, much less let in or attempt to relive. Kate Nolan didn't experience flashbacks and nightmares until 2001, when she made a return trip to France, visiting Normandy. Standing in the sand on Utah Beach close to the water where she nearly drowned, Kate could see the destruction and the dead bodies, hear the distant thump of artillery, and smell the smoke of burning vehicles. She was back there again. Once home, Kate joined a veterans' support group, where she was the only woman veteran. She still couldn't sleep more than three hours a night.

PTSD didn't just affect those in uniform. Holocaust survivors and those who hid, rescued, or helped them, spies and Resistance fighters — everyone exposed to the sudden shock of extreme violence, constant fear of death, or imprisonment and loss of personal freedom — also suffered. For hundreds of thousands who had traveled those war years, the fear, stress, and anxiety they had endured stayed with them for life.

Hilda Eisen discovered another path to healing. She and her husband Harry were active with survivor groups in California and found comfort in their shared stories. These were not the stories of their years of suffering, the camps, or the deprivations. They shared stories from their youth, what life had been like in Eastern Europe before the war, the schools they went to, the friends they had, and family life. They spoke Yiddish, made home-cooked dishes from childhood, and supported a variety of Zionist causes. These were bittersweet experiences that they shared in their get-togethers. Later, both Hilda and Harry would give testimony about their experiences as Resistance fighters during the war.

The women who did highly classified work were sworn to secrecy, and they continued to hold their service secrets close. Some did remain friends through the years, exchanged letters and pictures, and talked about their families. But they never discussed their service. Others simply tried to move away, pushing themselves forward, carrying all their experiences — that heady excitement of the early days, their successes, fears, and failures — with them. For some, it was pride of accomplishment. For others, it was heavy baggage that had scarred them. Most unit war files, such as the records of the WASP, the codebreakers, and other organizations, were sealed for thirty-five years. Following the war, women's contributions were all but unknown and their legacy nonexistent. That was about to change.

"From the beginning, all the women had

been connected, whether they liked it or not, building on one another's successes, saddled with one another's failures, and pressing on together." And it was together that they persisted.

CHAPTER 17

NO MORE FIRSTS

"We do not have to become heroes overnight. Just a step at a time, meeting each thing that comes up, seeing it is not as dreadful as it appears, discovering that we have the strength to stare it down."

FORMER FIRST LADY ELEANOR ROOSEVELT AS QUOTED IN
THE AMERICAN INTEREST

By the 1980s, nearly forty years on from VE day, the girls who stepped out of line began to be recognized for their contributions in World War II. Surprisingly, they found themselves being embraced as the trailblazers they were. Maybe their wartime actions typically weren't as dramatic as those of the men fighting battles, bombing the enemy, or taking prisoners. Their achievements couldn't be measured in numbers — miles covered, bullets expended, or ships sunk.

But their roles, often ignored or taken for granted, were just as important to the overall effort. Those contributions could be measured through the sometimes unmeasurable — a double negative — in saved lives, families reunited, and disasters averted. After the war, many of these women who stepped out of line had to take a step back.

As they began to emerge from the shadows, reconnecting with their past and with each other, new generations wanted to connect with them. Suddenly, they were the role models.

The veterans were interviewed and feted. Diet Eman wrote an autobiography. So did Kate McIntosh, Charity Adams Early, Mary Previte, and the Cook sisters. Alice Marble wrote two. Ida Cook even signed with the Maurice Frost lecture agency and for many years gave talks about her wartime experiences, using the title: "Two Against Hitler." It was clear she was just as interested in other topics, including romance novels or her favorite subject of all — opera. Mary Taylor Previte continued to work with at-risk juveniles and pursue her political career in New Jersey.

Hilda and Harry Eisen gave testimony about their lives with the Resistance to the U.S. Holocaust Memorial Museum and the

Mary Eisen Cramer, daughter of Hilda and Harry Eisen, shown here in Poland in 2018, visiting the monument to her family, erected by her parents. Photo courtesy of Michael Rubinstein.

Shoah Foundation. Even as they moved forward with their lives, they resolved never to forget the past. None of us can ever forget what happened to them, and to six million Jews who were killed in the Holocaust. In 2019, their daughter visited the family's ancestral home of Izbica, Poland, and Chelmno, the death camp where her parents' families perished.

Dame Mary Barraco gave her testimony to the Holocaust Commission of the United Jewish Federation of Tidewater, Virginia. Mary, Diet Eman, and the Cook sisters were named Righteous Among Nations by the Yad Vashem Holocaust Memorial Authority in Jerusalem. When the Cook sisters were honored in 1965, they were two of only four British citizens to have their names included with luminaries such as Oscar Schindler. A plaque now marks the site of the Cook sisters' childhood home in Sunderland, a coal mining city in northeast England.

The National Holocaust Memorial Museum was dedicated in Washington, DC, in April 1993. Hilda and Harry Eisen were on hand for that event, having been among the first donors to support its construction. They clutched flickering candles that chilly spring day and stood in silent witness as President Bill Clinton christened the museum "a place of deep sadness and a sanctuary of bright hope." Ruth Gruber participated in the dedication of the Safe Haven Holocaust Refugee Shelter Museum at Fort Ontario, New York, on October 6, 2002. The museum is housed in the old Administration Building, where she once had an office. While we can never forget what happened to them, we must remember what they did to make a difference.

Stories about the codebreakers were the last to resurface. In the 1980s, a London stage play, "Breaking the Code," was the first to tell the story about British codebreakers at Bletchley Park. Later, another play and then a movie, both titled *The Imitation Game* gained a global audience and greater appreciation for their secret work. Betty Bemis Robarts learned the truth about her meaningful service in 1995 at a Sugar House reunion. But it wasn't until 2017 that the book *Code Girls* told the full story of the American Army and Navy women involved with codebreaking work in Washington.

Awards continued to accumulate. Dame Mary Barraco was knighted by the King of Belgium. A number of others received international awards, including Ruth Gruber and Kate Nolan. Virginia Hall had received the Distinguished Service Cross in 1945, but nothing further in her lifetime.

She continued to keep her past service and her secrets close. In 2012, Stephanie Czech Rader was presented with the OSS Society's inaugural Virginia Hall award. The Army posthumously awarded her the Legion of Merit. Hilda Eisen was busy building an entirely new life, a journey that took her a lifetime.

Veteran communities and groups were being recognized too. As these veterans shared their stories and their advice, they also supported new generations of women through their examples of drive, determination, and a stubborn refusal to give up. But their gifts went beyond personal example. They shared other important lessons, including that of mentorship. Stephanie Czech Rader's high school teacher saw something in her that merited a hand up — that teacher recommended her for acceptance into Cornell. Charity Adams Earley's college dean recommended her for the first class of women officers in the newly formed WAC Corps. Women in the OSS had an advocate in Major General William J. Donovan. Ruth Gruber had Secretary of the Interior Harold Ickes as her mentor. While many of the women had their champions and advocates, many others had to soar alone. Hilda Eisen, Diet Eman, and Mary Barraco were nearly destroyed by the persecution they endured and the deaths of their loved ones. Yet they emerged stronger than could have ever been imagined and continued to bear witness, sharing their struggle and promoting their love of freedom and opportunity in America. They purposefully sought opportunities to speak out to influence others through their stories.

Others remained quietly in the background, enjoying some semblance of their prewar lives, but continued their involvement in their communities, veterans' groups, and local civic organizations. These women who had already given so much continued to give back.

The WASP pilots received the Congressional Gold Medal for their wartime service in 2009. The OSS members received their Medal in 2016, with Marion Frieswyk in attendance along with a few other remaining veterans. In 2019, a bill was introduced in Congress to award the Gold Medal to the Six Triple Eight.

Many of the women appeared in documentaries. Diet Eman was featured in several documentary programs about the Dutch Resistance. Ruth Gruber was the subject of a documentary produced by the National Center for Jewish Film. Released in 2009,

Ahead of Time: The Extraordinary Journey of Ruth Gruber, won numerous awards for Best Documentary. Lincoln Penny Films produced a documentary about Charity Adams and her unit from WWII titled *The Six Triple Eight: No Mail, Low Morale.* It was released in April 2019.

The story of the dramatic rise of the WASP and their rapid fall received a great deal of attention in the entertainment media. There have been at least twelve dramatized stories about WASPs in television programs and as secondary story lines in feature films, including several about the Wonder Woman herself, Alice Marble. There have been at least five documentaries, with two new productions underway as of 2021, one entitled *CAF Rise Above: WASP.* The documentary is a project of the Commemorative Air Force (CAF) and Hemlock Films. A second project is titled *Coming Home: Fight for Legacy,* a documentary by Red Door films. At least twenty books have been written about the WASPs, some featuring the stories of individual women, others focusing on the program itself and its impacts. One book produced for young readers was *Yankee Doodle Gals: Women Pilots of World War II.* A National Geographic book published in 2001 featured a foreword by astronaut Eileen

Collins. She made the connection between the pilots' service and her own dreams of flying. She said, "Although the WASP program was short-lived, the outstanding performance of those pilots helped open up opportunities for women in my generation and generations to come."

Nurses were featured in dozens of documentaries. Women codebreakers were included in documentaries about Bletchley Park, but there was little mention of their role in American documentaries. The few documentaries about women spies in WWII primarily focused on the heroines of the French Resistance.

Major feature films were slower to come. In 2001, the TV movie *Haven* told the story of Ruth Gruber's odyssey with the 1,000 Jewish refugees on their way to Oswego, New York. By 2017, there were reports of a major feature film in production to tell the story of the Cooks. Another production was announced in 2017, this one to tell the incredible story of Alice Marble — tennis star, spy, and equal rights advocate.

Seventy-five years after the end of the second World War, the last remaining members of the Greatest Generation are departing this earth. Stephanie Czech Rader and Millie Rexroat, who both passed away at the age of 100, now rest in hallowed ground at Arlington National Cemetery. Kate Nolan joined them there in July 2020. Many of their contemporaries lie there as well. Following the end of the war, a soldier from the 26th Infantry Division wrote, "No war is really over until the last veteran is dead." We are approaching that sobering benchmark now. It gives more urgency to telling the stories of these remarkable people and enhancing our understanding of their contributions to our lives today.

Women of the Greatest Generation challenged, then changed the status quo. When the doors of opportunity closed to them following World War II, the pipeline behind them stopped. New generations were left to find their own way. They discovered these women who had forged a new path before them and held them up as role models to be emulated and thanked. The courage displayed by the Girls Who Stepped Out of Line gave hope to girls growing up who wanted to challenge themselves and make a difference. For these new generations, the struggle continues to achieve acceptance at a level that is neither remarkable nor without peer. When it is no longer unique or unusual that women have achieved a certain position, been elected, or been selected as

A statue of a WASP pilot stands on the grounds of the U.S. Air Force Academy in Colorado Springs, Colorado — a silent role model for generations of women pilots yet to come. U.S. Air Force photo.

care, doors that went beyond nursing to include all medical fields. Yet it took a generation to crack open the doors to medical school. It wasn't until 2017 that the number of women enrolling in medical school edged past that of men. According to the Association of American Medical Colleges (AAMC), women make up more than half of the 21,000-plus enrollees. That is a significant jump, considering that in 1965, only one enrollee in ten was a woman. Yet, even now, women doctors earn 26 percent less than their male counterparts.

The struggle for acceptance has been particularly daunting in the tight-knit aviation community. In 1960, one out of every 21,417 pilots with an "other than student" license was a woman. Today that number is even more surprising. Now it is one out of every 5,623. Certainly, this is progress, but not even close to parity. Why not one out of every two? Or even three? Given that the U.S. population is 51 percent female, that is logical.

Millie Rexroat and her fellow WASPs would have seen the challenges women continue to face in pursuit of flight training as all too familiar. But those they influenced and mentored became their champions in return. Senator Martha McSally, a former

the "first," then more will flood through the open doors. Achievement becomes the norm, not the exception.

In 1980, the first women graduated from military service academies. That first class of women cadets stood up proudly in the summer of 1976 and entered the halls where they had never been welcomed before. They were scorched and scathed during their four years of trailblazing, but they survived. They knew the impact it would have on those following them if they failed. Since those "firsts," the number of women applying has gradually continued to rise.

It wasn't until 2013 that the Naval Academy began a mentorship program for female midshipmen. Until that time, there simply weren't enough women on the staff and faculty to create such a program. By the fall of 2019, the admittance rate was 26.2 percent.

More than 224,000 women serve in the armed forces today. It has been a slow chipping away at military culture and convention to push for more change. Eventually, more women were promoted to senior leadership positions in the majority of career fields. Once combat arms positions opened to women, they began to explore the infantry and other functional fields previously closed to them. At first, the old axiom still held: "When you stand up, you stick out." The woman who chooses to make the military a career now is often not the "unicorn" any longer. She is not the only woman in the room.

Kate Nolan at the Women in Military Service to America Memorial in October 2007. Here she's surrounded by new generations of women who serve in uniform. Photo courtesy of the Nolan family.

But a trickle of "firsts" doesn't necessarily cause a flood. At least not immediately. Women continued chipping at the glass ceiling, knocking down one sharp, bloody sliver of institutional discrimination at a time. At first it was access to military schools, the ones that granted "credibility" badges, the silver wings of a pilot, or the coveted ranger

tab. Virginia Hall, Kate McIntosh, and Marion Frieswyk are all considered heroes in the Special Operations Forces (SOF) community. But they are not particularly well known outside of that community or in the intelligence arena.

An examination of cartography today as a field of science yields little information about women like Marion Frieswyk who excelled in the field. A Wikipedia list of 200-plus famous cartographers includes the names of only two women. A British list of the top ten female cartographers includes "the unknown cartographer" as number ten. These unknowns were the women who made maps for the British military in World War II. One former staffer in the Ordnance Survey Office recalled, "There were hundreds of drawing and photo writing people there and most were female. What bothered me was that these ladies . . . were better at it than me. It was a relief to join the Army."

Katie Nolan and her contemporaries served in a role that was once considered to be "women's work." But the work of a nurse in a field hospital during combat could in no way be compared to serving as a hom[e] health nurse in peacetime. Their servic[e] in all types of emergency and high-stak[es] situations opened doors for women in heal[th]

Air Force pilot, met many of the WASP pilots at aviation conferences early in her career. She said, "I was in the 9th class of women allowed to attend the Air Force Academy and one of only two women in my pilot training class, so I was getting used to competing and succeeding in the very male-dominated military world . . . Finally, I met some women who could relate to what I was going through a generation later!"

In military aviation, the combat exclusion policy (preventing women from serving in front line units) was lifted in 1993. It was not changed for all military specialties until 2013. Chairman of the Joint Chiefs of Staff General Martin Dempsey wrote to then Secretary of Defense Panetta, "The time has come to rescind the direct combat exclusion rule for women and to eliminate all unnecessary gender-based barriers to service."

From air to space, the first women astronauts weren't chosen to be part of the space program until 1978 when NASA selected six women, one of whom, Sally Ride, became the first woman in space. Ten years later, Mae Jemison, the first African American woman, was selected. It was ten years before another, Stephanie Wilson, would make the team. When she made the cut in 1990, Colonel Eileen Collins said, "I remembered the

WASPs and felt a great responsibility to do a good job so there would be more opportunities for women in the future." By March 2020, sixty-five women had flown in space, including astronauts, cosmonauts, payload specialists, and space station crew members. Another first — the first all-female spacewalk — took place in November 2019.

In 1987, Congress passed a law proclaiming March as Women's History Month. Since that time, women leaders in a number of fields have been featured in lectures, on news programs, and in lists — of firsts.

Charity Adams Earley knew what it was like to be a Black woman who was first in just about everything she did in the Army. She learned exactly what it took to succeed. The formula was more than education, desire, and persistence. It took resilience. According to a *Harvard Business Review* article from 2018, the ingredients for success are emotional intelligence, authenticity, and agility. Charity Adams would undoubtedly agree. She used every tool available to her to prove that she was the right person to be selected for a job, the best qualified to command, and in retirement, to be the leader that many businesses and boards coveted — and needed — to help them be successful. There is no doubt that her success as a commander and the mission success of her unit, the Six Triple Eight, was considered, along with the wartime service of African American men, in creating a policy change. On July 26, 1948, President Harry S. Truman signed Executive Order 9981, establishing the President's Committee on Equality of Treatment and Opportunity in the Armed Services, integrating the segregated military.

Hilda Eisen and her husband Harry started their small business in their kitchen, washing and boxing eggs from their first investment of 100 chickens. That they were able to grow that tiny backyard business into a multimillion-dollar enterprise is a testament to their hard work and the power of the American dream. In 2019, the Center for American Progress reported that 27 percent of small business owners are women. That number continues to grow at the rate of about four percent a year. There were thirty-three women CEOs on the *Fortune* 500 list in 2019. Only two African American women have made that list. It is more striking to note that the number of Black women running small businesses has exploded. While the number of women-owned businesses grew an impressive 58 percent from 2007 to 2018, the number of companies owned by Black women grew by an astounding 164 percent.

Else Mayer-Lismann was a Jewish refugee from Germany. Ida and Louise Cook helped her mother Mitia emigrate to Britain just before the war, and then the whole family joined her, including Else. Else's father died soon after arriving in London, but Mitia found work as a teacher and Else followed in her footsteps before launching a career lecturing about the pleasures of opera. One of her students already had an impressive knowledge of opera when they met in the 1980s, Prince Charles. He later recalled their meeting and their long-term friendship. "I remain forever indebted to her for her uniquely invaluable tutoring . . . It was a privilege and a blessing to have known her."

From the heady experience of a former refugee providing counsel to a prince, to an ongoing legacy of dominance on the court, the impacts of these women continued to multiply.

In 1947, Althea Gibson was a rising Black tennis star. She continued to win tournaments and had an amazing career ahead of her, but she wasn't invited to participate in the U.S. National Championships (the U.S. Open), a Grand Slam event, because of her race. She didn't have the requisite number of points to score an invitation, and the only way to get them was by playing tournaments at all-white clubs, where she was not allowed. Alice Marble saw what was happening and stepped in. She had zero tolerance for racism and took on the establishment full force.

Later, Althea would pay it forward and provide encouragement and support to Serena and Venus Williams. In 2006, Venus Williams followed Alice's example, calling out inequality in the sport she loved. She wrote an op-ed for the *London Times,* remarking on the disparity in prize money for men and women at Wimbledon. She wrote, "I'm disappointed . . . the home of tennis is sending a message to women across the world that we are inferior." Six months later, Wimbledon announced the same prize money would be awarded to players of both sexes. Alice Marble's legacy continues to echo down through the generations and into other professional women's sports as well.

Ruth Gruber continued her long career as a witness to history. Becoming involved in her stories, her fate intertwined with the themes of rescue and survival. Her own story continues to serve as a lesson for young journalists today. In recent years, a nonprofit organization, Fellowships at Auschwitz for the Study of Professional Ethics

(FASPE), began a series of programs for young professionals to explore ethical issues in professions, using the historical lens of World War II. The fellowship for young journalists has had them travel to Eastern Europe to study how so many journalists in World War II missed the rise of Hitler and became enablers at best, or coconspirators at worst. Each student profiles a prominent journalist of the time and presents that person's perspectives to the others. Ruth Gruber is one. Participants visit the Reichstag in Berlin, standing near where the Nazi Party began to flex its power in the 1930s. Perhaps close to where a young Ruth Gruber once stood, witnessing the first stirrings of a coming storm. There is still much to learn from her journey.

Mary Taylor Previte made the leap from a school board to a run for assemblywoman in 1998, serving in the New Jersey State Assembly until 2006. She entered politics at a time when the number of women in government and politics was steadily increasing. It felt natural for her to take her place in the state assembly, and she found the processes of lawmaking and cooperation with her peers to be no different than dealing with parents and teachers when she ran for a seat on the local school board. She was a tireless advocate for women and children, inspiring generations of young girls to have hope for the future.

A record number of women ran for public office in 2020. There were 127 women in Congress in 2020, making up 23 percent of the 525 members. That figure was 19 percent just three years ago. Forty-seven members were women of color. Women's representation continues to grow.

A "troublemaker with a gavel," Rep. Nancy Pelosi is in her second term as Speaker of the House of Representatives. She may often be the only woman at the table but has definitely paved the way for many others. She said, "But as I say to the women, nobody ever gives away power. If you want to achieve that, you go for it. But when you get it, you must use it."In November 2020, Senator Kamala Harris became the first woman and the first woman of color elected to the office of vice president of the United States. In her acceptance speech, she said, "While I may be the first woman in this office, I will not be the last, because every little girl watching tonight sees that this is a country of possibilities."

There is mixed news in other professional fields. As of March 2020, women earn 48.5 percent of all law degrees but represent only

22 percent of partners and 19 percent of equity partners. Of the nine seats on the Supreme Court, three are held by women justices. And while the "brass ceiling" was broken in the Army in 2008 with the first woman four-star general, there have been none since. [Publisher's Note: Since original publication, a second female four-star general has been confirmed, in 2021.] When the pipeline hasn't been prepared or developed, that high ceiling is repaired or replaced by the status quo. Then it becomes even harder to break through for that woman who is second. Or third.

Even so, we are nearly past the era of the "first." Certainly, by this point in our history, seventy-five years after the end of the Second World War, there should be no more firsts. There should be no more ceilings to break. Yet there are. The remaining firsts are the biggest challenges — such as the first woman U.S. president. Women in a number of other countries have already crashed through these ceilings. An Oxford-educated chemist, Margaret Thatcher became the first female prime minister in Britain in 1979, over thirty years ago. Another chemist, Angela Merkel, was elected chancellor of Germany in 2005. In New Zealand there have been three women appointed as prime minister since 1997. The current PM is also the youngest; Jacinda Ardern was appointed in 2017 at the age of thirty-seven.

Achievement by women shouldn't be the exception. It should be the norm. That is what equal opportunity really means. In 2020, the National Commission on Military, National and Public Service recommended that women should be eligible for the draft and required to register at the age of eighteen. After three years of study, the commission realized that "the male-only military draft excluded women from a fundamental civic obligation, reinforces gender stereotypes about women's roles and omits a skilled population from being called into military service during emergencies." The report aims to make a "service year" a rite of passage for young Americans and boost standards for civic education in public schools.

The girls who stepped out of line have stepped into their rightful place in history. There's no forgetting them now. Perhaps more importantly, their belated recognition and the growing acknowledgment of their achievements and struggles have had a lasting influence. They didn't wait for opportunity to knock. These women pried the doors open themselves. And we must remember, the girls who stepped out of line were volunteers. Every last one of them. Over 400,000 women found a way to contribute to the cause in the United States during WWII, from farm to factory to uniform. Thousands more served overseas. For those who took that first step over the line, quitting was never an option.

They aren't just unsung heroes who downplayed their contributions and their impact. Whether their jobs were large or small, their contributions were made in the cause of freedom, and they knew it. As these women began to march forward, we were all swept forward by their sacrifices. We stand on their shoulders. Because they stepped out of line.

CHAPTER 18

IT STARTS TODAY

"We can't save the world by playing by the rules, because the rules have to change. Everything needs to change — and it has to start today."

GRETA THUNBERG

Seventy-five years from now, who will we look to as our role models from the first half of the twenty-first century? Will there be too many names to count? Will we find seminal leaders in an era with no more "firsts," or will there continue to be leaders who rise up in the skirmishes and battles in society's longstanding fight against cultural bias, racism, and anti-Semitism? According to the U.S. Holocaust Memorial Museum, "The world is experiencing the largest Humanitarian crisis since the end of World War II and the Holocaust. Syria, Afghanistan, and South Sudan account for more than half the 25 million refugees around the world today."

Will women be willing and able to take the lead to help — to stand up and stick out? Who will take the risk to step out of line?

We don't know their names yet. At least not all of them. But we do know some who have clearly solidified their place in our future history. They have already made significant impacts on our lives, our culture, and our society. And their trials, their challenges, and how they met them have already turned our heads, forcing us to pay attention to their life lessons as examples for future generations. This we know too: they will come from varied backgrounds, many from humble beginnings, immigrants or refugees, or orphans or children of pain, hunger, and addiction.

We will marvel at the contrast between their backgrounds and their accomplishments. Some will face discrimination, online bullying, or hate mail. Others will be controversial for the stands they take. And there will be those who simply want to do their jobs, the jobs they have trained for, rehearsed, and craved their entire lives, even when that job appears to be unorthodox or still something uncommon for women to do. They will humble us with their passion, amaze us with their drive, and awaken us to become our best selves through their example.

Like the girls who stepped out of line, many of them will be very young when they begin to express their passion. They will be focused, fearless, and able to get results — for themselves and for others who follow.

One young trailblazer is Greta Thunberg. At fifteen, the Swedish schoolgirl walked out of class and started her "School Strike for Climate" campaign. By 2019, hundreds of thousands of teenagers from over 100 countries joined her in delivering the same blunt message to world leaders — climate change has to be addressed *now*. She's spoken to the Pope and addressed the United Nations, the European Union, British Parliament, and the U.S. Congress. "You're not trying hard enough. Sorry," she told a group of senators in one task force meeting. If leaders fail to act, she warns, "their irresponsible behavior will no doubt be remembered in history as one of the greatest failures of mankind."

Another is Malala Yousafzai, a Pakistani high school student who was riding on a school bus when she was shot in the head by a Taliban would-be assassin. She was fifteen years old. Malala never backed down, and she didn't give up. She said later, "I realized the essence and importance of duty when terrorism came into our lives, when the right to education was taken away. I realized I had the duty to do something." Upon her recovery, she became an activist for girls' education and is the cofounder of the Malala Fund. In 2014, at age seventeen, she became the youngest-ever recipient of the Nobel Peace Prize.

A major upset on Court Number One resulted in a total uproar at the Wimbledon tennis championships in 2019 and showed us yet another young woman taking steps out of line. Fifteen-year old Coco Gauff burst onto the international scene, taking down Venus Williams in a surprisingly hard-fought match. Her poise and confidence led her to the fourth round where she lost, while twenty-three-time Grand Slam Champion Serena Williams advanced. Coco said she always admired the Williams sisters. But the young player, still learning to compete at the highest level, enjoys spending time with Serena at other tournaments and playing against her in practice. In a multigenerational lineup of mentoring and professional support that can be traced from Coco to Serena, then back to Althea Gibson, and finally to Alice Marble, the teenager is definitely in the right place at the right time. "She's just impressive all around," Serena said about her young practice partner and future competitor. "I was nowhere near her level at fifteen, either on the court or off the court. Not even close."

Elizabeth Smart was abducted from her home in Salt Lake City at the age of fourteen. She was held captive by a religious fanatic and his wife for nearly nine months. Drugged, forced to drink alcohol, and raped multiple times, Elizabeth survived through sheer force of will and her faith. Following her escape, she went on to become an author and an advocate for children who survived trauma. In her book, *My Story*, she said, ". . . I wanted to share my story. I wanted others to know what had happened to me . . . I wanted them to know how I got through it and that they can get through it too . . . I want to help them realize that life is still worth living. I want them to realize that there is always hope! We should never give up." Her personal example of not only survival but also determination hearkens back to the stories of Hilda Eisen, Mary Barraco, Diet Eman, and Mary Previte. Like them, Elizabeth Smart had the drive to create and embrace her future happiness, and the will to leave the past behind. Her story stands as a sterling example to thousands struggling to recover from past abuse. She tells audiences what she learned of resilience: "Never be afraid to speak out. Never be afraid to live your life. Never let your past dictate your future."

At age sixteen, Cyntoia Brown Long was sentenced to life in prison for murdering a man who sex-trafficked her. Granted clemency, she was released fifteen years later, in August 2019. While in prison, she earned an associate's and then a bachelor's degree and began to work with at-risk youth. Her memoir, *Free Cyntoia,* was published in October 2019. She's now happily married and a motivational speaker. "I'm committed to the same fight that got me free," she said recently. "I definitely think that there's a need for reform, not just in prison, but in sentencing and the way justice is handed out in our country. I'm committed to fighting for all the other people who are just like me," Cyntoia said.

Beyond the youth of today, women continue to break barriers and live their dreams, following in the footsteps of the girls who stepped out of line. Danielle Outlaw became the first African American police commissioner for Philadelphia in February 2020. She previously served as the first Black police chief in Portland, Oregon. She believes in progressive policing, that there can be humanity within authority, and is focused on how policing needs to change in the future. She has a tattoo on her arm of a quote from Shakespeare's *Midsummer Night's Dream:* "Though she be but little, she is fierce." Danielle belongs to the Human and Civil Rights Committee of the International Association of Chiefs of Police (IACP) and cites Rosa Parks as her cultural mentor because "Her one act influenced others to perform many." In an early interview after assuming the new position with Philadelphia, she talked about her mode of operations, stating, "Build trust, move with urgency, and take risks." In June 2020, she marched in the streets of Philadelphia with peaceful protesters following George Floyd's murder.

Rep. Ilhan Omar has been serving in Congress since 2017. She is the first Somali American, the first naturalized citizen from Africa, and the first nonwhite woman to hold elective office from Minnesota. Controversial from the moment she arrived at the House of Representatives, many of her statements have been misinterpreted as provocative or excessively inflammatory. In an interview with *Teen Vogue* in 2018, she gave advice to young women on how to deal with discrimination and chart their own paths. She said, "It's okay to know that we never need permission or an invitation to stand up or work on creating positive change in our communities."

In 2018, Beth Ford became the first openly gay woman to be named CEO of a *Fortune 500* company. Her thirty-four-year career spans six industries and seven companies. As CEO of Land O'Lakes, she is a passionate advocate of farm-to-table agriculture. In 2019, *Fortune* magazine named her one of the world's fifty greatest leaders. In an interview with *Fortune,* she was asked her views on resilience. Beth said, "Everybody has failures in their life and in their career. I certainly can point to many. Resilience is so central, confidence is so central to a career that you learn from that (failure) and then you move forward. And I fear sometimes that some young women I've spoken to are concerned to step out because they're afraid of failure. Resilience allows you to learn the lesson."

Aimee Mullins was born without shin bones. Both of her legs were amputated below the knee before she turned one. Aimee became a star athlete, the first female amputee in history to compete in NCAA track and field events. She later competed in the Paralympics, prompting *Sports Illustrated* to name her "one of the coolest women in sports." An inspirational public speaker, advocate for women, model, and actress, her TED talks have been translated into forty-two languages and garnered millions of views. She was in and out of hospitals as a child. "I haven't had an easy life, but at some point, you have to take responsibility for yourself and shape who it is that you want to be. I have no time for moaners. I like to chase my dreams and surround myself with other people who are chasing their dreams too."

Captain Lindsay Gordon Heisler graduated from West Point in 2012. By December 2015, she was serving as the copilot and gunner of an Apache helicopter while deployed to Afghanistan. She and her pilot engaged enemy forces on the ground to support a Ranger unit in its extraction from the engagement. With fire coming at them from all directions, Lindsay continued to draw fire away from the Rangers on the ground. In October 2019, she received the West Point Association of Graduates Nininger Award for Valor at Arms. At the Academy to receive the award, she said, "Understand that . . . it is not about you: it's about making every soldier in your platoon successful and enabling them as a team to accomplish their mission." She also received the Distinguished Flying Cross for courage under fire.

Dr. Serena McCalla, a STEM educator and scientist, is the science resource co-ordinator for Jericho High School in New York. She holds a BA in biological sciences, an MS in hematology/microbiology, and a PhD in diagnostic testing in genetics, photosynthesis, and respiration. She is also the founder of iResearch Institute, which shares her research practices with educators and students around the world. In 2019, she led her students to win an unprecedented seven Grand Awards at the International Science and Engineering Fair. This "Olympics of Science Fairs" hosts 1,700 student competitors from seventy-eight countries. Dr. McCalla's students don't just come to win a prize; they come to change the world. In a National Geographic 2018 documentary, *Science Fair,* Serena talked about her team, "I'm going to be so proud when one of them wins the Nobel Prize," she said. "Because they will." She later explained a bit about her vision. "This next generation is not going to be about who can use their hands. It's going to be about who is most forward thinking."

Ramida "Jennie" Juengpaisal is a front-end developer and digital product designer at 5Lab in Thailand. She is an advocate for women in STEM fields and believes that technology can make a difference in society.

As the COVID-19 pandemic grew, she became frustrated at the spread of fake news about the virus on social media and asked why there was no central website to curate information and data about the spread. The resulting website, designed to provide factual information about the virus, gained four million users within five days of launch. Jenny said, "I believe what I'm doing is important and data transparency is key."

Women of substance are excelling in every field, making a difference in their communities and across the globe. They are able to recognize when they have an opportunity to act, even if that opportunity arises through fate or happenstance. Some of those accidental achievers are already icons, respected for their accomplishments and their drive. Their gifts are marked by humor, common sense, and just a touch of self-deprecation. They create their own path and own their story.

There is only one leader in the world whose remarkable leadership spans the decades from the greatest generation to the next generation. And she reigns supreme. Great Britain's Queen Elizabeth is an icon of grace, service, and above all, servant leadership. Her father, King George VI, became king only after his older brother

Edward VIII abdicated the throne. She was thrust into the limelight as a young princess, served in uniform as a truck driver and auto mechanic in World War II, and shortly after her father's death a few years later, was crowned Queen, only the sixth woman in Britain's history to serve as such. She's led a nation, a commonwealth, and indeed the world, through every challenge imaginable. In 2012, she celebrated her Diamond Jubilee — sixty years on the throne. She has spoken often of the need to face life with courage. In one of her best-known speeches, she talked about the need for courage in everyday life. "Today we need a special kind of courage. Not the kind needed in battle, but a kind which makes us stand up for everything that we know is right, everything that is true and honest. We need the kind of courage that can withstand the subtle corruption of the cynics, so that we can show the world that we are not afraid of the future."

Along the future path, we will recognize the next generation of standouts by their humility, their humanity, and their insistence that "I was just doing my job"; the constant refrain that "I only played a small part"; their discomfort at recognition, applause, and rewards; and by their genuine gratitude for those who understand and support their

Queen Elizabeth accepts flowers from a young girl on her eightieth birthday, April 21, 2006. The Queen was on a walkabout in Windsor Town Center, celebrating with many young people who gathered there. Photo credit Geoff Caddick/EPA/Shutterstock.

life's mission. Undoubtedly, every one of them will marvel at being in the company of the others.

We will celebrate their empathy, their humanity, and their respect for all living things. They won't all be global figures. Most won't be celebrities. Some may not even be well known outside their hometown or community of practice. But in those circles, they will be heroes.

As we have come to know the women of the Greatest Generation, we have also realized that World War II isn't ancient history.

471

It happened yesterday. Their past isn't gone, receding into a golden mist until the thread that connects us fades, frays, and falls away. That can't happen as long as their heirs hold the line. From us back to them. From them forward to us, breathing life into the legacy for future generations.

We will know their names.

ACKNOWLEDGMENTS

If there is an overriding theme in these stories, it is one of faith. In an era of acceptable misogyny and racial prejudice, these women possessed the fierce drive and fortitude to overcome multiple barriers and succeed. They changed the settings for society's norms, forging new paths. They invented their own roles, their paths, themselves, and made our achievements possible.

I need to thank them all for their inspiration. Every one of them did things that have never been done before. Some of them did things that didn't even exist in human imagination until they created them. They led large organizations. They became pilots. They wrote the book on juvenile rehabilitation, counterespionage, and special operations procedures. Some created entirely new career fields like cartography and psychological operations. They pried the doors open.

Others survived the attempted genocide of

473

an entire people. They went on to become entrepreneurs, caregivers extraordinaire, and impassioned advocates of freedom and faith. We can never forget the pain they endured, the example they set, and the inspiration they gave so freely.

More battled racial discrimination, anti-Semitism, and gender bias. They stood up and stuck out. They made a difference when it counted. Some felt they played a minor role in the bigger picture of service during wartime. What they did mattered, even if they didn't realize it themselves. A very few had a national platform, based on their considerable talents and reach. Whether in documenting injustice on a global scale or fighting to desegregate professional sports, their selflessness was considerable. They set the example in persistence.

I would also like to thank the families and friends of these remarkable women for speaking with me, sharing stories, and helping me to honor their loved ones. May God bless, and Angels keep them.

The girls who stepped out of line not only made history, they created the future.

NOTES

Introduction

"Women make excellent workers": L. H. Sanders, "Eleven Tips on Getting More Efficiency Out of Women Employees," *Mass Transportation* magazine, July 1943, 244.

"With one third": "World War II Veterans by the Numbers," Department of Veterans Affairs, VA Fact Sheet, 2003, http://dig.abclocal.go.com/ktrk/ktrk_120710_WWIIvetsfactsheet.pdf.

"Over 16 million men": Asher Kohn, "It's Amazing Just How Many Americans Served in World War II," Timeline.com, May 8, 2016, https://timeline.com/its-amazing-just-how-many-americans-served-in-world-war-ii-18d197a685ca.

"There are many hundreds": Frank Moore, *Women of the War* (Hartford, CT: S. S. Scranton & Company, 1867), v.

"The story of the war": Moore, *Women of the War*, vi.

"They were recognized": Elizabeth Cobbs, *The Hello Girls: America's First Women Soldiers* (Cambridge, MA: Harvard University Press, 2017), 306.

"They did not have": Stephen E. Ambrose, *D-Day June 6, 1944: The Climactic Battle of World War II* (New York: Simon & Schuster, 1994), 488.

Chapter 1

"When my life": "Alice Marble," *Encyclopedia of World Biography,* accessed July 10, 2020 from Encyclopedia.com, https://www.encyclopedia.com/people /sports-and-games/sports-biographies /alice-marble.

"My mother didn't": Alice Marble and Dale Leatherman, *Courting Danger: My Adventures in World-Class Tennis, Golden-Age Hollywood, and High-Stakes Spying* (New York: Saint Martin's Press, 1991), xii.

"Her mother began": Arnold B. Cheyney, *Athletes of Purpose: 50 People Who Changed the Face of Sports* (Culver City, CA: Good Year Books, 2000), 64.

"Queen of Swat": "Hall of Fame Inductees: Alice Marble," International Tennis Hall of Fame, https://www.tennisfame.com/hall of-famers/inductees/alice-marble.

"played like a man": Julie Cart, "Women's

Pioneer Alice Marble Dies: Tennis: As a National Champion in the '30s, She Played a Serve and Volley Game," *Los Angeles Times,* December 14, 1990, https://www.latimes.com/archives/la-xpm-1990-12-14-sp-6452-story.html.

"She was the first": "Alice Marble," *Encyclopedia of World Biography,* s.v.

"With a little": Marble and Leatherman, *Courting Danger: My Adventures in World-Class Tennis, Golden-Age Hollywood, and High-Stakes Spying,* 146.

"What's left to": Marble and Leatherman, *Courting Danger: My Adventures in World-Class Tennis, Golden-Age Hollywood, and High-Stakes Spying,* 170.

"Later she donated": "Women and Tennis: Lesson 1: Alice Marble and Helen Hull Jacobs," International Tennis Hall of Fame, https://cdn0.scrvt.com/c2465e9022ba94 6df66d1244a69b1c75/47fc203b06b9aa11 /2fd265ca17cb/Women_and_Tennis_ Lesson_1.pdf.

"Her loss to Mary": "1941 H2H Tour — Marble, Hardwick, Budge, Tilden," Former Pro Player Talk, Tennis Warehouse, September 29, 2017, https://tt.tennis-warehouse.com/index.php?threads/1941-h2h-tour-marble-hardwick-budge-tilden.6 00809/.

"Clara Barton, Dolly": Marble and Leatherman, *Courting Danger: My Adventures in World-Class Tennis, Golden-Age Hollywood, and High-Stakes Spying,* 177.

"The first issue": Roy Thomas, *Wonder Woman: The War Years 1941–1945* (New York: Chartwell Books), 125.

"Her creation, stories": Bryan Cronin, "Comic Book Legends Revealed #333," CBR.com, September 23, 2011, https://www.cbr.com /comic-book-legends-revealed-333/.

"She also entertained": Marble and Leatherman, *Courting Danger: My Adventures in World-Class Tennis, Golden-Age Hollywood, and High-Stakes Spying,* 168.

"My husband and I": Marble and Leatherman, *Courting Danger: My Adventures in World-Class Tennis, Golden-Age Hollywood, and High-Stakes Spying,* 189.

"We regret to inform": Marble and Leatherman, *Courting Danger: My Adventures in World-Class Tennis, Golden-Age Hollywood, and High-Stakes Spying,* 196.

"It was time": Marble and Leatherman, *Courting Danger: My Adventures in World-Class Tennis, Golden-Age Hollywood, and High-Stakes Spying,* 200.

"I felt I had": Marble and Leatherman, *Courting Danger: My Adventures in World-Class Tennis, Golden-Age Hollywood, and*

High-Stakes Spying, 207.

"At present, we do not": Isabel Vincent, *Hitler's Silent Partners: Swiss Banks, Nazi Gold, and the Pursuit of Justice* (New York: William Morrow and Company 1997), 112–113.

"We can accept": Eleni Schirmer, "The Mighty Pens of Women's Tennis: The Letter Legacy of Alice Marble and Venus Williams," Women's History Month, 2016, ESPN, March 17, 2016, https://www.espn.com/espnw/voices/story/_/id/14999091/letter-legacy-alice-marble-venus-williams.

"If tennis is": Beverly Wettenstein, "Let Us Remember Alice Marble, the Catalyst for Althea Gibson to Break the Color Barrier," *Huffington Post,* August 30, 2007, https://www.huffpost.com/entry/let-us-remember-alice-mar_b_62571.

"Then there is": Susana Polo, "Alice Marble: Tennis Celebrity, Wonder Woman Writer and Spy?" TheMarySue.com, September 23, 2011, https://www.themarysue.com/alice-marble-wonder-woman/.

"She was fortunate": Wettenstein, "Let Us Remember Alice Marble, the Catalyst for Althea Gibson to Break the Color Barrier."

"I have been": Alice Marble, *The Road to Wimbledon* (London: W. H. Allen, 1946), 166.

"both perfectly plausible": Robert Weintraub,

The Divine Miss Marble: A Life of Tennis, Fame, and Mystery (New York: Dutton, 2020), 307.

"Nuance and enigma": Weintraub, *The Divine Miss Marble: A Life of Tennis, Fame, and Mystery,* 389.

Chapter 2

"You're going to": James R. Hagerty, "Polish Holocaust Survivor Heeded Brutal Advice, Then Moved On," *Wall Street Journal,* December 16, 2017, https://www.wsj.com/articles/polish-holocaust-survivor-heeded-brutal-advice-then-moved-on-1513350000.

"She used the": Mary Eisen Cramer, "The Eisen Family Story," video presentation at Norco College, April 27, 2012, https://www.youtube.com/watch?v=Tzn6e857GL0.

"Everyone Hilda knew": Robert Kuwalek and Weronika Litwin, "Izbica: A Story of a Place," Foundation for the Preservation of Jewish Heritage in Poland, 2007, http://fodz.pl/download/fodz_izbica_broszura_EN.pdf.

"Following the First": "Izbica Ghetto," Holocaust Education & Archive Research Team, 2007, http://www.holocaustresearchproject.org/ghettos/izbica/izbica.html.

"Russia took the": "Records Relating to the Katyn Forest Massacre at the National

Archives," U.S. Foreign Policy Research, The National Archives, April 8, 2020, https://www.archives.gov/research/foreign-policy/katyn-massacre.

"We just closed": Hagerty, "Polish Holocaust Survivor Heeded Brutal Advice."

"It was filth": Hagerty, "Polish Holocaust Survivor Heeded Brutal Advice."

"Of the more": Debbie Cenziper, *Citizen 865: The Hunt for Hitler's Hidden Soldiers in America* (New York: Hachette Books, 2019), 142.

"The killing often": Cenziper, *Citizen 865: The Hunt for Hitler's Hidden Soldiers in America*, 58.

"You survive if": "Interview with Hilda Eisen," USC Shoah Foundation, Visual History Archive, June 18, 2001, https://collections.ushmm.org/search/catalog/vha51694.

"They picked up": "Partisan Groups in the Parczew Forests," Holocaust Encyclopedia, U.S. Holocaust Memorial Museum, https://encyclopedia.ushmm.org/content/en/article/partisan-groups-in-the-parczew-forests.

"There was no": Maura Turcotte, "Holocaust Survivor and Philanthropist Mourned," *Park LaBrea News,* December 21, 2017, https://beverlypress.com/2017/12/holocaust-survivor-and-philanthropist-mourned.

"Day is day": "Interview with Hilda Eisen."

"I'll tell you": "Interview with Hilda Eisen."

"Together they shuffled": Dennis McClellan, "Harry Eisen Dies at 95; Norco Ranch Founder," *Los Angeles Times*, July 29, 2012, https://www.latimes.com/local/obituaries/la -me-harry-eisen-20120730-story.html.

"The situation was": Ruth Gruber, *Witness: One of the Great Correspondents of the Twentieth Century Tells Her Story* (New York: Schocken Books, 2007), 88.

"I talked Jewish": Hagerty, "Polish Holocaust Survivor Heeded Brutal Advice."

"How did they": McClellan, "Harry Eisen Dies at 95; Norco Ranch Founder."

"Until 2005, Norco": "Hilda Eisen, Holocaust Survivor, Philanthropist, 100," *Jewish Journal,* December 7, 2017, https://jewish journal.com/culture/lifestyle/obituaries /228445/hilda-eisen-holocaust-survivor -philanthropist-100/.

"In 2014, the organization": The 1939 Society, https://www.the1939society.org/about /?history.

"The nonprofit donated": "Bonded by Ghetto," *Jewish Journal,* April 24, 2003, https:// jewishjournal.com/news/nation/7791/.

"That act made": Beverly Beyette, "A Modern Day Schindler Faces the Consequences," *Los Angeles Times,* August 19, 1998, https://www.latimes.com/archives/la

-xpm-1998-aug-19-ls-14350-story.html.

"By 1998, a lawsuit": Barry Meier, "Jewish Groups Fight for Spoils of Swiss Case," *New York Times,* November 29, 1998, https://www.nytimes.com/1998/11/29/world/jewish-groups-fight-for-spoils-of-swiss-case.html?pagewanted=all&src=pm.

"They were able": "Hilda Eisen, Holocaust Survivor, Philanthropist, 100."

"We are the eyewitnesses": McClellan, "Harry Eisen Dies at 95; Norco Ranch Founder."

"In 2016, Hilda": "Hilda Eisen, Holocaust Survivor, Philanthropist, 100."

"They were touched": Hagerty, "Polish Holocaust Survivor Heeded Brutal Advice."

"They always said": Hagerty, "Polish Holocaust Survivor Heeded Brutal Advice."

Chapter 3

"They gave me": Adam Bernstein, "Stephanie Rader, Undercover Spy in Postwar Europe, Dies at 100," *Washington Post,* January 21, 2016, https://www.washingtonpost.com/national/stephanie-rader-undercover-spy-in-postwar-europe-dies-at-100/2016/01/21/7e2e873a-c067-11e5-bcda-62a36b394160_story.html.

"But Stephanie was": *Office of Strategic Services (OSS) Organization and Functions* training booklet, OSS Schools

and Training Branch, June 1945, http://www.ibiblio.org/hyperwar/USG/JCS/OSS/OSS-Functions/#:~:text=%2D%2D4%2D%2D-,OSS%20Organization, responsible%20for%20a%20particular%20 function.&-text=The%20two%20large%20 OSS%20functions,administered%20 by%20two%20deputy%20directors.

"People in that generation": Petula Dvorak, "A Female Spy Finally Gets the Recognition She Deserved 70 Years Ago," *Washington Post,* June 2, 2016, https://www.washingtonpost.com/local/a-female-spy -finally-gets-the-recogntion-she-deserved -70-years-ago/2016/06/02/eb5dd046-2826 -11e6-a3c4-0724e8e24f3f_story.html.

"The OSS Society": Bernstein, "Stephanie Rader, Undercover Spy."

"Like many of those": Dvorak, "A Female Spy."

"The award is": Amy Tikkanen, ed., "The Legion of Merit," *Encyclopedia Britannica,* July 20, 1998, https://www.britannica.com /topic/Legion-of-Merit.

"When you get to": Bernstein, "Stephanie Rader, Undercover Spy."

"Stephanie graduated with": Dvorak, "A Female Spy."

"They were interested": "The Virginia Hall Award: Major Stephanie Czech Rader,

USA," The OSS Society (Video), 2012. https://www.youtube.com/watch?v=e IFW3xEYvvw.

"The Intelligent Services": Office of Strategic Services (OSS) Organization and Functions training booklet.

"Unfortunately, the creation": "The Office of Strategic Services, America's First Intelligence Agency, an End and a Beginning," *Central Intelligence Agency Library,* June 28, 2008, https://www.cia.gov/library /publications/intelligence-history/oss/art10 .htm.

"A study in despair": Arthur Bliss Lane, *I Saw Poland Betrayed: An American Ambassador Reports to the American People* (Western Islands: Bobs Merrill Co., 1948), 251.

"He gave her": Lane, *I Saw Poland Betrayed: An American Ambassador Reports to the American People,* 189, 190.

"They gave me": Bernstein, "Stephanie Rader, Undercover Spy."

"Her outstanding qualifications": Shane Harris, "Will America's 100-Year-Old Female Spy Finally Be Recognized for the Hero She Is?" *Daily Beast,* June 26, 2017, https:// www.thedailybeast.com/will-americas-100 -year-old-female-spy-finally-be-recognized -for-the-hero-she-is.

"The Cold War": Richard F. Staar, "Elections

in Communist Poland," *Midwest Journal of Political Science,* vol. 2, no. 2 (May 1958), 200–201, https://www.jstor.org/stable/2108 857?seq=1.

"Together, Bill and": "William Staats Rader, Brigadier General U.S. Air Force," Arlington National Cemetery website, August 23, 2006, http://www.arlingtoncemetery.net /wsrader.htm.

"Stephanie and Bill": Bernstein, "Stephanie Rader, Undercover Spy."

"He was buried": "William Staats Rader, Brigadier General U.S. Air Force."

"After I found": Dvorak, "A Female Spy."

"She was tough": Alexandra Genova, "Groundbreaking Female Spy Finally Gets Legion of Merit on the Day of Her Funeral for Her Services in WWII," *Daily Mail,* June 5, 2016, https://www.dailymail.co.uk/news /article-3619267/Groundbreaking-WWII -era-spy-buried-Arlington.html.

"Stephanie was a": Jose Beduya and Joe Wilensky, "WWII Era Spy Stephanie Czech Rader '37 Dies at Age 100," *Ezra Update,* Cornell University, January 2016, http://ezramagazine.cornell.edu/Update /Jan16/EU.Stephanie.Rader.html.

"In 2012, the OSS": "What the Heck Was I Gonna Do with a Dumb Gun? The Derring-Do of Stephanie Czech Rader,"

News & Information, Central Intelligence Agency website, June 28, 2017, https:// www.cia.gov/news-information/featured -story-archive/2017-featured-story-archive /stephanie-czech-rader.html.

"Membership in this": "Membership," Special Forces Association website, https:// www.specialforcesassociation.org/about /membership/.

"Stephanie Rader was": "Senator Warner Announces Legion of Merit to Be Awarded Posthumously to WWII Era Spy Stephanie Rader," News, Senator Mark Warner homepage, May 26, 2016, https:// www.warner.senate.gov/public/index.cfm /2016/5/sen-warner-announces-legion-of -merit-to-be-awarded-posthumously-to -ww2-era-u-s-spy-stephanie-rader.

"Stephanie chose the": Shane Harris and Andrew Desiderio, "America's Toughest Lady Spy Laid to Rest," *Daily Beast,* April 13, 2017, https://www.thedailybeast .com/americas-toughest-lady-spy-laid-to -rest?ref=scroll.

Chapter 4

"It was then": Elizabeth P. McIntosh, "Honolulu after Pearl Harbor: A Report Published for the First Time, 71 Years Later," *Washington Post,* December 6,

2012, https://www.washingtonpost.com /opinions/honolulu-after-pearl-harbor -a-report-published-for-the-first-time-7 1-years-later/2012/12/06/e9029986-3d69 -11e2-bca3-aadc9b7e29c5_story.html.

"The Hermit was": Gene Santoro, "At War With the Enemy's Mind: Conversation with Betty McIntosh," *World War II Magazine,* June 2013, https://www.historynet .com/war-enemys-mind-conversation -betty-mcintosh.htm.

"Something brand-new": Ann Todd, *OSS Operation Black Mail: One Woman's Covert War Against the Imperial Japanese Army* (Annapolis, MD: Naval Institute Press), 2017, 149.

"It was a": "Spy Girl Betty McIntosh Turns 100 Years Old," Central Intelligence Agency News and Information, March 3, 2015, https://www.cia.gov/news -information/featured-story-archive/2015 -featured-story-archive/201cspy-girl201d -betty-mcintosh-turns-100-years-old .html.

"Then, from the": McIntosh, "Honolulu after Pearl Harbor: A Report Published for the First Time, 71 Years Later."

"It was then": McIntosh, "Honolulu after Pearl Harbor: A Report Published for the First Time, 71 Years Later."

"Wouldn't you like": Tom Neven, "Women in SOF: A Historical Perspective — 'Undercover Girl' Betty McIntosh," *Tip of the Spear* (MacDill AFB, FL), February 2019, 6.

"toughening up": Dr. John Whiteclay Chambers II, "Office of Strategic Services Training During World War II," *Studies in Intelligence* vol. 54, no. 2 (June 2010), 1–26, https://www.cia.gov/library/center-for-the-study-of-intelligence/csi-publications/csi-studies/studies/vol.-54-no.-2/pdfs-vol.-54-no.-2/Chambers-OSS%20Training%20in%20WWII-with%20notes-web-19Jun.pdf.

"We fired guns": Jeff Silverman, "Spies in the Clubhouse: The Intelligence That Won World War II May Not Have Been Accumulated in the Hallways of Power, But along the Fairways of Congressional," U.S. Golf Association, 2011, 79–82, https://www.osssociety.org/pdfs/SpiesUSO.pdf.

"The gun weighed": Linda McCarthy, *Betty McIntosh: OSS Spy Girl* (Front Royal, VA: History Is a Hoot, Inc., 2012), 143.

"an open-face-sandwich": Elizabeth P. MacDonald, *Undercover Girl* (New York: The McMillan Company, 1947), 39.

"I went back": MacDonald, *Undercover Girl,* 51.

"'Black' information was": "Chapter 2: Wartime Organization for Unconventional Warfare," *The OSS (1942–1945),* The National Park Service, 69–70, https://www.nps.gov/parkhistory/online_books/oss/chap2.pdf.

"They didn't salute": "Spy Girl Betty McIntosh Turns 100 Years Old."

"The tide of": MacDonald, *Undercover Girl,* 83.

"Surrenders increased": Elizabeth P. McIntosh, *Sisterhood of Spies: Women of the OSS* (Annapolis, MD: Naval Institute Press, 1998), 207–208.

"persuasion through subversion": MacDonald, *Undercover Girl,* 304.

"Someday, I knew": MacDonald, *Undercover Girl,* 114.

"The three became": McIntosh, *Sisterhood of Spies: Women of the OSS,* 234.

"He jumped to safety": Adam Bernstein, "Elizabeth McIntosh: Journalist Who Became an Agent for the Office of Strategic Services Whose Efforts Were Crucial in the War in the East," *The Independent,* June 16, 2015, https://www.independent.co.uk/news/people/news/elizabeth-mcintosh-journalist-who-became-an-agent-for-the-office-of-strategic-services-whose-efforts-10322016.html.

"I felt very badly": "Decades after Duty in OSS and CIA, 'Spy Girls' Find Each Other in Retirement," *The Record,* July 2, 2011, https://www.therecord.com/news/world/2011/07/02/decades-after-duty-in-oss-and-cia-spy-girls-find-each-other-in-retirement.html.

"Seven man OSS": MacDonald, *Undercover Girl,* 230.

"The beloved cocker spaniel": McIntosh, *Sisterhood of Spies: Women of the OSS,* 237.

"There were only": MacDonald, *Undercover Girl,* 199.

"Then Richard was": C. Peter Chen, "Richard Heppner," World War II Database, June 2015, https://ww2db.com/person_bio.php?person_id=901.

"She took on": "Spy Girl Betty McIntosh Turns 100 Years Old."

"Betty finally agreed": "Spy Girl Betty McIntosh Turns 100 Years Old."

"She was back": Bob Bergin, *OSS Undercover Girl Elizabeth P. McIntosh: An Interview* (Fairfax, VA: Banana Tree Press, 2012), 236.

"I guess I developed": "Spy Girl Betty McIntosh Turns 100 Years Old."

"Well he was": Adam Bernstein, "Elizabeth McIntosh: Spy Whose Lies Helped Win a War, Dies at 100," *Washington Post,* June

8, 2015, https://www.washingtonpost.com /national/elizabeth-mcintosh-spy-whose -lies-helped-win-a-war-dies-at-100/2015 /06/08/6ed48900–0dfd–11e5-adec -e82f8395c032_story.html.

"The war meant": Santoro, "At War With the Enemy's Mind: Conversation with Betty McIntosh."

"We cannot afford": McIntosh, *Sisterhood of Spies: Women of the OSS,* 255–256.

"Like siblings separated": Todd, *OSS Operation Black Mail: One Woman's Covert War Against the Imperial Japanese Army,* 208.

"She said later": Linda McCarthy, email message to author, May 6, 2020.

"[the] CIA is": "Spy Girl Betty McIntosh Turns 100 Years Old."

"I'm glad I was": "Spy Girl Betty McIntosh Turns 100 Years Old."

Chapter 5

"I must have liberty": Sonia Purnell, *A Woman of No Importance: The Untold Story of the American Spy Who Helped Win World War II* (New York: Penguin Random House, 2019), 8.

"Her horrified friends": Judith L. Pearson, *Wolves at the Door: The True Story of America's Greatest Female Spy* (Guilford, CT: The Lyons Press, 2005), 8–9.

"That much was real": Pearson, *Wolves at the Door: The True Story of America's Greatest Female Spy,* 12.

"'Cuthbert' was a": Ian Shapira, "As Nazis Closed In, Spy Fled Across Mountains on Her Wooden Leg," *Washington Post,* July 11, 2017, https://www.washingtonpost.com/news/retropolis/wp/2017/07/11/the-nazis-were-closing-in-on-a-spy-known-as-the-limping-lady-she-fled-across-mountains-on-a-wooden-leg/.

"An SOE agent": Purnell, *A Woman of No Importance: The Untold Story of the American Spy Who Helped Win World War II,* 31.

"Tall, with shining": Gordon Thomas and Greg Lewis, *Shadow Warriors of World War II: The Daring Women of the OSS and SOE* (Chicago: Chicago Review Press, 2017), 32.

"The Limping Lady": McIntosh, *Sisterhood of Spies: Women of the OSS,* 113.

"The message itself": Dave Roos, "World War II's 'Most Dangerous' Allied Spy Was a Woman with a Wooden Leg," History.com, February 27, 2019, https://www.history.com/news/female-allied-spy-world-war-2-wooden-leg.

"I'd give anything": Shapira, "As Nazis Closed In, Spy Fled Across Mountains on Her Wooden Leg."

"The woman who limps": McIntosh, *Sisterhood of Spies: Women of the OSS,* 114.

"She went on": Nancy Polette, *The Spy with the Wooden Leg: The Story of Virginia Hall* (St. Paul, MN: Elva Resa Publishing, 2012), 83.

"I am living": McIntosh, *Sisterhood of Spies: Women of the OSS,* 119.

"I preferred to": MacDonald, *Undercover Girl,* 199.

"Using a wireless": Purnell, *A Woman of No Importance: The Untold Story of the American Spy Who Helped Win World War II,* 242.

"Virginia and her team": Cate Lineberry, "Wanted: The Limping Lady: The Intriguing and Unexpected True Story of America's Most Heroic — and Most Dangerous — Female Spy," *Smithsonian Magazine,* February 1, 2007, https://www.smithsonianmag.com/history/wanted-the-limping-lady-146541513/.

"She would spend": Beryl E. Escott, Squadron Leader, *The Heroines of SOE: Britain's Secret Women in France F Section* (Stroud, Gloucestershire, UK: The History Press, 2010), 38.

"In a subdued": Tom Neven, "Virginia Hall: The Limping Lady." *Tip of the Spear* (MacDill AFB, FL), February 2019, 4.

"The citation read": "Citation for Virginia

Hall for the Distinguished Service Cross," DocsTeach, The National Archives, 1945, https://www.docsteach.org/documents/document/citation-for-virginia-hall-for-the-distinguished-service-cross.

"It was just": Lineberry, "Wanted: The Limping Lady."

"Women were made": Jacqueline R., "The Petticoat Panel: A 1953 Study of the Role of Women in the CIA's Career Service," Special Report Prepared at the Request of the Central Intelligence Agency, Approved for Release October 30, 2013, https://www.cia.gov/library/readingroom/docs/2003-03-01.pdf.

"She included": Jacqueline R., "The Petticoat Panel."

"Former CIA officer": Jacqueline R., "The Petticoat Panel."

"The British ambassador": Steve Balestrieri, "Virginia Hall, the Famous 'Limping Lady' of the OSS," SOFREP.com, July 13, 2017, https://sofrep.com/specialoperations/virginia-hall-famous-limping-lady-oss/.

"I stand on": Sonja Purnell, "Virginia Hall Was America's Most Successful Female WWII Spy. But She Was Almost Kept from Serving," *Time,* April 9, 2019, https://time.com/5566062/virginia-hall/.

"In one of her": "Activity Report of Virginia

Hall," DocsTeach, The National Archives, September 30, 1944, https://www.docsteach.org/documents/document/activity-report-of-virginia-hall.

Chapter 6

"Some people say": Mary Taylor Previte, "America Has Heroes: I Know Their Names," Weihsien-Paintings.org, undated, http://www.weihsien-paintings.org/Mprevite/text/HowIFoundMyWeihsienHeroes.htm.

"The only place": Kate Morgan, "Ten Questions: Mary Previte," *SJ Magazine,* September 2005, https://sjmagazine.net/september-2015/survivor.

"The day after": Michael Bristow, "Growing up in a Japanese WW2 Internment Camp in China," BBC News, August 17, 2015, https://www.bbc.com/news/world-asia-33709730.

"It became the largest": He Na and Ju Chuanjiang, "Weihsien: Life and Death in the Shadow of the Empire of the Sun," *China Daily,* February 20, 2014, https://www.chinadaily.com.cn/2014-02/20/content_17293388.htm.

"All prisoners were": Na and Chuanjiang, "Weihsien: Life and Death in the Shadow of the Empire of the Sun."

"The school also": Na and Chuanjiang, "Weihsien: Life and Death in the Shadow of the Empire of the Sun."

"One of her": Mary Taylor Previte, "A Song of Salvation at Weihsien Prison Camp," WeihsienPaintings.org, August 25, 1985, http://weihsien-paintings.org/Mprevite /inquirer/MPrevite.htm.

"You could be": Morgan, "Ten Questions: Mary Previte."

"Later she recalled": Katharine Q. Seelye, "Mary Previte, Grateful Survivor of a Concentration Camp, Dies at 87," *New York Times,* November 24, 2019, https:// www.nytimes.com/2019/11/24/us/mary -previte-dead.html.

"She added": Bristow, "Growing up in a Japanese WW2 Internment Camp in China."

"War and hate": Na and Chuanjiang, "Weihsien: Life and Death in the Shadow of the Empire of the Sun."

"I don't think": Morgan, "Ten Questions: Mary Previte."

"At 400 feet": Alan Bauer, "8-17-45 'I've Been in Love with America from That Day to This," *Haddonfield Sun,* May 11–17, 2005, https:// web.archive.org/web/20050514125504 /http://www.haddonfieldsun.com/news _story.php?newsId=6&edition=2.

"They were angels": Kristen A. Graham,

"Mary T. Previte, Former N.J. Assembly-woman and Concentration Camp Survivor, Dies at 87," *Philadelphia Inquirer,* November 18, 2019, https://www.inquirer.com/news/mary-taylor-previte-obituary-south-jersey-assemblywoman-concentration-camp-20191118.html.

"The moment the Japanese": Mary Taylor Previte, "Ted Nagaki, an American Hero," Japanese American Veterans Association (JAVA.com), April 22, 2013, http://javadc.org/news/feature/tad-nagaki-an-american-hero-a-eulogy-by-mary-taylor-previte/.

"Everyone was": NPR Staff, "After Long Wait for Combat, Tad Nagaki Became POW Liberator," WBUR News, May 28, 2013, https://www.wbur.org/npr/186899875/after-long-wait-for-combat-tad-nagaki-became-pow-liberator.

"Later she recalled": Previte, "America Has Heroes: I Know Their Names."

"When they reached": Morgan, "Ten Questions: Mary Previte."

"He was actually": MacDonald, *Undercover Girl,* 231.

"Mary didn't know": Bauer, "8-17-45 'I've Been in Love with America from That Day to This."

"His sketches": William A. Smith, "In Weihsien Prison Camp," *Asia,* July 1946, http://www

.weihsien-paintings.org/StanleyFairchild /Sketches/asia.htm.

"*Just after the camp*": MacDonald, *Undercover Girl*, 231.

"*down the block*": Mary Taylor Previte, *Hungry Ghosts: One Woman's Mission to Change their World*, self-published, 1994, 2011, 522.

"*That's when I learned*": Previte, "Ted Nagaki, an American Hero."

"*Mary remembered screaming*": Mary Taylor Previte, *Hungry Ghosts: One Woman's Mission to Change Their World*, self-published, 1994, 2011, 536.

"*Later, her younger brother*": Theodora Aggeles, review of *How Jane Won: 55 Successful Women Share How They Grew from Ordinary Girls to Extraordinary Women*, HowJaneWon.com, March 25, 2001, http:// www.seejanewin.com/HowJaneWon.htm.

"*Mary taught English*": Graham, "Mary T. Previte."

"*Bruce Stout*": Graham, "Mary T. Previte."

"*We discovered*": David Bianculli and Terry Gross, "'We Took Terror Out of Their Lives:' Remembering Youth Advocate Mary Previte," National Public Radio (NPR), December 6, 2019, https://www .npr.org/2019/12/06/785479653/we-took -terror-out-of-their-lives-remembering

-youth-advocate-mary-previte.

"Some kid will say": Bianculli and Gross,
" 'We Took Terror Out of Their Lives.' "

"What keeps you going": Bianculli and Gross,
" 'We Took Terror Out of Their Lives.' "

"Let me tell you": Previte, "Ted Nagaki, an
American Hero."

"Notably, Mary served": Graham, "Mary T.
Previte.' "

"She sponsored legislation": Philip Murphy,
Governor, New Jersey Executive Order
No. 93, November 22, 2019.

"She cared about": Graham, "Mary T.
Previte."

"But his heart": Previte, "America Has Heroes:
I Know Their Names."

"My heart said": Previte, "America Has
Heroes: I Know Their Names."

"A number of them": Patrick Lion, "A Kiss 71
Years in the Making," *Daily Mail,* July 28,
2016, https://www.dailymail.co.uk/news
/article-3712872/A-kiss-71-years-making
-American-prisoner-war-meets-thanks
-Chinese-man-rescued-1500-Japanese
-Second-World-War-camp-searching-18
-years.html.

"My world was full": Previte, *Hungry Ghosts:
One Woman's Mission to Change Their
World,* 769.

"Upon her death": Philip Murphy, Governor,

New Jersey Executive Order No. 93, November 22, 2019.

"Some people say": Previte, "America Has Heroes: I Know Their Names."

Chapter 7

"I was trembling": Ruth Gruber, *Inside of Time: My Journey from Alaska to Israel* (New York: Avalon Publishing Group, 2003), 231.

"Standing alone": Gruber, *Inside of Time*, 163.

"Our next speaker": Gruber, *Inside of Time*, 149.

"She was a woman": Gruber, *Inside of Time*, 149.

"You're right": Emily Langer, "Ruth Gruber, Who Accompanied 1,000 Jews to the Shores of the United States During the Holocaust, Dies at 105," *Washington Post,* November 19, 2016, https://www.washingtonpost.com/national/ruth-gruber-who-accompanied-1000-jews-to-the-shores-of-the-united-states-during-the-holocaust-dies-at-105/2016/11/17/da16277c-ad12-11e6-8b45-f8e493f06fcd_story.html.

"Mr. Secretary": Gruber, *Inside of Time: My Journey from Alaska to Israel,* 228.

"Ruth heard": Ruth Gruber, *Witness: One of the Great Correspondents of the Twentieth*

Century Tells Her Story (New York: Schocken Books, 2007), 67.

"The others were cargo": Nava Atlas, "Ruth Gruber: Journalist, Documentary Photographer, Humanitarian," Literary-LadiesGuide.com, October 30, 2016, https://www.literaryladiesguide.com/trailblazing-journalists/ruth-gruber-journalist-documentary-photographer-humanitarian/.

"Years later": Advance Media NY Editorial Board, "Ruth Gruber Documented Injustice, Then Did Something about It (Editorial)," Syracuse.com, October 22, 2019, https://www.syracuse.com/opinion/2016/11/ruth_gruber_safe_haven_witness_to_injustice_humanitarian_editorial.html.

"While the majority": Diane Bernard, "Jews Fleeing the Holocaust Weren't Welcome in the U.S. Then FDR Finally Offered a Refuge to Some," *Washington Post,* May 1, 2019, https://www.washingtonpost.com/history/2019/05/01/jews-fleeing-holocaust-werent-welcome-us-then-fdr-finally-offered-refuge-some/.

"To her it was": Ruth Gruber, *Haven: The Dramatic Story of 1,000 World War II Refugees and How They Came to America* (New York: Open Road, 2002), 113.

"Later, she recalled": Karen Michel, "A Woman of Photos and Firsts, Ruth Gruber at 100," WBUR News, National Public Radio, October 15, 2001, https://www.wbur.org/npr/141325143/a-woman-of-photos-and-firsts-ruth-gruber-at-100.

"Ruth even taught": Gruber, *Haven*, 115.

"A rabbi offered": Atlas, "Ruth Gruber: Journalist, Documentary Photographer, Humanitarian."

"This is all": Gruber, *Haven*, 147.

"They were stateless": Bernard, "Jews Fleeing the Holocaust Weren't Welcome in the U.S."

"Imagine having bedsheets": Gruber, *Witness: One of the Great Correspondents of the Twentieth Century Tells Her Story*, 85.

"That opened the door": Atlas, "Ruth Gruber: Journalist, Documentary Photographer, Humanitarian."

"Would your mother": Gruber, *Haven*, 173.

"On September 20, 1944": Gruber, *Witness: One of the Great Correspondents of the Twentieth Century Tells Her Story*, 70.

"Of the 982": Advance Media NY Editorial Board, "Ruth Gruber Documented Injustice, Then Did Something about It (Editorial)."

"Many refugees chanted": Gruber, *Inside of Time: My Journey from Alaska to Israel*, 98.

503

"He'd held the job": "Harold L. Ickes," University of Virginia, MillerCenter.org, undated, https://millercenter.org/president /fdroosevelt/essays/ickes-1933-harold -secretary-of-the-interior.

"She continued to serve": Barbara Seaman, "Ruth Gruber 1911–2016," *Jewish Women: A Comprehensive Historical Encyclopedia,* Jewish Women's Archive, February 27, 2009, https://jwa.org/encyclopedia/article /gruber-ruth.

"In 1998, she received": Seaman, "Ruth Gruber 1911–2016."

"The museum library": Seaman, "Ruth Gruber 1911–2016."

"Speaking about the refugees": Advance Media NY Editorial Board, "Ruth Gruber Documented Injustice, Then Did Something about It (Editorial)."

"Ruth said": Gruber, *Inside of Time: My Journey from Alaska to Israel,* 158.

Chapter 8

"I have never": "Dame Mary Barraco," What We Carry, Holocaust Commission of the United Jewish Federation of Tidewater, 2020, https://holocaustcommission .jewishva.org/home-page/what-we-carry /dame-mary-barraco.

"We were required": "Dame Mary Barraco,"

Holocaust Commission of the United Jewish Federation of Tidewater.

"Then Mary shepherded": Katherine Hafner, "Dame Mary Barraco, World War II Resistance Fighter Who Suffered Nazi Torture, Dies in Virginia Beach at 96," *Virginian Pilot,* December 12, 2019, https://www.pilotonline.com/news/obituaries/vp-nw-mary-barraco-obit-20191212-au 232fbla5d4xg3rmzajtf3haq-story.html.

"Their freedom": Tobi Walsh, "Families, Veterans Mark D-Day Anniversary at Bedford Memorial," *Lynchburg News & Advance,* June 6, 2015, https://www.roanoke.com/news/families-veterans-mark-d-day-anniversary-at-bedford-memorial/article_edc3e858–9fbd-5061-bde2-caabc2426ca2.html.

"I have such": "Dame Mary Barraco," Holocaust Commission of the United Jewish Federation of Tidewater.

"I heard the roaring": Walsh, "Families, Veterans Mark D-Day Anniversary at Bedford Memorial."

"It was a brazen": Tina Kish, "Dame Mary Barraco Dies in Virginia Beach at 96," Non-Commissioned Officers Association (NCOA) News, December 13, 2019, https://ncoausa.org/dame-mary-barraco-dies-in-virginia-beach-at-96/.

"Special agents watched": "Dame Mary Sigillo Barraco," *Virginia Pilot,* December 8, 2019, https://www.legacy.com/obituaries/piloton line/obituary.aspx?n=mary-sigillo-barraco &pid=194655717&fhid=15635.

"For me to live": "Dame Mary Barraco," Holocaust Commission of the United Jewish Federation of Tidewater.

"Not only were": Kish, "Dame Mary Barraco Dies in Virginia Beach at 96."

"Virginia Beach recognized": Donnie Bales, "Sopa (Soup) for the Soul: Passing on the Torch of Freedom," Virginia Tech School of Performing Arts News, January 5, 2018, https://www.performingarts.vt.edu/index .php/blog/view/sopa-soup-for-the-soul -passing-on-the-torch-of-freedom.

"He said, 'She was'": Bales, "Sopa (Soup) for the Soul: Passing on the Torch of Freedom."

"You can only get": Hafner, "Dame Mary Barraco, World War II Resistance Fighter Who Suffered Nazi Torture, Dies in Virginia Beach at 96."

"On her obituary page": "Dame Mary Barraco," Holocaust Commission of the United Jewish Federation of Tidewater.

"It is only after": Bales, "Sopa (Soup) for the Soul: Passing on the Torch of Freedom."

Chapter 9

"Because there were": Harrison Smith, "Dutch Resistance Hero Saved Jews in World War II," *Washington Post,* September 8, 2019, https://www.washingtonpost.com/local /obituaries/diet-eman-dutch-resistance-hero-who-saved-jews-during-world-war -ii-dies-at-99/2019/09/05/65faf2be-cfe7 -11e9-8c1c-7c8ee785b855_story.html.

"By the time": Brigit Katz, "Diet Eman, the Dutch Resistance Fighter Who Helped Jews Escape the Nazis, Has Died at 99," *Smithsonian Magazine,* September 9, 2019, https://www.smithsonianmag.com /smart-news/diet-eman-dutch-resistance -fighter-who-found-shelter-jews-has-died -99-180973066/.

"It was only the": Smith, "Dutch Resistance Hero Saved Jews in World War II."

"Now the country's": "The Netherlands," Holocaust Encyclopedia, U.S. Holocaust Memorial Museum, https://encyclopedia.ushmm .org/content/en/article/the-netherlands.

"But as Diet": James C. Schaap, "The Diet Eman Story, Part I," *The Banner: Weekly Publication of The Christian Reformed Church* (Grand Rapids, MI), November 8, 1993, 10.

"In the beginning": Smith, "Dutch Resistance Hero Saved Jews in World War II."

"He was sent": Diet Eman with James C. Schaap, *Things We Couldn't Say* (Grand Rapids, MI: William B. Eerdmans Publishing Company, 1994), 180.

"I felt as though": Eman with Schaap, *Things We Couldn't Say*, 185.

"Diet said": Kathryn J. Atwood, *Women Heroes of World War II: 26 Stories of Espionage, Sabotage, Resistance, and Rescue* (Chicago: Chicago Review Press, 2011), 98.

"She knew then": James C. Schaap, "The Diet Eman Story, Part III," *The Banner: Weekly Publication of The Christian Reformed Church* (Grand Rapids, MI), November 22, 1993, 10.

"They were Jews": Mitchell Bard, "Concentration Camps: Vught (Herzogenbusch)," Jewish Virtual Library, undated, https://www.jewishvirtuallibrary.org/vught-concentration-camp.

"Corrie had her own": Eman with Schaap, *Things We Couldn't Say*, 254.

"In her memoir": Katz, "Diet Eman, the Dutch Resistance Fighter Who Helped Jews Escape the Nazis, Has Died at 99."

"It was a message": Max Lucado, *Unshakable Hope: Building Our Lives on the Promises of God* (Nashville, TN: Thomas Nelson, 2018), 44.

"He looked Diet": Eman with Schaap, *Things We Couldn't Say*, 279.

"Later, Diet recalled": Eman with Schaap, *Things We Couldn't Say*, 372.

"Hein wrote": Katz, "Diet Eman, the Dutch Resistance Fighter Who Helped Jews Escape the Nazis, Has Died at 99."

"Love conquers all": Smith, "Dutch Resistance Hero Saved Jews in World War II."

"I began to receive": Eman with Schaap, *Things We Couldn't Say*, 369.

"She moved again": Rossella Tercatin, "Dutch Heroine Who Saved Dozens of Jews in World War II Dies at 99," *Jerusalem Post,* September 9, 2019, https://www.jpost.com/Diaspora/Dutch-heroine-who-saved-dozens-of-Jews-in-World-War-II-dies-at-99-600987.

"There she worked": Chris Meehan, "Diet Eman Praised for Her Courage," Christian Reformed Church News, September 10, 2019, https://www.crcna.org/news-and-views/diet-eman-praised-her-courage.

"With her newfound time": Eman with Schaap, *Things We Couldn't Say,* 389.

"Diet thought about it": Katz, "Diet Eman, the Dutch Resistance Fighter Who Helped Jews Escape the Nazis, Has Died at 99."

"My conscience": Eman with Schaap, *Things We Couldn't Say,* 377.

"Although she'd only spoken": Meehan, "Diet Eman Praised for Her Courage."

"It was about": James C. Schaap, "Diet Eman 1920-2019," Stuff in the Basement, https://siouxlander.blogspot.com/2019/09/diet-eman-1920-2019.html.

"It was as Corrie": Corrie Ten Boom, *The Hiding Place* (Grand Rapids, MI: Chosen Books, 1971 and 1984).

"In risking your safety": Atwood, *Women Heroes of World War II: 26 Stories of Espionage, Sabotage, Resistance, and Rescue,* 101.

"Israel's Holocaust memorial": Christine Manby, "Diet Eman Dutch Resistance Fighter Who Saved Many Lives in the Second World War," *The Independent,* September 19, 2019, https://www.independent.co.uk/news/obituaries/diet-eman-death-netherlands-resistance-second-world-war-nazis-a909.

"She was honored": Katz, "Diet Eman, the Dutch Resistance Fighter Who Helped Jews Escape the Nazis, Has Died at 99."

"She was a fierce": Schaap, "Diet Eman 1920–2019."

"She accompanied": James C. Schaap, "The Diet Eman Story, Part VIII," *The Banner: Weekly Publication of The Christian Reformed Church* (Grand Rapids, MI), December 27, 1993, 12.

"In the postscript": Smith, "Dutch Resistance Hero Saved Jews in World War II."

"By the time": Jeffrey Schaeffer and Angela Charlton, Associated Press, "Holocaust Survivors Share Their Stories So the Memories Will Endure," *Mercury News,* December 23, 2019, https://www.mercurynews.com/2019/12/23/holocaust-survivors-share-their-stories-so-the-memories-will-endure/.

"Fifty-eight percent": David Brennan, "One-Third of Americans Don't Believe 6 Million Jews Were Murdered During the Holocaust," *Newsweek,* April 12, 2018, https://www.newsweek.com/one-third-americans-dont-believe-6-million-jews-were-murdered-during-holocaust-883513.

"Though an army": Psalm 27, Bible Gateway, https://www.biblegateway.com/passage/?search=Psalm+27&version=NIV.

Chapter 10

"We were lucky": Ida Cook, *Safe Passage: The Remarkable True Story of Two Sisters Who Rescued Jews from the Nazis* (Ontario: Harlequin, 2008), 183.

"Years later, Ida said": "The Opera Loving Sisters Who 'Stumbled' into Heroism," BBC News, January 28, 2017, https://www.bbc.com/news/uk-england-tyne-38732779.

"The brazen ruse": Dr. Yvette Alt Miller, "Ida and Louise Cook's Remarkable Rescue Mission," Aish.com, November 18, 2017, https://www.aish.com/jw/s/Ida-and -Louise-Cooks-Remarkable-Rescue -Mission.html.

"It was just": Cook, *Safe Passages,* 103.

"The friend opened": "The Opera Loving Sisters Who 'Stumbled' into Heroism."

"As Ida once exclaimed": Cook, *Safe Passage,* 147.

"It was just": Margaret Talbot, "Ida and Louise Cook, Two Unusual Heroines of the Second World War," *The New Yorker,* September 3, 2019, https://www.new yorker.com/books/second-read/ida-and -louise-cook-two-unusual-heroines-of-the -second-world-war.

"If our jewelry": Cook, *Safe Passage,* 183.

"But after the Kristallnacht": U.S. Holocaust Memorial Museum, "Kristallnacht (The Night of Broken Glass, November 9–10, 1938)," Holocaust Encyclopedia, October 18, 2019, https://encyclopedia.ushmm.org /content/en/article/kristallnacht.

"After all": Louise Carpenter, "Ida and Louise: 'They Had Lived for Art,' " *Granta,* July 2, 2007, https://granta.com/ida-and-louise/.

"Finally, her mother": Cook, *Safe Passage,* 127.

"And on such details": Cook, *Safe Passage,* 190.

"I see them now": Cook, *Safe Passage,* 192.

"She continued": Josh Farley, "WWII Documents Reveal Importance of Air Raid Wardens," AP News, July 29, 2018, apnews.co m/35969cd5c1de47118d8c0d7c240521a6 /WWII-documents-reveal-importance-of -air-raid-wardens.

"The British program host": Anne Sebba and Doreen Montgomery, "Ida Cook 1904-1986," Big Red Book: Celebrating Television's *This Is Your Life,* undated, https:// www.bigredbook.info/a_novel_life.html.

"One was Viorica": Paul Gruber, ed., *The Metropolitan Opera Guide to Recorded Opera* (New York: W. W. Norton & Company, 1993), 526.

"Ida's response": Sebba and Montgomery, "Ida Cook 1904–1986."

"The sisters got her": "The Righteous Among Nations Database," Yad Vashem: The World Holocaust Remembrance Center, undated, https://righteous.yadvashem.org /?searchType=righteous_only&language =en&itemId=4021818&ind=NaN.

"Even now": Cook, *Safe Passage,* 16.

"Some days": Anne Sebba, forward to *Safe Passage: The Remarkable True Story of Two Sisters Who Rescued Jews from the Nazis,* 18.

"Twenty-five Britons": Heidi Blake, "Unsung British Heroes of the Holocaust Awarded Medals," *The Telegraph,* March 10, 2010, https://www.telegraph.co.uk/history/britain-at-war/7407251/Unsung-British-heroes-of-the-Holocaust-awarded-medals.html.

"And on January": Tony Henderson, "The Story of Inspirational Sisters Who Saved Jewish Escapees from Nazi Germany," ChronicleLive, January 17, 2017, https://www.chroniclelive.co.uk/news/north-east-news/story-inspirational-sisters-who-saved-12464531.

"She said, 'they were'": Anne Sebba, forward to *Safe Passage, 18.*

Chapter 11

"I can't recall": Katie Sanders, "The Women Whose Secret Work Helped Win World War II," *New York Times Magazine,* March 6, 2019, https://www.nytimes.com/2019/03/06/magazine/intelligence-world-war-ii-oss-women.html.

"The team started": Sanders, "The Women Whose Secret Work Helped Win World War II."

"Henry gave me": Sanders, "The Women Whose Secret Work Helped Win World War II."

"That topographic map": Lawrence Dudley, "Who the Spies Really Were," *The Strand Magazine,* December 8, 2019, https://strand mag.com/who-the-spies-really-were/.

"As demand": "Marion Frieswyk: The First Female Cartographer," Central Intelligence Agency News and Information, November 10, 2016, https://www .cia.gov/news-information/featured-story -archive/2016-featured-story-archive/first -female-intel-cartographer.html.

"My parents": Sanders, "The Women Whose Secret Work Helped Win World War II."

"I moved to Worcester": Sanders, "The Women Whose Secret Work Helped Win World War II."

"I said yes": Sanders, "The Women Whose Secret Work Helped Win World War II."

"She said, 'I can't'": Sanders, "The Women Whose Secret Work Helped Win World War II."

"No one ever knew": "Marion Frieswyk: The First Female Cartographer."

"It also meant": "Marion Frieswyk: The First Female Cartographer."

"Maps were critical": "The Big Three," The National WWII Museum, undated, https://www.nationalww2museum.org /war/articles/big-three.

"By the time": Jeremy W. Crampton, *Mapping:*

A Critical Introduction to Cartography and GIS (West Sussex, UK: Wiley Blackwell, 2010).

"Maps as propaganda": Maria Popova, "Magnificent Maps: Cartography as Power, Propaganda, and Art," Brainpickings. org, April 17, 2012, https://www.brain pickings.org/2012/04/17/magnificent-maps -cartography-as-power-propaganda-and -art/.

"The role": Michael N. DeMers, "The Role of Geographers in the Office of Strategic Services" (PowerPoint presentation), University of New Mexico, December 3, 2019, https://www.slideshare.net/akadrgadget /geographers-and-the-oss.

"One historian said": Kirk H. Stone, "Geography's Wartime Service," *Annals of the Association of American Geographers,* vol. 69, no. 1, 1979, 89, https://www.tandfonline.com /doi/abs/10.1111/j.1467–8306.1979.tb01 233.x.

"The theater didn't open": Mark Jones, "The Curtain Rises Again at Ford's Theatre," Boundary Stones (WETA local history blog), January 30, 2018, https://blogs. weta.org/boundarystones/2018/01/30 /curtain-rises-again-fords-theatre.

"Following retirement": "Henry Frieswyk Dies at 76," *Washington Post,* May 7,

1997, https://www.washingtonpost.com/archive/local/1997/05/07/henry-frieswyk-dies-at-76/1c4ce4dc-30ee-46fa-a80e-804614a7939e/.

"Cartographers know": Sanders, "The Women Whose Secret Work Helped Win World War II."

"Only by decisions": Charles Pinck, "75th Anniversary Speech," OSS Society presentation, June 16, 2017, https://m.osssociety.org/pdfs/75TH_ANNIVERSARY_SPEECH.pdf.

"Asked about her work": Missy Ryan, "After a Long Wait World War II Spy service Honored for Daring Acts That Helped Secure Allied Victory," *Stars and Stripes,* March 28, 2018, https://www.stripes.com/news/us/after-a-long-wait-world-war-ii-spy-service-honored-for-daring-acts-that-helped-secure-allied-victory-1.519293.

"She was featured": Judith Tyner, *Women in American Cartography: An Invisible Social History* (Lanham, MD: Lexington Books, 2020), 60–61.

"It explained": "The Central Intelligence Agency Will Be Recruiting at Mary Washington on Thursday March 21," University of Mary Washington, https://cas.umw.edu/geography/2019/02/26/the-central-intelligence-agency-will-be-recruiting-at

-mary-washington-on-thursday-march-21
st/.

"The CIA's 2019 tribute": Tom Neven, "Marion Frieswyk: The First Female OSS Intelligence Cartographer," *Tip of the Spear* (MacDill AFB, FL), February 2019, 10.

Chapter 12

"The work that we": "Betty Bemis Robarts Collection" (AFC/2001/001/35024), Veterans History Project, American Folklife Center, Library of Congress, http://memory.loc.gov/diglib/vhp/story/loc.natlib.afc2001001.35024/.

"Betty was a part": John A. N. Lee, Colin Burke, and Deborah Anderson, "The US Bombes, NCR, Joseph Desch, and 600 WAVES: The First Reunion of the US Naval Computing Machine Laboratory," *IEEE Annals of the History of Computing,* vol. 22, no. 3, July–September 2000, 6, doi.org/10.1109/85.859524.

"Betty was one of": "Women's History Month: Betty Robarts," National Museum of the Mighty Eighth Air Force, undated, https://www.mightyeighth.org/betty-robarts/.

"Her father drove her": "Hall of Fame: Betty Bemis Robarts, 1986," Minnesota State High School Swim Coaches Association (MSHSCA) Swimming and Diving, https://

sites.google.com/view/mshscaswimdive
/hall-of-fame/hall-of-fame-members.

"The Riviera team won": "Hall of Fame: Betty Bemis Robarts, 1986."

"She made the women's": Leslie Moses, "Pooler's Mighty Eighth Museum Seeks 26,000 Handmade Poppies for Wall of Valor," *Savannah Morning News,* April 21, 2018, https://www.savannahnow.com/entertain mentlife/20180421/poolers-mighty-eighth -museum-seeks-26000-handmade-poppies -for-wall-of-valor.

"She said, 'I was'": "Dayton's WWII Role no Longer a Secret," *Dayton Daily News,* August 28, 2016, https://www.dayton dailynews.com/news/local-military /dayton-wwii-role-longer-secret/4pX g9x4wEWAmYZaFD5f8ZO/.

"You know Betty": Stephen Prudhomme, "World War II Vet Made Waves in the Navy and Pool," *Spirit Newspapers,* November 5, 2015, http://thespiritnewspaper .com/world-war-ii-vet-made-waves-in-the -navy-and-pool-p8666–1.htm.

"The Navy rented": "Navigating the WAVES in World War II," *The Sextant,* Naval History and Heritage Command, November 6, 2014, https://usn history.navylive.dodlive.mil/2014/11/06 /navigating-the-waves-in-world-war-ii/.

"She learned": Kathleen Broome Williams, *Grace Hopper: Admiral of the Cyber Sea* (Annapolis, MD: Naval Institute Press, 2012), 22.

"We are learning": "Navigating the WAVES in World War II."

"More than 86,000": Donna Cipolloni, "Remembering Navy WAVES During Women's History Month," Department of Defense News Service, March 3, 2017, https://www.defense.gov/Explore /News/Article/Article/1102371 /remembering-navy-waves-during -womens-history-month/#:~:text=On%20 July%2030%2C%201942%2C%20 President,male%20personnel%20for%20 sea%20duty.

"The Navy's cryptanalysis": Megan Harris, "Breaking Codes and Glass Ceilings in Wartime Washington," Folklife Today, American Folklife Center & Veterans History Project, Library of Congress, Marcy 14, 2018, https://blogs.loc .gov/folklife/2018/03/breaking-codes-and -glass-ceilings-in-wartime-washington/.

"In the Pacific decryption": Liza Mundy, *Code Girls: The Untold Story of the American Women Code Breakers of World War II* (New York: Hachette Books, 2017), 190.

"When the lecture": Stephen Budiansky, *Battle*

of Wits: The Complete Story of Codebreaking in World War II (New York: Simon & Schuster, 2000), 263.

"In the following days": Mundy, *Code Girls: The Untold Story of the American Women Code Breakers of World War II,* 17.

"Period": Moses, "Pooler's Mighty Eighth Museum Seeks 26,000 Handmade Poppies for Wall of Valor."

"Don't think we won't": "Betty Bemis Robarts Collection."

"If they didn't know": Mundy, *Code Girls: The Untold Story of the American Women Code Breakers of World War II,* 260.

"One of the Navy": "Soldering the Bombe Wheels: Betty Bemis Robarts," November 21, 2017, https://www.youtube.com /watch?v=SR_UXvpJHRo.

"I got pretty good": Prudhomme, "World War II Vet Made Waves in the Navy and Pool."

"There was a diagram": Mundy, *Code Girls: The Untold Story of the American Women Code Breakers of World War II,* 263; "Deborah Anderson: An Oral History Conducted in 2013 by Kelsey Irvin," IEEE History Center, Hoboken, NJ, https://ethw .org/Oral-History:Deborah_Anderson.

"Their ability": Lee, Burke, and Anderson, "The US Bombes, NCR, Joseph Desch,

and 600 WAVES," 10.

"Once the results": "History of the Nebraska Avenue Complex," Department of Homeland Security, undated, https://www.dhs.gov/history-nac.

"In nearby Virginia": "Code Girls and Arlington Hall: A Diverse History," Arlington Public Library, https://library.arlingtonva.us/2017/10/24/code-girls-and-arlington-hall-a-diverse-history/.

"Gradually": Mundy, *Code Girls: The Untold Story of the American Women Code Breakers of World War II*, 288; "Deborah Anderson: An Oral History."

"Ed and other": "Edward Watson Robarts," *Savannah Morning News*, August 24, 2009, legacy.com/obituaries/savannah/obituary.aspx?n=edward-watson-robarts&pid=1318 17333.

"She hitched": Mundy, *Code Girls: The Untold Story of the American Women Code Breakers of World War II*, 346.

"On Valentine's Day": Sam Bauman, "WWII Veteran Shares Her Love Story Ahead of Valentine's Day," WTOC News, February 13, 2020, https://www.wtoc.com/2020/02/13/wwii-veteran-shares-her-love-story-ahead-valentines-day/.

"They went on": "Hall of Fame: Betty Bemis Robarts, 1986."

"Its more for me": Tim Guidera, "WTOC Senior Active: Betty Robarts," WTOC News, October 21, 2013, https://www.wtoc.com/story/23747880/senior-active-betty-robarts/.

"The secrecy oath": Jason Fagone, *The Woman Who Smashed Codes: A True Story of Love, Spies, and the Unlikely Heroine Who Outwitted America's Enemies* (New York: Harper Collins, 2017), 319.

"I believe": Mundy, *Code Girls: The Untold Story of the American Women Code Breakers of World War II*, 31.

"In fact, the program": Lee, Burke, and Anderson, "The US Bombes, NCR, Joseph Desch, and 600 WAVES," 11.

"You talk about": "Deborah Anderson: An Oral History."

"At the Reunion's farewell": "Keeping the Secret: The WAVES and NCR," Dayton History Books Online, https://www.daytonhistorybooks.com/page/page/1482151.htm.

"Their contributions": Lee, Burke, and Anderson, "The US Bombes, NCR, Joseph Desch, and 600 WAVES," 11.

"I cried": "Dayton's WWII Role No Longer a Secret."

"I only wish": "Betty Bemis Robarts Collection."

"Twenty-four years": Kaylah Jackson, "WWII

Women Code Breakers Hold First Reunion in over 70 Years," ConnectingVets.com, March 25, 2019, https://connectingvets.radio.com/articles/womens-history-month-female-wwii-veterans-have-their-first-reunion-over-70-years?fbclid=IwAR1LxKAXqKQgxMBwvJ97p5TNFJQ_T08CIDxnGGqis3YbM9hhd73IHN5ufdI.

"It's hard for me": "Dayton's WWII Role No Longer a Secret."

Chapter 13

"Worry about": Steve Long, "WWII WASP with Pine Ridge Roots: 'A Long the Way,'" KEVN Black Hills Fox, March 1, 2016, https://www.blackhillsfox.com/content/news/WWII-WASP-with-Pine-Ridge-roots--A-Long-the-Way-370746721.html

"There were two": "History of Reagan National Airport," Reagan National website, undated, https://www.flyreagan.com/dca/history-reagan-national-airport.

"She looked": Aliana Beautiful Bald Eagle, "Millie Rexroat: A Pioneer for Women in Aviation and in Life," *West River Eagle,* May 29, 2019, https://www.westrivereagle.com/articles/millie-rexroat-a-pioneer-for-women-in-aviation-and-in-life/.

"My mother": Long, "WWII WASP with

Pine Ridge Roots: 'A Long the Way.'"

"In 1939, she wrote": Patricia O'Connell Pearson, *Fly Girls: The Daring American Women Pilots Who Helped Win WWII* (New York: Simon & Shuster, 2018), 246.

"This is not": Eleanor Roosevelt, "My Day, September 1, 1942," *The Eleanor Roosevelt Papers Digital Edition* (2017), https://www2.gwu.edu/~erpapers/myday/display doc.cfm?_y=1942&_f=md056279.

"They were also": "WW2 Spitfire Pilot Mary Ellis Given Freedom of Isle of Wight," BBC News, January 18, 2018, https://www.bbc.com/news/uk-england-hampshire-42731003.

"Classes included": Beautiful Bald Eagle, "Millie Rexroat: A Pioneer for Women in Aviation and in Life."

"After all": Pearson, *Fly Girls: The Daring American Women Pilots Who Helped Win WWII*, 74.

"During advanced training": Beautiful Bald Eagle, "Millie Rexroat: A Pioneer for Women in Aviation and in Life."

"after the snake incident": Amy Nathan, *Yankee Doodle Gals: Women Pilots of World War II* (Washington, DC: National Geographic Society, 2001), 36.

"wishing well": Nathan, *Yankee Doodle Gals: Women Pilots of World War II*, 42.

"What could be better?": Ola Mildred

Rexroat, "Ola Rexroat Oral History Interview," Woman's Collection, Texas Woman's University, September 8, 2006, https://twudigital.contentdm.oclc.org /digital/collection/p214coll2/search/search term/Oral%20History!Rexroat/field /colleb!all/mode/exact!all/conn/and!all /order/nosort/ad/asc.

"Dahl, a former": Walton Rawls, *Disney Dons Dogtags: The Best of Disney Military Insignia from World War II* (New York: Abbeville Publishing Group, 1992), 29-30.

"Fifi": Maureen Russell, "Women Airforce Service Pilots (WASP)," The Women of Action Network (WON), undated, http://www.woa.tv/articles/hi_wasp.html.

"Hazel Ying Lee": Nathan, *Yankee Doodle Gals: Women Pilots of World War II,* 27.

"Seventy years later": Nathan, *Yankee Doodle Gals: Women Pilots of World War II,* 27.

"Worry about": Long, "WWII WASP with Pine Ridge Roots: 'A Long the Way.'"

"big problem for me": Nick Penzenstadler, "Last Surviving South Dakota WASP, 'Sexy Rexy,' Recalls World War II Service," *Rapid City Journal,* Nov. 11, 2010, https://rapidcityjournal.com/news/last-surviving -south-dakota-wasp-sexy-rexy-recalls -world-war-ii-service/article_a61be93c -ed44-11df-8e3e-001cc4c002e0.html.

"There was prejudice": Long, "WWII WASP with Pine Ridge Roots: 'A Long the Way.'"

"These planes": Pearson, *Fly Girls: The Daring American Women Pilots Who Helped Win WWII,* 105.

"I'm very happy": Katherine Sharp Landdeck, *The Women with Silver Wings: The Inspiring True Story of the Women Airforce Service Pilots of World War II* (New York: Crown Publishers, 2020), 244.

"When we needed you": Beautiful Bald Eagle, "Millie Rexroat: A Pioneer for Women in Aviation and in Life."

"We were devastated": Beautiful Bald Eagle, "Millie Rexroat: A Pioneer for Women in Aviation and in Life."

"WASP records were sealed": Susan Stamberg, "Female WWII Pilots: The Original Fly Girls," *Morning Edition,* National Public Radio (NPR), March 9, 2010, https://www.npr.org/2010/03/09/123773525/female-wwii-pilots-the-original-fly-girls.

"It's the first time": Pete Mecca, "A Veteran's Story," *Clayton News Daily,* March 3, 2019, https://www.news-daily.com/features/a-veteran-s-story/article_6db721ab-5fc7-521a-b1fb-ab84e2753cd8.html.

"G.I. Bill Improvement Act": Long, "WWII WASP with Pine Ridge Roots: 'A Long the Way.'"

"Along with the museum": Travis Monday, *Wings, WASP & Warriors* (Morrisville, NC: Lulu Enterprises, 2005), 156.

"Our service": Beautiful Bald Eagle, "Millie Rexroat: A Pioneer for Women in Aviation and in Life."

"loving, caring person": "Ola Mildred Rexroat: The Only Native American Woman to Serve in the Women Airforce Service Pilots," White Wolf Pack, http://www.whitewolfpack.com/2016/11/ola-mildred-rexroat-only-native.html.

"I counted": Erin Miller, *Final Flight Final Fight: My Grandmother, the WASP, and Arlington National Cemetery* (Silver Spring, MD: 4336 Press, 2019), iii.

"Everything my mother": Airman 1st Class Donald C. Knechtel, "Ellsworth AFB Airfield Ops Building Renamed in Honor of WASP," Air Force News, October 4, 2017, https://www.edwards.af.mil/News/Air-Force-News/Air-Force-Features/Article/1333839/ellsworth-afb-airfield-ops-building-renamed-in-honor-of-wasp/.

"If I had to": Long, "WWII WASP with Pine Ridge Roots: 'A Long the Way.'"

"I'm sure": Landdeck, *The Women with Silver Wings: The Inspiring True Story of the Women Airforce Service Pilots of World War II*, 244.

Chapter 14

"It felt like": Kate Nolan, "Kate Nolan, WWII Combat Nurse," interview by Susan Stamberg, National Public Radio (NPR), May 28, 2004, https://www.npr.org/templates /story/story.php?storyId=191374.

"Flight nurses routinely": Evelyn M. Monahan and Rosemary Neidel-Greenlee, *And If I Perish: Frontline U.S. Army Nurses in World War II* (New York: Anchor Books, 2003), 389.

"We didn't have time": Katherine Nolan, "Interview with Katherine Nolan," interview by James Triesler, The Veterans of the Battle of the Bulge Conference, September 2009, http://www.ittookawar.com /Interviews/Nolan%20Interview/Nolan _Interview.htm.

"It was a lot": Nolan, "Interview with Katherine Nolan."

"They had Rolls-Royce": Nolan, "Interview with Katherine Nolan."

"We were with Patton": Nolan, "Interview with Katherine Nolan."

"We got hit": Nolan, "Interview with Katherine Nolan."

"The Chain of Evacuation": Judith A. Bellafaire, *The Army Nurse Corps: A Commemoration of World War II Service*, U.S. Army Center for Military History, January

1, 1993, https://history.army.mil/books/wwii/72–14/72–14.HTM.

"You have to get": Nolan, "Kate Nolan, WWII Combat Nurse."

"We had done it": Nolan, "Kate Nolan, WWII Combat Nurse."

"Of course, we had": Nolan, "Interview with Katherine Nolan."

"He started bossing": Nolan, "Interview with Katherine Nolan."

"Quickly the cots": Nolan, "Kate Nolan, WWII Combat Nurse."

"The patients made": Nolan, "Kate Nolan, WWII Combat Nurse."

"Red Ball": David P. Colley, "On the Road to Victory: The Red Ball Express," History Net.com, undated, https://www.historynet.com/red-ball-express.

"Headlights blazing": Nolan, "Kate Nolan, WWII Combat Nurse."

"five major campaigns": "Katherine M. Flynn Nolan Collection (AFC/2001/001/63598)," Veterans History Project, American Folklife Center, Library of Congress, http://memory.loc.gov/diglib/vhp/bib/63598.

"a real love story": Telephone conversation with Steve Nolan, May 9, 2020.

"It felt like": Nolan, "Kate Nolan, WWII Combat Nurse."

"Her uncle had saved": "Battle of the Bulge

Remembered: Kate Nolan," Honor and Remembrance (video by Brett Flashnik), The American Legion, undated, https://www.legion.org/honor/battleofthebulge.

"I know exactly": Susan Stamberg, "Mother, Son Share Experiences of War," *Morning Edition,* National Public Radio (NPR), September 24, 2007, https://www.npr.org /templates/story/story.php?storyId=14627960.

"over half served": Linda Ford, "A Look Back: Worcester Hahnemann Hospital School of Nursing (WHHSON)," WHHSON Legacy site, September 10, 2010, http://whhson.tripod.com/our_history.htm.

"Another grandson became": Email from Kate Nolan's daughter, Mary Battaglia, April 24, 2020.

Chapter 15

"I have opened": Charity Adams Earley, *One Woman's Army: A Black Officer Remembers the WAC* (College Station, TX: Texas A&M University Press, 1989), 214.

"I had learned": Earley, *One Woman's Army: A Black Officer Remembers the WAC,* 100.

"ten percenters": Dr. Kelly A. Spring, "Charity Adams Earley," National Women's History Museum, 2017, https://www .womenshistory.org/education-resources /biographies/charity-earley.

"it was time": Spring, "Charity Adams Earley."

"Later she said": Earley, *One Woman's Army: A Black Officer Remembers the WAC*, 120.

"vote of confidence": Cheryl Mullenbach, *Double Victory: How African American Women Broke Race and Gender Barriers to Help Win World War II* (Chicago: Chicago Review Press, 2017), 110.

"There's only one": Charity Adams Earley, "LTC Charity Adams, Oral History, 1990," interview by Brig. General (Ret) Pat Foote, Women's Army Corps Museum History Project, 1990, https://www.you tube.com/watch?v=L3snVXlW5ng.

"Too late": Earley, *One Woman's Army: A Black Officer Remembers the WAC*, 139.

"A second contingent": Kathleen Fargey, "6888th Central Postal Directory Battalion," U.S. Army Center of Military History, February 2014, https://history.army .mil/html/topics/afam/6888thPBn/index .html.

"Charity established": Early, "LTC Charity Adams, Oral History, 1990."

"seven million Americans": Kathleen Fargey, "Women of the 6888th Central Postal Directory Battalion," The Buffalo Soldier Educational and Historical Committee, February 14, 2014, https://www

.womenofthe6888th.org/the-6888th.

"It was tedious": Shahan Russell, "Charity Edna Adams — the Highest Ranking African-American Woman During WWII," War History Online, March 18, 2018, https://www.warhistoryonline.com /world-war-ii/charity-edna-adams-woman -wwii.html.

"The general backed down": Joseph Williams, "Meet Charity Adams Earley, the Highest-Ranking African American Female Officer of World War II," Allthatsinteresting.com, January 9, 2020, https://allthatsinteresting .com/charity-adams-earley.

"White GIs": Early, "LTC Charity Adams, Oral History, 1990."

"I'm so sorry": Earley, *One Woman's Army: A Black Officer Remembers the WAC,* 155.

"People are people": Earley, *One Woman's Army: A Black Officer Remembers the WAC,* 156.

"beauty salon": Carole Sears Botsch, "Charity Edna Adams Earley," African-Americans and South Carolina, University of South Carolina, June 10, 2002, https://polisci .usca.edu/aasc/earley.htm.

"Again, the Six Triple": Fargey, "6888th Central Postal Directory Battalion."

"When that silver oak": Russell, "Charity Edna Adams — The Highest Ranking

African-American Woman During WWII."

"I'd been": Early, "LTC Charity Adams, Oral History, 1990."

"fought the greatest": Col. Cole Kingseed, "The GI Generation: Valor Was Common Through the Ranks." *ARMY* Magazine, vol. 70, no. 5 (April 2020), 48–50.

"they moved back": Williams, "Meet Charity Adams Earley, the Highest-Ranking African American Female Officer of World War II."

"She served": Botsch, "Charity Edna Adams Early."

"Both of her": Spring, "Charity Adams Earley."

"They knew": Brenda L. Moore, *To Serve My Country, To Serve My Race: The Story of the Only African-American WACs Stationed Overseas During World War II* (New York: New York University Press, 1996), 200–201.

"Their greatest legacy": Neil Genzlinger, "Millie Veasey, Part of Trailblazing Unit in WWII, Dies at 100," *New York Times,* March 21, 2018, https://www.nytimes.com/2018/03/21/obituaries/millie-veasey-part-of-trailblazing-unit-in-wwii-dies-at-100.html.

"She remarked": Earley, *One Woman's Army: A Black Officer Remembers the WAC,* back cover.

"When I talk": Richard Goldstein, "Charity Adams Earley, Black Pioneer in Wacs, Dies at 83," *New York Times,* January 22, 2002, https://www.nytimes.com/2002/01/22/us /charity-adams-earley-black-pioneer-in -wacs-dies-at-83.html.

"My mother was always": Beth A. Warrington, "New Monument Honors All-Female, African American Battalion," Army University Press (U.S. Army), February 4, 2019, https://www.army.mil/article/216907/new _monument_honors_all_female_african _american_battalion.

"The legacy": "Sen. Moran Announces Award for Women of 6888th Central Postal Directory Battalion," *The Times — Pottawatomie County, KS,* March 8, 2019, http://www.wamegotimes.com/politics/sen -moran-announces-award-for-women-of -th-central-postal/article_086bc6ba-41cf -11e9-888f-131ce5ea7ec7.html.

"The film continued": The Six Triple Eight: No Mail, No Morale, Lincoln Penny Films, 2019, http://lincolnpennyfilms.com/index .php/the-six-triple-eight.

Chapter 16

"Many of us": Eleanor Roosevelt, "Speech on V-J Day — August 18, 1945," Iowa State University, Carrie Chapman Catt Center for

Women and Politics, March 21, 2017, https://
awpc.cattcenter.iastate.edu/2017/03/21
/speech-on-v-j-day-aug-18-1945/.

"General Eisenhower felt": Stephen E. Ambrose, *D-Day June 6, 1944: The Climactic Battle of World War II* (New York: Simon & Schuster, 1994), 488.

"Public opinion wouldn't": Tim O'Melia, "Ladies Courageous Flew into Blue in WWII," *Palm Beach Post-Times* (Palm Beach, CA), October 2, 1976.

"starred in a movie": *Pat and Mike*, directed by George Cukor (Burbank, CA: MGM, June 13, 1952).

"He emphasized": James R. Clapper and Trey Brown, *Facts and Fears: Hard Truths From a Life in Intelligence* (New York: Penguin Random House, 2018), 18.

"Mothers told": "WW2: Did the War Change Life for Women?" BBC Teach, 2020, https://www.bbc.co.uk/teach/did-ww2-change-life-for-women/zbktwty.

"The first wave": History.com Editors, "Baby Boomers," A&E Television Networks, June 7, 2019, https://www.history.com/topics/1960s/baby-boomers-1.

"Equality of rights": The Learning Network, "March 22, 1972: Equal Rights Amendment for Women Passed by Congress," *New York Times Learning Network*, March

22, 2012, https://learning.blogs.nytimes.com/2012/03/22/march-22-1972-equal-right-amendment-for-women-passed-by-congress/.

"couldn't sleep": Nolan, "Kate Nolan, WWII Combat Nurse."

"For hundreds": History.com Editors, "PTSD and Shell Shock," A&E Television Networks, August 21, 2018, https://www.history.com/topics/inventions/history-of-ptsd-and-shell-shock.

"From the beginning": Keith O'Brien, *Fly Girls: How Five Daring Women Defied All Odds and Made Aviation History* (New York: Houghton Mifflin Harcourt, 2018), 246.

Chapter 17

"a place of deep": Henry Allen, "Holocaust Museum Dedicated with Hope," *Washington Post*, April 23, 1993, https://www.washingtonpost.com/archive/politics/1993/04/23/holocaust-museum-dedicated-with-hope/95ee7fd4-9fc2-48e3-9950-4fdf55832365/.

"The museum is housed": "Our Story," Safe Haven Holocaust Refugee Shelter Museum, undated, https://www.safehavenmuseum.com/story.

"In the 1980s": Hugh Whitmore, *Breaking the Code* (New York: Samuel French,

1987), https://www.concordtheatricals.com/p/2217/breaking-the-code.

"Released in 2009": "Ahead of Time: The Extraordinary Journey of Ruth Gruber," The National Center for Jewish Film, Brandeis University, 2009, http://www.jewishfilm.org/Catalogue/films/aheadoftime.htm.

"It was released": The Six Triple Eight: No Mail, No Morale, Lincoln Penny Films, 2019, http://lincolnpennyfilms.com/index.php/the-six-triple-eight.

"The documentary": General Aviation News Staff, "Filming Begins on WASP Documentary," General Aviation News, August 11, 2018, https://generalaviationnews.com/2018/08/11/filming-begins-on-wasp-documentary/.

"Although the WASP": Amy Nathan, *Yankee Doodle Gals: Women Pilots of World War II* (Washington, DC: National Geographic Society, 2001), 5.

"By 2017": Dalya Alberge, "Spy Mystery of British Sisters Who Helped Jewish Refugees Flee the Nazis," *The Guardian,* November 4, 2017, https://www.theguardian.com/world/2017/nov/05/ida-louise-cook-sisters-helped-jewish-refugees-flee-nazis-spy-mystery-film.

"Another production": "Courting Danger," IMDb Announcement, June 7, 2017,

https://www.imdb.com/title/tt6731098/.

"It gives more urgency": Rick Atkinson, "V-E Day Forged a World Still Worth Defending," *Wall Street Journal,* May 1, 2020, https:// www.wsj.com/articles/v-e-day-forged-a -world-still-worth-defending-11588341627.

"By the fall": Michael Melia, "Nominations to Military Academies on the Rise for Women," Associated Press, July 23, 2019, https://www.military.com/daily-news /2019/07/23/nominations-military- academies-rise-women.html.

"There were hundreds": "The Women Who Shaped The World," The Future Mapping Company, August 31, 2019, https://futuremaps.com/blogs/news/the -women-who-shaped-the-world.

"one out of every 5,623": Mireille Goyer, "Five Decades of American Female Pilots Statistics: How Did We Do?" Women of Aviation Week, March 2010, https:// womenofaviationweek.org/five-decades -of-women-pilots-in-the-united-states -how-did-we-do/.

"Given that": "Quick Facts, Women in the Civilian Labor Force 2014–2018," United States Census Bureau, https://www.census .gov/quickfacts/fact/table/US/LFE046218.

"I was in the 9th": Miller, *Final Flight Final Fight: My Grandmother, the WASP, and*

Arlington National Cemetery, iii.

"The time has come": Ernesto Londoño, "Pentagon Removes Ban on Women in Combat," *Washington Post,* January 24, 2013, https://www.washingtonpost.com/world/national-security/pentagon-to-remove-ban-on-women-in-combat/2013/01/23/6cba86f6-659e-11e2-85f5-a8a9228e55e7_story.html.

"I remembered the WASPs": Nathan, *Yankee Doodle Gals: Women Pilots of World War II,* 5.

"Another first": Michael Johnson, ed., "Celebrating Women's History Month: Most Recent Female Astronauts," NASA.gov., April 14, 2020, https://www.nasa.gov/mission_pages/station/research/news/whm-recent-female-astronauts.

"ingredients for success": Laura Morgan Roberts, Anthony J. Mayo, Robin J. Ely, and David A. Thomas, "Beating the Odds," *Harvard Business Review,* vol. 96, no. 2, March–April 2018, https://hbr.org/2018/03/beating-the-odds.

"On July 26": "Executive Order 9981: Desegregation of the Armed Forces (1948)," National Archives & Records Administration, https://www.ourdocuments.gov/doc.php?flash=false&doc=84.

"That number continues": Judith Warner,

Nora Ellmann, and Diana Boesch, "The Women's Leadership Gap," Center for American Progress, November 20, 2018, https://www.americanprogress.org/issues/women/reports/2018/11/20/461273/womens-leadership-gap-2/.

"I remain": Serena Davies, "The Refugee Who Taught Prince Charles to Love opera," *The Telegraph,* May 25, 2020, https://www.telegraph.co.uk/opera/what-to-see/refugee-taught-prince-charles-love-opera/.

"Six months later": Eleni Schirmer, "The Mighty Pens of Women's Tennis: The Letter Legacy of Alice Marble and Venus Williams," Women's History Month, 2016, ESPN, March 17, 2016.

"There is still": "Fellowships at Auschwitz for the Study of Professional Ethics (FASPE): Our Mission History," FASPE.com, 2020, https://www.faspe-ethics.org/about-us/#missionhistory.

"Forty-seven": "Women in the U.S. Congress 2020," Center for American Women and Politics (CAWP), Eagleton Institute of Politics, Rutgers University, 2020, https://cawp.rutgers.edu/women-us-congress-2020.

"But as I say": Karen Tumulty, "A Troublemaker with a Gavel," *Washington Post,* March 25, 2020, https://www.washingtonpost.com/opinions/2020/03/25/how

-nancy-pelosis-unlikely-rise-turned-her
-into-most-powerful-woman-us-history/?ar
c404=true.

"As of March": Warner, Ellmann, and Boesch,
"The Women's Leadership Gap."

"An Oxford-educated chemist": "Margaret
Thatcher Sworn in as Britain's First Female
Prime Minister: This Day in History, May
4, 1979," A&E Television Networks, May
1, 2020, https://www.history.com/this-day
-in-history/margaret-thatcher-sworn-in.

"Another chemist": CNN Editorial Research, "Angela Merkel Fast Facts,"
CNN World, July 10, 2020, https://
www.cnn.com/2012/12/30/world/europe
/angela-merkel---fast-facts.

"The current PM": Uri Friedman, "New
Zealand's Prime Minister May Be the
Most Effective Leader on the Planet,"
The Atlantic, April 19, 2020, https://www
.theatlantic.com/politics/archive/2020/04
/jacinda-ardern-new-zealand-leadership
-coronavirus/610237/.

"The report aims": Nikki Wentling, "Commission: Women Should Be Eligible for
the Draft," *Stars and Stripes,* March 25,
2020, https://www.stripes.com/news/us
/commission-women-should-be-eligible
-for-the-draft-1.623651.

"In November 2020": Lisa Lerer and

Sydney Ember, "Kamala Harris Makes History as First Woman and Woman of Color as Vice President," *New York Times,* November 7, 2020, https://www.nytimes.com/2020/11/07/us/politics/kamala-harris.html.

Chapter 18

"We can't save": Jessica Corbett, "Teen Climate Activist to Crowd of Thousands: 'We Can't Save the World by Playing by the Rules Because the Rules Have to Change,'" Common Dreams, October 20, 2018, https://www.commondreams.org/news/2018/10/20/teen-climate-activist-crowd-thousands-we-cant-save-world-playing-rules-because-rules.

"The world is": Adena Bernstein Astrowsky, *Living Among the Dead: My Grandmother's Holocaust Survival Story of Love and Strength* (Oegstgeest, Netherlands: Amsterdam Publishers, 2020), 233.

"You're not trying": Lauren Gambino, "Greta Thunberg to Congress: 'You're Not Trying Hard Enough. Sorry.'" *The Guardian,* September 17, 2019, https://www.theguardian.com/environment/2019/sep/17/greta-thunberg-to-congress-youre-not-trying-hard-enough-sorry.

"their irresponsible behavior": The Week

Staff, "Greta Thunberg's Climate Crusade," *The Week,* May 4, 2019, https://theweek.com/articles/839011/greta-thunbergs-climate-crusade.

"I realized the essence": Malala Yousafzai, "Duty," The Columnists, *WSJ. Magazine,* June 8, 2020, 6.

"I was nowhere near": Taku Mushonga, "Serena Williams and Coco Gauff: From Inspiration to Dance Partners," SportRazzi.com, January 22, 2020, https://sportrazzi.com/2020/01/serena-williams-and-coco-gauff-from-inspiration-to-dance-partners-watch-video/.

"I wanted to share": Elizabeth Smart, *My Story* (New York: St. Martin's Griffin, 2013), 316.

"Never be afraid": Margaret Talbot, "Gone Girl: The Extraordinary Resilience of Elizabeth Smart," *The New Yorker,* October 14, 2013, https://www.newyorker.com/magazine/2013/10/21/gone-girl-2.

"I definitely think": Elena Nicolaou, "Cyntoia Brown-Long Has Been Thriving Since Her Prison Release," *O: The Oprah Magazine,* April 29, 2020, https://www.oprahmag.com/entertainment/a32288695/where-is-cyntoia-brown-now.

"Her one act": Michael Coard, "8 Things You Didn't Know about Philadelphia's

New Police Chief," *Philadelphia Tribune,* January 6, 2020, https://www.phillytrib .com/commentary/michaelcoard/coard -8-things-you-didnt-know-about-phillys -new-police-chief/article_ff1edaf7-2c2b -5862-a067-618401b2ff7c.html.

"Build trust": Sharrie Williams, "Sharrie Williams Talks to Commissioner Danielle Outlaw about her Vision for the Philadelphia Police Department," WPVI TV, Philadelphia, PA, February 13, 2020, https://6abc .com/commissioner-danielle-outlaw -police-philadelphia-portland/5924995/.

"In June 2020": Elizabeth Wolfe and Saeed Ahmed, "Danielle Outlaw Was the First African-American Woman to Be Portland's Police Chief. Now She's Philadelphia's First Black Female Commissioner," CNN News, December 31, 2019, https:// www.cnn.com/2019/12/31/us/danielle -outlaw-first-african-american-woman -police-commissioner-trnd/index.html.

"It's okay to know": Azmia Magane, "Congresswoman-Elect Ilhan Omar Shares Advice for Young People and How She Deals with Islamophobia," *Teen Vogue,* November 9, 2018, https://www.teenvogue.com/story /ilhan-omar-shares-how-she-deals-with -islamophobia.

"Everybody has failures": Susie Gharib, "Land

O' Lakes CEO Beth Ford Says 'Resilience' Is Key to Her Success," *Fortune,* February 19, 2019, https://fortune.com/2019/02/19/land-o-lakes-ceo-beth-ford-leadership-on-leading/.

"I haven't had": "Aimee Mullins Quotes and Sayings," Inspiringquotes.us, https://www.inspiringquotes.us/author/6316-aimee-mullins.

"Distinguished Flying Cross": Brandon O'Connor, "Capt Lindsay Heisler Receives 2019 Nininger Award for Actions in Afghanistan," *Army News Service,* October 28, 2019, https://www.army.mil/article/229085/capt_lindsay_heisler_receives_2019_nininger_award_for_actions_in_afghanistan.

"I'm going to be": Science Fair, National Geographic Documentary Film, October 19, 2018, https://films.nationalgeographic.com/science-fair/.

"This next generation": Gayle Jo Carter, "How One Woman Inspired Seven Grand Awards in Science," Aspireforequality.com, January 15, 2019, https://www.aspireforequality.com/newsandviews/2019/01/15/serena-mccallas-inspiring-greatness/.

"I believe": Ramida Juengpaisal, "I Am Generation Equality: Ramida 'Jennie' Juengpaisal, Designer and Developer of a COVID-19

Tracker in Thailand," UNWomen.org, April 22, 2020, https://www.unwomen.org /en/news/stories/2020/4/i-am-generation -equality-ramida-juengpaisal.

"Today we need": "Queen Elizabeth II: Christmas Broadcast," December 25, 1957, https:// www.royal.uk/christmas-broadcast-1957.

BIBLIOGRAPHY AND REFERENCES

Books

Ambrose, Stephen E. *D-Day: June 6, 1944: The Climactic Battle of World War II*. New York: Simon & Schuster, 1994.

Atwood, Kathryn J. *Women Heroes of World War II: 26 Stories of Espionage, Sabotage, Resistance, and Rescue*. Chicago: Chicago Review Press, 2011.

Bell, Richard. *The Last Veterans of World War II: Portraits and Memories*. Atglen, PA: Schiffer Publishing Ltd., 2017.

Bellafaire, Judith A., *The Army Nurse Corps: A Commemoration of World War II Service*. Washington, DC: U.S. Army Center for Military History, January 1, 1993.

Bergin, Bob. *OSS Undercover Girl Elizabeth P. McIntosh: An Interview*. Fairfax, VA: Banana Tree Press, 2012.

Bernstein Astrowsky, Adena. *Living Among the Dead: My Grandmother's Holocaust Survival Story of Love and Strength*. Oegstgeest,

Netherlands: Amsterdam Publishers, 2020.

Boom, Corrie Ten. *The Hiding Place*. Grand Rapids, MI: Chosen Books, 1971 and 1984.

Budiansky, Stephen. *Battle of Wits: The Complete Story of Codebreaking in World War II*. New York: Simon & Schuster, 2000.

Camp, Dick. *Shadow Warriors: The Untold Stories of American Special Operations During World War II*. Minneapolis, MN: Zenith Press, 2013.

"Chapter 2: Wartime Organization for Unconventional Warfare," *The OSS (1942–1945)*, The National Park Service.

Cheyney, Arnold B. *Athletes of Purpose: 50 People Who Changed the Face of Sports*. Culver City, CA: Good Year Books, 2000.

Clapper, James R., and Trey Brown. *Facts and Fears: Hard Truths from a Life in Intelligence*. New York: Penguin Random House, 2018.

Cobbs, Elizabeth. *The Hello Girls: America's First Women Soldiers*. Cambridge, MA: Harvard University Press, 2017.

Cook, Ida. *Safe Passage: The Remarkable True Story of Two Sisters Who Rescued Jews from the Nazis*. Ontario: Harlequin, 2008.

Crampton, Jeremy W. *Mapping: A Critical*

Introduction to Cartography and GIS. West Sussex, UK: Wiley Blackwell, 2010.

DeBrosse, Jim, and Colin Burke. *The Secret in Building 26: The Untold Story of How America Broke the Final U-Boat Code*. New York: Random House, 2005.

Distel, Barbara, and Ruth Jakusch. *Concentration Camp Dachau 1933–1945*. Brussels, Belgium: Comité International de Dachau, 1978.

Earley, Charity Adams. *One Woman's Army: A Black Officer Remembers the WAC*. College Station, TX: Texas A&M University Press, 1995.

Eman, Diet. *The Things We Couldn't Say*. Grand Rapids, MI: Wm. B. Eerdmans Publishing Co., 1994.

Escott, Beryl E., Squadron Leader. *The Heroines of SOE: Britain's Secret Women in France F Section*. Stroud, Gloucestershire, UK: The History Press, 2010.

Fagone, Jason. *The Woman Who Smashed Codes: A True Story of Love, Spies, and the Unlikely Heroine Who Outwitted America's Enemies*. New York: Harper Collins, 2017.

Gralley, Craig. *Hall of Mirrors: Virginia Hall: America's Greatest Spy of World War II*. Pisgah Forest, NC: Chrysalis Press, 2019.

Gruber, Paul, ed. *The Metropolitan Opera*

Guide to Recorded Opera. New York: W. W. Norton & Company, 1993.

Gruber, Ruth. *Haven: The Dramatic Story of 1,000 World War II Refugees and How They Came to America*. New York: Open Road Integrated Media, 2002.

Gruber, Ruth. *Inside of Time: My Journey from Alaska to Israel*. New York: Avalon Publishing Company, 2003.

Gruber, Ruth. *Witness: One of the Great Correspondents of the Twentieth Century Tells Her Story*. New York: Schocken Books, 2007.

Landdeck, Katherine Sharp. *The Women with Silver Wings: The Inspiring True Story of the Women Airforce Service Pilots of World War II*. New York: Crown Publishing, 2020.

Lane, Arthur Bliss. *I Saw Poland Betrayed: An American Ambassador Reports to the American People*. Western Islands: Bobs Merrill Co., 1948.

Lucado, Max. *Unshakable Hope: Building Our Lives on the Promises of God*. Nashville, TN: Thomas Nelson, 2018.

Marble, Alice. *Courting Danger: My Adventures in World-Class Tennis, Golden-Age Hollywood, and High-Stakes Spying*. New York: Saint Martin's Press, 1991.

Marble, Alice. *The Road to Wimbledon*. London: W. H. Allen, 1946.

MacDonald, Elizabeth P. *Undercover Girl*. New York: The McMillan Company, 1947.

McCarthy, Linda. *Betty McIntosh: OSS Spy Girl*. Front Royal, VA: History Is a Hoot, Inc., 2012.

McIntosh, Elizabeth P. *The Role of Women in Intelligence. Intelligence Professional Series Number Five*. McLean, VA: The Association of Former Intelligence Officers, 1989.

McIntosh, Elizabeth P. *Sisterhood of Spies: Women of the OSS*. Annapolis, MD: Naval Institute Press, 1998.

McKay, Sinclair. *The Lost World of Bletchley Park: An Illustrated History of the Wartime Codebreaking Centre*. London: Aurum Press, 2013.

Miller, Erin. *Final Flight Final Fight: My Grandmother, the WASP, and Arlington National Cemetery*. Silver Spring, MD: 4336 Press, 2019.

Milton, Giles. *Churchill's Ministry of Ungentlemanly Warfare: The Mavericks Who Plotted Hitler's Defeat*. London: Picador, 2017.

Mitchell, Don. *The Lady Is a Spy: Virginia Hall, World War II Hero of the French Resistance*. New York: Scholastic Focus, 2019.

Monahan, Evelyn M., and Rosemary Neidel-Greenlee. *And If I Perish: Frontline U.S. Army Nurses in World War II*. New York: Random House, 2004.

Monday, Travis. *Wings, WASP & Warriors*. Morrisville, NC: Lulu Enterprises, 2005.

Moore, Brenda L. *To Serve My Country, To Serve My Race: The Story of the Only African-American WACs Stationed Overseas During World War II*. New York: New York University Press, 1996.

Moore, Frank. *Women of the War*. Hartford, CT: S.S. Scranton & Company, 1867.

Moorehead, Caroline. *Village of Secrets: Defying the Nazis in Vichy, France*. New York: Harper Collins, 2014.

Morden, Bettie J. *The Women's Army Corps, 1945–1978*. Washington, DC: Office of the Chief of Military History, Department of the Army, 1990.

Mullenbach, Cheryl. *Double Victory: How African American Women Broke Race and Gender Barriers to Help Win World War II*. Chicago: Chicago Review Press, 2017.

Mundy, Liza. *Code Girls: The Untold Story of the American Women Code Breakers of World War II*. New York: Hachette Books, 2017.

Nathan, Amy. *Yankee Doodle Gals: Women Pilots of World War II*. Washington, DC: National Geographic Society, 2001.

O'Brien, Keith. *Fly Girls: How Five Daring Women Defied All Odds and Made Aviation History*. New York: Houghton Mifflin Harcourt, 2018.

Office of Strategic Services (OSS) Organization and Functions training booklet. OSS Schools and Training Branch, June 1945.

Pearson, Judith L. *Wolves at the Door: The True Story of America's Greatest Female Spy.* Guilford, CT: The Lyons Press, 2005.

Pearson, Patricia O'Connell. *Fly Girls: The Daring American Women Pilots Who Helped Win WWII.* New York: Simon & Schuster, 2018.

Polette, Nancy. *The Spy with the Wooden Leg: The Story of Virginia Hall.* St. Paul, MN: Elva Resa Publishing, LLC, 2012.

Previte, Mary Taylor. *Hungry Ghosts: One Woman's Mission to Change Their World.* Self-published, 1994, 2011.

Purnell, Sonia. *A Woman of No Importance: The Untold Story of the American Spy Who Helped Win World War II.* New York: Penguin Random House, 2019.

Rawls, Walton. *Disney Dons Dogtags: The Best of Disney Military Insignia from World War II.* New York: Abbeville Publishing Group, 1992.

Rose, Sarah. *D-Day Girls: The Spies Who Armed the Resistance, Sabotaged the Nazis, and Helped Win World War II.* New York: Crown Books, 2019.

Shults, Tammie Jo. *Nerves of Steel: How I Followed My Dreams, Earned My Wings, and*

Faced My Greatest Challenge. Nashville, TN: W. Publishing Company, 2019.

Smart, Elizabeth. *My Story.* New York: St. Martins Griffin, 2013.

Sutin, Jack and Rochelle. *Jack and Rochelle: A Holocaust Story of Love and Resistance.* Saint Paul, MN: Graywolf Press, 1995.

Thomas, Gordon, and Greg Lewis. *Shadow Warriors of World War II: The Daring Women of the OSS and SOE.* Chicago: Chicago Review Press, 2017.

Thomas, Roy. *Wonder Woman: The War Years 1941–1945.* New York: Chartwell Books, 2015.

Todd, Ann. *OSS Operation Black Mail: One Woman's Covert War Against the Imperial Japanese Army.* Annapolis, MD: Naval Institute Press, 2017.

Treadwell, Mattie E. *The United States Army in World War II: Special Studies: The Women's Army Corps.* Washington, DC: Office of the Chief of Military History, Department of the Army, 1954.

Turgel, Gena. *I Light a Candle.* London: Grafton Books, 1987.

Tyner, Judith. *Women in American Cartography: An Invisible Social History.* Lanham, MD: Lexington Books, 2020.

Vincent, Isabel. *Hitler's Silent Partners: Swiss Banks, Nazi Gold, and the Pursuit of Justice.*

New York: William Morrow and Company, Inc. 1997.

Waller, Douglas. *Wild Bill Donovan: The Spymaster Who Created the OSS and Modern American Espionage.* New York: Simon & Schuster, 2011.

Weintraub, Robert. *The Divine Miss Marble: A Life of Tennis, Fame, and Mystery.* New York: Dutton, 2020.

Williams, Kathleen Broome. *Grace Hopper: Admiral of the Cyber Sea.* Annapolis, MD: Naval Institute Press, 2012.

Yellin, Emily. *Our Mother's War: American Women at Home and at the Front During World War II.* New York: Simon & Schuster, 2004.

Yu, Maochun. *OSS in China: Prelude to Cold War.* Annapolis, MD: Naval Institute Press, 1996.

Articles

"1941 H2H Tour — Marble, Hardwick, Budge, Tilden." Former Pro Player Talk, Tennis Warehouse, September 29, 2017.

"Activity Report of Virginia Hall." DocsTeach, The National Archives, September 30, 1944.

Advance Media NY Editorial Board. "Ruth Gruber Documented Injustice, Then Did Something about It (Editorial)." Syracuse .com, October 22, 2019.

"Aimee Mullins Quotes and Sayings." Inspiringquotes.us.

Alberge, Dalya. "Spy Mystery of British Sisters Who Helped Jewish Refugees Flee the Nazis." *The Guardian,* November 4, 2017.

"Alice Marble." *Encyclopedia of World Biography,* accessed July 10, 2020 from Encyclopedia.com.

Allen, Henry. "Holocaust Museum Dedicated with Hope." *Washington Post,* April 23, 1993.

Atkinson, Rick. "V-E Day Forged a World Still Worth Defending." *Wall Street Journal,* May 1, 2020.

Atlas, Nava. "Ruth Gruber: Journalist, Documentary Photographer, Humanitarian." LiteraryLadiesGuide.com, October 30, 2016.

Bales, Donnie. "Sopa (Soup) for the Soul: Passing on the Torch of Freedom." Virginia Tech School of Performing Arts News, January 5, 2018.

Balestrieri, Steve. "Virginia Hall, the Famous 'Limping Lady' of the OSS." SOFREP.com, July 13, 2017.

Bard, Mitchell. "Concentration Camps: Vught (Herzogenbusch)," Jewish Virtual Library, undated.

Bauer, Alan. "8-17-45 'I've Been in Love with America from That Day to This."

Haddonfield Sun, May 11–17, 2005.

Bauman, Sam. "WWII Veteran Shares Her Love Story ahead of Valentine's Day." WTOC News, February 13, 2020.

Beautiful Bald Eagle, Aliana. "Millie Rexroat: A Pioneer for Women in Aviation and in Life." *West River Eagle,* May 29, 2019.

Beduya, Jose, and Joe Wilensky. "WWII Era Spy Stephanie Czech Rader '37 Dies at Age 100." *Ezra Update,* Cornell University, January 2016.

Bernard, Diane. "Jews Fleeing the Holocaust Weren't Welcome in the U.S. Then FDR Offered a Refuge to Some." *Washington Post,* May 1, 2019.

Bernstein, Adam. "Stephanie Rader, Undercover Spy in Postwar Europe, Dies at 100." *Washington Post,* January 21, 2016.

Bernstein, Adam. "Elizabeth McIntosh: Journalist Who Became an Agent for the Office of Strategic Services Whose Efforts Were Crucial in the War in the East." *The Independent,* June 16, 2015.

Bernstein, Adam. "Elizabeth McIntosh, Spy Whose Lies Helped Win a War, Dies at 100." *Washington Post,* June 8, 2015.

"Betty Bemis Robarts Collection" (AFC/2001/001/35024). Veterans History Project, American Folklife Center, Library of Congress.

Beyette, Beverly. "A Modern Day Schindler Faces the Consequences." *Los Angeles Times,* August 19, 1998.

"The Big Three." The National WWII Museum, undated.

Blake, Heidi. "Unsung British Heroes of the Holocaust Awarded Medals." *The Telegraph,* March 10, 2010.

"Bonded by Ghetto." *Jewish Journal,* April 24, 2003.

Botsch, Carole Sears. "Charity Edna Adams Earley." African-Americans and South Carolina, University of South Carolina, June 10, 2002.

Brennan, David. "One-Third of Americans Don't Believe 6 Million Jews Were Murdered During the Holocaust." *Newsweek,* April 12, 2018.

Carpenter, Louise. "Ida and Louise: 'They Had Lived for Art." *Granta,* July 2, 2007.

Cart, Julie. "Women's Pioneer Alice Marble Dies: Tennis: As a National Champion in the 30's, She Played a Serve and Volley Game." *Los Angeles Times,* December 14, 1990.

Carter, Gayle Jo. "How One Woman Inspired Seven Grand Awards in Science." Aspireforequality.com, January 15, 2019.

"The Central Intelligence Agency Will Be Recruiting at Mary Washington on

Thursday March 21." University of Mary Washington, February 26, 2019.

Chambers II, Dr. John Whiteclay. "Office of Strategic Services Training During World War II." *Studies in Intelligence* vol. 54, no. 2 (June 2010): 1–26.

Chen, C. Peter. "Richard Heppner." *World War II Database,* June 2015.

Cipolloni, Donna. "Remembering Navy WAVES During Women's History Month." Department of Defense News Service, March 3, 2017.

CNN Editorial Research. "Angela Merkel Fast Facts." CNN World, July 10, 2020.

Coard, Michael. "8 Things You Didn't Know about Philadelphia's New Police Chief." *Philadelphia Tribune,* January 6, 2020.

"Code Girls and Arlington Hall: A Diverse History." Arlington Public Library, undated.

Colley, David P. "On the Road to Victory: The Red Ball Express." HistoryNet.com, undated.

Corbett, Jessica. "Teen Climate Activist to Crowd of Thousands: 'We Can't Save the World by Playing by the Rules Because the Rules Have to Change." Common Dreams, October 20, 2018.

"Courting Danger." IMDb Announcement, June 7, 2017.

Cronin, Bryan. "Comic Book Legends Revealed #333." CBR.com, September 23, 2011.

"Dame Mary Sigillo Barraco." *Virginia Pilot,* December 8, 2019.

Davies, Serena. "The Refugee Who Taught Prince Charles to Love Opera." *The Telegraph,* May 25, 2020.

"Dayton's WWII Role No Longer a Secret." *Dayton Daily News,* August 28, 2016.

"Deborah Anderson: An Oral History Conducted in 2013 by Kelsey Irvin." IEEE History Center, Hoboken, NJ.

"Decades after Duty in OSS and CIA, 'Spy Girls' Find Each Other in Retirement." *The Record,* July 2, 2011.

DeMers, Michael N. "The Role of Geographers in the Office of Strategic Services" (PowerPoint presentation), University of New Mexico, December 3, 2019.

Dudley, Lawrence. "Who the Spies Really Were." *The Strand Magazine,* December 8, 2019.

Dvorak, Petula. "Female Spy Finally Gets the Recognition She Deserved 70 Years Ago," *Washington Post,* June 2, 2016.

"Edward Watson Robarts." *Savannah Morning News,* August 24, 2009.

Fargey, Kathleen. "6888th Central Postal Directory Battalion." U.S. Army Center of

Military History, February 2014.

Fargey, Kathleen. "Women of the 6888th Central Postal Directory Battalion." The Buffalo Soldier Educational and Historical Committee, February 14, 2014.

Farley, Josh. "WWII Documents Reveal Importance of Air Raid Wardens." AP News, July 29, 2018.

"Fellowships at Auschwitz for the Study of Professional Ethics (FASPE): Our Mission History." FASPE.com, 2020.

Ford, Linda. "A Look Back: Worcester Hahnemann Hospital School of Nursing (WHHSON)." WHHSON Legacy site, September 10, 2010.

Friedman, Uri. "New Zealand's Prime Minister May Be the Most Effective Leader on the Planet." The Atlantic, April 19, 2020.

Gambino, Lauren. "Greta Thunberg to Congress: 'You're Not Trying Hard Enough. Sorry.'" The Guardian, September 17, 2019.

General Aviation News Staff. "Filming Begins on WASP Documentary." General Aviation News, August 11, 2018.

Genova, Alexandra. "Groundbreaking Female Spy Finally Gets Legion of Merit on the Day of Her Funeral for Her Services in WWII." Daily Mail, June 5, 2016.

Genzlinger, Neil. "Millie Veasey, Part of Trailblazing Unit in WWII, Dies at 100."

New York Times, March 21, 2018.

Gharib, Susie. "Land O' Lakes CEO Beth Ford Says 'Resilience' Is Key to Her Success." *Fortune* magazine, February 19, 2019.

Goldstein, Richard. "Charity Adams Earley, Black Pioneer in Wacs, Dies at 83." *New York Times,* January 22, 2002.

Goyer, Mireille. "Five Decades of American Female Pilots Statistics: How Did We Do?" Women of Aviation Week, March 2010.

Graham, Kristen A. "Mary T. Previte, Former N.J. Assemblywoman and Concentration Camp Survivor, Dies at 87." *Philadelphia Inquirer,* November 18, 2019.

Guidera, Tim. "WTOC Senior Active: Betty Robarts." WTOC News, October 21, 2013.

Hafner, Katherine. "Dame Mary Barraco, World War II Resistance Fighter Who Suffered Nazi Torture, Dies in Virginia Beach at 96." *Virginian Pilot,* December 12, 2019.

Hagerty, James R. "Polish Holocaust Survivor Heeded Brutal Advice, Then Moved On." *Wall Street Journal,* December 16, 2017.

"Hall of Fame: Betty Bemis Robarts, 1986." Minnesota State High School Swim Coaches Association (MSHSCA) Swimming and Diving.

"Hall of Fame Inductees: Alice Marble." International Tennis Hall of Fame.

"Harold L. Ickes." University of Virginia, MillerCenter.org, undated.

Harris, Megan. "Breaking Codes and Glass Ceilings in Wartime Washington." *Folklife Today*. American Folklife Center & Veterans History Project, Library of Congress, March 14, 2018.

Harris, Shane. "Will America's 100-Year-Old Female Spy Finally Be Recognized for the Hero She Is?" *Daily Beast,* June 26, 2017.

Harris, Shane, and Andrew Desiderio. "America's Toughest Lady Spy Laid to Rest." *Daily Beast,* April 13, 2017.

Henderson, Tony. "The Story of Inspirational Sisters Who Saved Jewish Escapees from Nazi Germany." ChronicleLive, January 17, 2017.

"Henry Frieswyk Dies at 76." *Washington Post,* May 7, 1997.

"Hilda Eisen, Holocaust Survivor, Philanthropist, 100." *The Jewish Journal,* December 7, 2017.

History.com Editors. "Baby Boomers." A&E Television Networks, June 7, 2019.

History.com Editors. "PTSD and Shell Shock." A&E Television Networks, August 21, 2018.

"History of the Nebraska Avenue Complex."

Department of Homeland Security, undated.

Jackson, Kaylah. "WWII Women Code Breakers Hold First Reunion in over 70 Years." ConnectingVets.com, March 25, 2019.

Johnson, Michael, ed. "Celebrating Women's History Month: Most Recent Female Astronauts." NASA.gov, April 14, 2020.

Jones, Mark. "The Curtain Rises Again at Ford's Theatre." *Boundary Stones* (WETA local history blog), January 30, 2018.

Juengpaisal, Ramida. "I Am Generation Equality: Ramida 'Jennie' Juengpaisal, Designer and Developer of a COVID-19 Tracker in Thailand." UNWomen.org, April 22, 2020.

"Katherine M. Flynn Nolan Collection (AFC/2001/001/63598)." Veterans History Project, American Folklife Center, Library of Congress.

"Keeping the Secret: The WAVES and NCR." Dayton History Books Online.

Kingseed, Cole, Colonel. "The GI Generation: Valor Was Common Through the Ranks." *ARMY* Magazine, vol. 70, no. 5 (April 2020): 48–50.

Kish, Tina. "Dame Mary Barraco Dies in Virginia Beach at 96." Non-Commissioned Officers Association (NCOA) News, December 13, 2019.

Knechtel, Donald C., Airman 1st Class. "Ellsworth AFB Airfield Ops Building Renamed in Honor of WASP." *Air Force News,* October 4, 2017.

Kuwalek, Robert, and Weronika Litwin. "Izbica: A Story of a Place." Foundation for the Preservation of Jewish Heritage in Poland, 2007.

Langer, Emily. "Ruth Gruber, Who Accompanied 1,000 Jews to the Shores of the United States during the Holocaust, Dies at 105." *Washington Post,* November 19, 2016.

The Learning Network. "March 22, 1972: Equal Rights Amendment for Women Passed by Congress." *New York Times Learning Network,* March 22, 2012.

Lee, John A. N., Colin Burke, and Deborah Anderson. "The US Bombes, NCR, Joseph Desch, and 600 WAVES: The First Reunion of the US Naval Computing Machine Laboratory." *IEEE Annals of the History of Computing,* vol. 22, no. 3, July–September 2000: 1–15.

Lineberry, Cate. "Wanted: The Limping Lady: The Intriguing and Unexpected True Story of America's Most Heroic — and Most Dangerous Female Spy." *Smithsonian Magazine,* February 2007.

Lion, Patrick. "A Kiss 71 Years in the

Making." *Daily Mail,* July 28, 2016.

Londoño, Ernesto. "Pentagon Removes Ban on Women in Combat." *Washington Post,* January 24, 2013.

Long, Steve. "WWII WASP with Pine Ridge Roots: 'A Long the Way.'" KEVN Black Hills Fox, March 1, 2016.

Magane, Azmia. "Congresswoman-Elect Ilhan Omar Shares Advice for Young People and How She Deals With Islamophobia." *Teen Vogue,* November 9, 2018.

Manby, Christine. "Diet Eman: Dutch Resistance Fighter Who Saved Many Lives in the Second World War." *The Independent,* September 19, 2019.

"Margaret Thatcher Sworn in as Britain's First Female Prime Minister: This Day in History, May 4, 1979." A&E Television Networks, May 1, 2020.

"Marion Frieswyk: The First Female Cartographer." Central Intelligence Agency News and Information, November 10, 2016.

McClellan, Dennis. "Harry Eisen Dies at 95; Norco Ranch Founder." *Los Angeles Times,* July 29, 2012.

McIntosh, Elizabeth P. "Honolulu after Pearl Harbor: A Report Published for the First Time, 71 Years Later." *Washington Post,* December 6, 2012.

Mecca, Pete. "A Veteran's Story." *Clayton News Daily,* March 3, 2019.

Meehan, Chris. "Diet Eman Praised for Her Courage." Christian Reformed Church News, September 10, 2019.

Meier, Barry. "Jewish Groups Fight for Spoils of Swiss Case." *New York Times,* November 29, 1998.

Melia, Michael. "Nominations to Military Academies on the Rise for Women." Associated Press, July 23, 2019.

Morgan, Kate. "Ten Questions: Mary Previte," *SJ Magazine,* September 2005.

Moses, Leslie. "Pooler's Mighty Eighth Museum Seeks 26,000 Handmade Poppies for Wall of Valor." *Savannah Morning News,* April 21, 2018.

Murphy, Philip, Governor. New Jersey Executive Order No. 93, November 22, 2019.

Mushonga, Taku. "Serena Williams and Coco Gauff: From Inspiration to Dance Partners." SportRazzi.com, January 22, 2020.

Na, He, and Ju Chuanjiang. "Weihsien: Life and Death in the Shadow of the Empire of the Sun." *China Daily,* February 20, 2014.

"Navigating the WAVES in World War II." *The Sextant,* Naval History and Heritage Command, November 6, 2014.

Neven, Tom. "Marion Frieswyk: The First

Female OSS Intelligence Cartographer." *Tip of the Spear,* February 2019: 10.

Neven, Tom. "Virginia Hall: The Limping Lady." *Tip of the Spear,* February 2019: 4.

Neven, Tom. "Women in SOF: A Historical Perspective — 'Undercover Girl' Betty McIntosh." *Tip of the Spear,* February 2019: 6.

Nicolaou, Elena. "Cyntoia Brown-Long Has Been Thriving Since Her Prison Release." *O: The Oprah Magazine,* April 29, 2020.

O'Connor, Brandon. "Capt Lindsay Heisler Receives 2019 Nininger Award for Actions in Afghanistan." *Army News Service,* October 28, 2019.

O'Melia, Tim. "Ladies Courageous Flew into Blue in WWII." *Palm Beach Post-Times,* October 2, 1976.

"Ola Mildred Rexroat: The Only Native American Woman to Serve in the Women Airforce Service Pilots." White Wolf Pack.

"Our Story." Safe Haven Holocaust Refugee Shelter Museum, undated.

"Partisan Groups in the Parczew Forests." Holocaust Encyclopedia, U.S. Holocaust Memorial Museum.

Penzenstadler, Nick. "Last Surviving South Dakota WASP, 'Sexy Rexy,' Recalls World War II Service." *Rapid City Journal,* November 11, 2010.

Pinck, Charles. "75th Anniversary Speech." OSS Society presentation, June 16, 2017.

Polo, Susana. "Alice Marble: Tennis Celebrity, Wonder Woman Writer and Spy?" TheMarySue.com, September 23, 2011.

Popova, Maria. "Magnificent Maps: Cartography as Power, Propaganda, and Art." Brainpickings.org, April 17, 2012.

Previte, Mary Taylor. "America Has Heroes: I Know Their Names." Weihsien-Paintings.org, undated.

Previte, Mary Taylor. "A Song of Salvation at Weihsien Prison Camp." Weihsien-Paintings.org, August 25, 1985.

Previte, Mary Taylor. "Ted Nagaki, an American Hero." Japanese American Veterans Association (JAVA.com), April 22, 2013.

Prudhomme, Stephen. "World War II Vet Made Waves in the Navy and Pool." *Spirit Newspapers,* November 5, 2015.

Purnell, Sonja. "Virginia Hall Was America's Most Successful Female WWII Spy. But She Was Almost Kept From Serving." *Time,* April 9, 2019.

"Queen Elizabeth II: Christmas Broadcast." December 25, 1957.

"Quick Facts, Women in the Civilian Labor Force 2014–2018." *United States Census Bureau.*

R., Jacqueline. "The Petticoat Panel: A 1953 Study of the Role of Women in the CIA's Career Service." Special Report Prepared at the Request of the Central Intelligence Agency, Approved for Release October 30, 2013.

"Records Relating to the Katyn Forest Massacre at the National Archives." U.S. Foreign Policy Research, the National Archives, April 8, 2020.

"The Righteous Among the Nations Database." Yad Vashem: The World Holocaust Remembrance Center, undated.

Roberts, Laura Morgan, Anthony J. Mayo, Robin J. Ely, and David J. Thomas. "Beating the Odds." *Harvard Business Review,* vol. 96, no. 2, March–April 2018.

Roosevelt, Eleanor. "My Day, September 1, 1942." *The Eleanor Roosevelt Papers Digital Edition* (2017).

Roosevelt, Eleanor. "Speech on V-J Day — August 18, 1945." Iowa State University, Carrie Chapman Catt Center for Women and Politics, March 21, 2017.

Russell, Maureen. "Women Airforce Service Pilots (WASP)." The Women of Action Network (WON), undated.

Russell, Shahan. "Charity Edna Adams — The Highest Ranking African-American Woman During WWII." War History

Online, March 18, 2018.

Ryan, Missy. "After a Long Wait World War II Spy Service Honored for Daring Acts That Helped Secure Allied Victory." *Stars and Stripes,* March 28, 2018.

Sanders, Katie. "The Women Whose Secret Work Helped Win World War II." *New York Times Magazine,* March 6, 2019.

Sanders, L. H. "Eleven Tips on Getting More Efficiency Out of Women Employees." *Mass Transportation,* July 1943.

Santoro, Gene. "At War with the Enemy's Mind: Conversation with Betty McIntosh." *World War II Magazine,* June 2013.

Schaap, James C. "Diet Eman 1920–2019," Stuff in the Basement.

Schaap, James C. "The Diet Eman Story, Part I." *The Banner: Weekly Publication of The Christian Reformed Church,* November 8, 1993: 10.

Schaap, James C. "The Diet Eman Story, Part III." *The Banner: Weekly Publication of The Christian Reformed Church,* November 22, 1993: 10.

Schaap, James C. "The Diet Eman Story, Part VIII." *The Banner: Weekly Publication of The Christian Reformed Church.* December 27, 1993: 12.

Schaeffer, Jeffrey, and Angela Charlton. "Holocaust Survivors Share Their Stories

So the Memories Will Endure." *Mercury News,* December 23, 2019.

Schirmer, Eleni. "The Mighty Pens of Women's Tennis: The Letter Legacy of Alice Marble and Venus Williams." Women's History Month, 2016, ESPN, March 17, 2016.

Seaman, Barbara. "Ruth Gruber 1911–2016." *Jewish Women: A Comprehensive Historical Encyclopedia,* February 27, 2009.

Sebba, Anne, and Doreen Montgomery. "Ida Cook 1904–1986." Big Red Book: Celebrating Television's *This is Your Life,* undated.

Seelye, Katharine Q. "Mary Previte, Grateful Survivor of a Concentration Camp, Dies at 87." *New York Times,* November 24, 2019.

"Sen. Moran Announces Award for Women of 6888th Central Postal Directory Battalion." *The Times — Pottawatomie County, KS,* March 8, 2019.

"Senator Warner Announces Legion of Merit to Be Awarded Posthumously to WWII Era Spy Stephanie Rader." News, Senator Mark Warner homepage, May 26, 2016.

Shapira, Ian. "As Nazis Closed In, Spy Fled Across Mountains on Her Wooden Leg." *Washington Post,* July 16, 2017.

Silverman, Jeff. "Spies in the Clubhouse:

The Intelligence That Won World War II May Not Have Been Accumulated in the Hallways of Power, But along the Fairways of Congressional." U.S. Golf Association, 2011: 79–82.

Smith, Harrison. "Dutch Resistance Hero Saved Jews in World War II." *Washington Post,* September 8, 2019.

Spring, Kelly A., Dr. "Charity Adams Earley." National Women's History Museum, 2017.

"Spy Girl Betty McIntosh Turns 100 Years Old." News & Information, Central Intelligence Agency, March 3, 2015.

Staar, Richard F. "Elections in Communist Poland." *Midwest Political Science Association,* vol. 2, no. 2 (May 1958): 200–201.

Stamberg, Susan. "Mother, Son Share Experiences of War." *Morning Edition,* National Public Radio (NPR), September 24, 2007.

Stamberg, Susan. "Female WWII Pilots: The Original Fly Girls." *Morning Edition,* National Public Radio (NPR), March 9, 2010.

Stone, Kirk H. "Geography's Wartime Service." *Annals of the Association of American Geographers,* vol. 69, no. 1, 1979: 89.

Talbot, Margaret. "Gone Girl: The Extraordinary Resilience of Elizabeth Smart." *The New Yorker,* October 14, 2013.

Talbot, Margaret. "Ida and Louise Cook, Two Unusual Heroines of the Second World War." *The New Yorker,* September 3, 2019.

Tercatin, Rossella. "Dutch Heroine Who Saved Dozens of Jews in World War II Dies at 99." *Jerusalem Post,* September 9, 2019.

Tikkanen, Amy, ed. "The Legion of Merit." *Encyclopedia Britannica,* July 20, 1998.

Tumulty, Karen. "A Troublemaker with a Gavel." *Washington Post,* March 25, 2020.

U.S. Holocaust Memorial Museum. "Kristallnacht (The Night of Broken Glass), November 9–10, 1938." Holocaust Encyclopedia, October 18, 2019.

Walsh, Tobi. "Families, Veterans Mark D-Day Anniversary at Bedford Memorial." *Lynchburg News & Advance,* June 6, 2015.

Warner, Judith, Nora Ellmann, and Diana Boesch. "The Women's Leadership Gap." Center for American Progress, November 20, 2018.

Warrington, Beth A. "New Monument Honors All Female, African American Battalion." Army University Press (U.S. Army), February 4, 2019.

The Week Staff. "Greta Thunberg's Climate Crusade." *The Week,* May 4, 2019.

Wentling, Nikki. "Commission: Women

Should Be Eligible for the Draft." *Stars and Stripes,* March 25, 2020.

Wettenstein, Beverly. "Let Us Remember Alice Marble, the Catalyst for Althea Gibson to Break the Color Barrier." *Huffington Post,* August 30, 2007.

"What the Heck Was I Gonna Do With a Dumb Gun? The Derring-Do of Stephanie Czech Rader." News & Information, Central Intelligence Agency, June 28, 2017.

"William Staats Rader, Brigadier General U.S. Air Force." Arlington National Cemetery website, August 23, 2006.

Williams, Joseph. "Meet Charity Adams Earley, the Highest-Ranking African American Female Officer of World War II." Allthatsinteresting.com, January 9, 2020.

Williams, Sharrie. "Sharrie Williams Talks to Commissioner Danielle Outlaw about Her Vision for the Philadelphia Police Department." WPVI TV, Philadelphia, PA, February 13, 2020.

Wolfe, Elizabeth, and Saeed Ahmed. "Danielle Outlaw was the First African-American Woman to Be Portland's Police Chief. Now She's Philadelphia's First Black Female Commissioner." CNN News, December 31, 2019.

"Women and Tennis: Lesson 1: Alice Marble

and Helen Hull Jacobs." International Tennis Hall of Fame, undated.

"Women in the U.S. Congress 2020." Center for American Women and Politics (CAWP), Eagleton Institute of Politics, Rutgers University, 2020.

"The Women Who Shaped the World." *The Future Mapping Company,* August 31, 2019.

"Women's History Month: Betty Robarts." National Museum of the Mighty Eighth Air Force, undated.

"World War II Veterans by the Numbers." Department of Veterans Affairs, VA Fact Sheet, 2003.

"WW2 Spitfire Pilot Mary Ellis Given Freedom of Isle of Wight." BBC News, January 18, 2018.

"WW2: Did the War Change Life for Women?" BBC Teach, 2020.

Yousafzai, Malala. "Duty." The Columnists, *WSJ.* magazine, June 8, 2020: 6.

Films and Documentaries

Ahead of Time: The Extraordinary Journey of Ruth Gruber. The National Center for Jewish Film, Brandeis University, 2009. (Ruth Gruber)

A Call to Spy. IFC Films, 2020. (Virginia Hall)

The Eisen Family Story. Video presentation by Mary Eisen Cramer at Norco College, April 27, 2012. (Hilda Eisen)

Dayton Codebreakers. American Public Television, 2006. (Betty Bemis Robarts)

Haven. Alliance Atlantis Communications, 2001. (Ruth Gruber)

Pat and Mike, MGM. (Alice Marble)

Safe Haven, a Story of Hope. Yesterday's News Inc., 2000. (Ruth Gruber)

Science Fair. National Geographic Documentary Film, October 19, 2018.

The Reckoning: Remembering the Dutch Resistance. Storytelling Pictures, 2007. (Diet Eman)

The Six Triple Eight: No Mail, No Morale. Lincoln Penny Films, 2019. (Charity Adams Earley)

The Virginia Hall Award: Major Stephanie Czech Rader, USA. The OSS Society, 2012. (Stephanie Czech Rader)

Screenplay

Whitmore, Hugh. *Breaking the Code.* New York: Samuel French, 1987.

Interviews

Barraco, Mary. "Dame Mary Barraco—What We Carry." The Holocaust Commission of the United Jewish Federation of Tidewater,

VA, 2016. https://holocaustcommission
.jewishva.org/home-page/what-we-carry
/dame-mary-barraco.

Early, Charity Adams. "LTC Charity
Adams, Oral History, 1990." By Brig.
General (Ret) Pat Foote. Women's
Army Corps Museum History Project,
1990. https://www.youtube.com/watch?v
=L3snVXlW5ng.

Eisen, Hilda. Testimony with the U.S. Shoah
Foundation, 2001. https://www.youtube
.com/watch?v=Daqe8Lad-z8.

Eman, Berendina Diet. U.S. Holocaust Museum, 2003. https://collections.ushmm
.org/search/catalog/irn514469.

Eman, Diet. "I Loved Psalm 27: A Conversation with Diet Eman." Manna Media,
July 19, 2013. https://www.youtube.com
/watch?v=OuYAKrc8bdE.

Eman, Diet. "Remembering Diet Eman:
A World War II Hero." Channel 8, News
at 6, September 5, 2019. https://www.you
tube.com/watch?v=29LqP0smTLY.

McIntosh, Elizabeth. "Women in the Office of Strategic Services." C-SPAN
Washington Journal, 2000. https://www.c
-span.org/video/?169597-4/women-office
-strategic-services.

Nolan, Kate. "Battle of the Bulge Remembered: Kate Nolan." Honor and

Remembrance. By Brett Flashnik. The American Legion, undated. https://www.legion.org/honor/battleofthebulge.

Nolan, Kate. "Kate Nolan, WWII Combat Nurse." *Morning Edition*. By Susan Stamberg. National Public Radio (NPR), May 28, 2004.

Previte, Mary. "This American Life." National Public Radio, 2015, www.thisamericanlife.org/radio-archives/episode/559/captains-log.

Previte, Mary. " 'We Took Terror Out of Their Lives:' Remembering Youth Advocate Mary Previte." *Fresh Air*. By David Bianculli and Terry Gross. National Public Radio, December 6, 2019. https://www.npr.org/2019/12/06/785479653/we-took-terror-out-of-their-lives-remembering-youth-advocate-mary-previte.

Rader, Stephanie Czech. By Jane Maliszewksi, September 2006. Arlington, VA. Oral History #074520, two tapes, collection of the Women in Military Service to America Memorial Foundation.

Rexroat, Ola. "Ola Rexroat Oral History Interview." Woman's Collection, Texas Woman's University, September 8, 2006, https://twudigital.contentdm.oclc.org/digital/collection/p214coll2/search/searchterm/Oral%20History!Rexroat/field

/colleb!all/mode/exact!all/conn/and!all
/order/nosort/ad/asc.

Robarts, Betty Bemis. Veterans History
Project, 2011. http://memory.loc.gov/diglib
/vhp/story/loc.natlib.afc2001001.35024/.

"Soldering the Bombe Wheels: Betty Bemis
Robarts." November 21, 2017, https://www
.youtube.com/watch?v=SR_UXvpJHRo.

Conversations/Correspondence with Author

Email from Sandra Frieswyk, Marion
Frieswyk's daughter, April 21, 2020.

Marion Frieswyk, by telephone, April 24,
2020.

Linda McCarthy, by telephone, April 24,
2020.

Email from Linda McCarthy, May 6, 2020.

Steve Nolan, Kate Nolan's son, by telephone,
May 9, 2020.

Email from Kate Nolan's daughter, Mary
Battaglia, April 24, 2020.

Lorna Catling, Virginia Hall's niece, by telephone, June 23, 2020.

Mary Gray, Diet Eman's granddaughter, by
telephone, August 2, 2020.

ABOUT THE AUTHOR

Mari K. Eder, retired U.S. Army Major General, is a renowned speaker, author, and thought leader on strategic communication and leadership. General Eder has served as director of public affairs at the George C. Marshall European Center for Security Studies and as an adjunct professor and lecturer in communications and public diplomacy at the NATO School and Sweden's International Training Command. She speaks and writes frequently on communication topics in universities and for international audiences and consults on communications issues. General Eder is the author of *Leading the Narrative: The Case for Strategic Communication.* Her latest communications book, *American Cyberscape,* was released in November 2020. When not writing, speaking, or traveling, she works with animal rescue groups and fosters dogs for adoption.

The employees of Thorndike Press hope you have enjoyed this Large Print book. All our Thorndike, Wheeler, and Kennebec Large Print titles are designed for easy reading, and all our books are made to last. Other Thorndike Press Large Print books are available at your library, through selected bookstores, or directly from us.

For information about titles, please call:

(800) 223-1244

or visit our website at:

http://gale.cengage.com/thorndike

To share your comments, please write:

Publisher
Thorndike Press
10 Water St., Suite 310
Waterville, ME 04901